ENDLESS EXPERIMENTS

Endless Experiments

ESSAYS ON THE HEROIC EXPERIENCE

IN AMERICAN ROMANTICISM

TODD M. LIEBER

OHIO STATE UNIVERSITY PRESS

COLUMBUS   1973

73-37

William Carlos Williams, IN THE AMERICAN GRAIN. Copyright 1925 by James Laughlin. Copyright 1933 by William Carlos Williams. Excerpts are reprinted by permission of New Directions Publishing Corporation.

William Carlos Williams, PATERSON. Copyright 1946, 1948, 1949, 1951, © 1958 by William Carlos Williams. Copyright © 1963 by Florence Williams. Excerpts are reprinted by permission of New Directions Publishing Corporation and Laurence Pollinger Limited, London, England.

Acknowledgment is hereby made to Alfred A. Knopf, Inc., for use of the copyrighted works of Wallace Stevens from THE NECESSARY ANGEL and THE COLLECTED POEMS OF WALLACE STEVENS.

Library of Congress Cataloging in Publication Data
Lieber, Todd M.
    Endless experiments
    1. American literature—19th century—History and criticism.
2. Romanticism—United States. 3. Heroes in literature.
I. Title.
PS208.L5   810'.9'353   72-10658
ISBN 0-8142-0180-6

Contents

Preface

In his now famous essay "On the Discrimination of Romanticisms," Professor Arthur O. Lovejoy observed that the term *Romanticism* "has come to mean so many things, that, by itself, it means nothing. It has ceased to perform the function of a verbal sign." [1] To the extent that Professor Lovejoy's statement is accurate, one assumes a certain risk in using *Romanticism* as the unifying term for a collection of essays, a risk of which I am well aware. However, although the word may lack real denotative meaning, it retains a wealth of connotative value; and, despite Professor Lovejoy's warning, there are some general characteristics of Romanticism that have been widely acknowledged and seem to be universally applicable. For example, the Romantic movements all represent, at least in their early stages, a reaction from the formal orthodoxy of a preceding period, a rebellion against the neoclassical emphasis on convention and the rigidity of a "given" external order, and an assertion of the freedom of the individual to control the forms of his own life. They are movements that respond to life with a sense of wonder and mystery, with a spirit that places less emphasis on logical, metaphysical, or theological consistency than on the intensity of momentary experience. The Romantics typically center this experience in the creative activity of imagination, the blending and unifying powers of the mind that enable man to shape and order his experience and realize the nature of its inner relationships. Romanticism is thus a way of looking at reality that places the self at the center of all existence, and serious romantic narrative tends to be preeminently a record of the dramatic experience of the individual personality encountering society and nature and exploring the depths of its own being.

In the same essay in which he pointed to the confusion brought about by the diversified use of "Romanticism," Professor Lovejoy suggested that, to restore some degree of utility to the word, each of the various Romanticisms, "after they are first thus roughly discriminated with respect to their representatives or their dates—should be resolved, by a more thorough and discerning analysis than is yet customary, into its elements—into the several ideas and aesthetic susceptibilities of which it is composed" (pp. 9–10). With the first of these tasks there is little difficulty in American literature. We know, so to speak, who our Romantics are, and all the earmarks of a Romantic movement can be found in the "tempest in a teapot" that took place in New England in the 1830s, when Romanticism is generally assumed to have blossomed in America. These essays are a partial response to Professor Lovejoy's second challenge: an attempt to apprehend the metaphysical structure of American Romanticism and to examine the manner in which the ideas become manifest in the dramatic experience of the Romantic hero. By *hero* I mean essentially the literary embodiment of a conception or image of the self, for in the works discussed here it is the drama of self that furnishes the material for the central "action" and thus becomes the heroic experience of the literature.

My thesis, stated simply, is that serious Romanticism in America grows out of the Puritan intellectual heritage and consequently is profoundly dualistic in nature, rooted in a deep sense of the distinctiveness of mind and object, spirit and matter, human and absolute, man and God. The Romantic aspiration is toward a harmony that reconciles these poles of experience, with imagination, as manifest in art, set forth as the prime vehicle for achieving this goal. But such a reconciliation is inherently unstable, always breaking down or growing stale, demanding endless experimentation in life and endless re-creation in art in order to keep it alive and meaningful. The need for such experimentation and re-creation forms the core of the experience of the American Romantic hero. He is typically a man in motion, both physically and psychologically, seeking harmony, but unable to accept any fixed vision as final or any single truth as absolute. His success comes in fleeting moments of imaginative vision; and between the peaks of experience when it is achieved, the Romantic consciousness ebbs and flows between the extremities of a universe conceived in dualistic terms. These dualities and the nature of this dramatic ebb and flow of consciousness are my central subjects.

The Introduction briefly traces the major issues in the development of Romanticism in the philosophical and religious thought of New England during the Transcendentalist period and outlines the basic dimensions of the Romantic vision as they are revealed in the thought of Ralph Waldo Emerson. From Emerson's writings I have abstracted a set of "ideal" tendencies to use in the body of the book as a means of studying the philosophical and religious tensions of Romanticism in their mythic and dramatic forms. The body of the book consists of a series of linked, interpretive essays dealing with particular works by Thoreau, Whitman, Melville, Poe, and William

Carlos Williams. In these essays I have attempted to see each work as a self-contained version of the drama of the Romantic self. Consequently, aside from necessary exposition, I have deemphasized the biographical and socio-cultural dimensions of the works—which have been discussed well and at some length by Perry Miller, R. W. B. Lewis, Leo Marx, and others—in order to allow a closer and more continuous scrutiny of the patterns of heroic consciousness and behavior within the works themselves, and of the metaphysical tensions implicit in these patterns. In the Epilogue I have returned to the less-confined format of the Introduction, focusing on the larger vision of the artist rather than on the internal dynamics of a single work. Again, however, I have limited myself to dealing with one man, Wallace Stevens, whose thought describes well the posture of the Romantic sensibility in the modern age.

My approach is intensive rather than extensive, focused on a single theme (though a theme, I believe, with wide importance for much modern literature), and based on a close reading and a detailed examination of a few major works. The book does not deal with many writers who have been strongly influenced by the Romantic tradition in America—Hawthorne, James, Hart Crane, Faulkner, Thomas Wolfe, and perhaps others, might have been included. But to have dealt with them would have made the study inordinately long and, at times, repetitive. The territory covered is, I think, broad enough to indicate the scope of the Romantic response and at the same time concise enough to allow for somewhat of a schematized presentation.

This study was begun as a doctoral dissertation at Case

Western Reserve University under the supervision of Roger B. Salomon, to whom I owe a special debt of gratitude for his valuable guidance and, especially, for his continuing support and encouragement. I would also like to thank Professor Henig Cohen, who read the manuscript and made several helpful suggestions; the administration of Simpson College, Indianola, Iowa, for financial assistance in preparing the manuscript; and my wife, Lori, whose patience and understanding were invaluable. There are, of course, other debts too numerous to mention.

ENDLESS EXPERIMENTS

Introduction

EMERSON

ENDLESS EXPERIMENTER

Nature delights to put us between extreme antagonisms,
and our safety is in the skill with which we keep the
diagonal line.—Emerson, *Society and Solitude*

But lest I should mislead any when I have my own head
and obey my whims, let me remind the reader that I am
only an experimenter. Do not set the least value on
what I do, or the least discredit on what I do not, as if
I pretended to settle any thing as true or false. I un-
settle all things. No facts are to me sacred; none are
profane; I simply experiment, an endless seeker with
no Past at my back.—Emerson, "Circles"

In September 1836, shortly after the celebration of the
second centennial of Harvard University, seven young
New Englanders met to create an informal society that
came to be known as the Transcendental Club. The
impetus for establishing such a group lay in a profound
dissatisfaction with the current state of philosophical opinion in America, a dissatisfaction that was manifest in a
review essay by one of the seven, Orestes A. Brownson,
which appeared in the current issue of the *Christian
Examiner*. In his essay Brownson rejected as inadequate
the two dominant philosophical orientations of the day

and praised the virtues of Victor Cousin, a French Idealist
philosopher whose writings had been controversial topics
in the intellectual circles of New England for quite a
while. Brownson first took to task the school of which
Locke was the figurehead, upon whose psychology the
whole Unitarian edifice had been constructed:

> The sensualist school admits and studies with great suc-
> cess the facts of the sensibility; but overlooking those
> of the activity and reason, or not making a sufficient
> account of them it mutilates the soul, and becomes
> false in its inductions.[1]

Brownson found the Lockean philosophy deficient because
it denied the role played by subjectivity in defining reality, but he was equally unwilling to accept the other extreme, represented for him by the ideas of Kant. A few
sentences later, he turned to the limitations of the Kantian
school:

> To deprive the reason of all but a subjective authority, to
> allow it no validity out of the sphere of our own per-
> sonality, is to deprive it of all legitimate authority. . . .
> If the reason have no authority out of the sphere of
> the personality, or of the individual consciousness in
> which its phenomena appear, it can reveal to us no es-
> sences which lie beyond ourselves. Such may be the laws
> of our nature, that we cannot help believing that we are,
> that there is an external world, and God; but . . . to
> this conclusion all are driven who assert the subjectivity
> of the reason. (p. 110)

Brownson realized that the Kantian emphasis on subjectivity, if carried to its ultimate conclusion, denied the
existence of all external reality, denied even the existence
of God.

The task that Brownson set for himself and his contemporaries was somehow to reconcile or to mediate between these apparently opposite approaches, one of which denied the essence of selfhood by "mutilating the soul," and the other denied the essence of everything that was not self by preventing man from ever escaping his own subjectivity. In Victor Cousin, Brownson felt he saw the first step toward his goal, a metaphysics that did not deny the self, external reality, or God. He concluded his essay by describing the "great mission" that lay ahead:

> We must be eclectics, excluding no element of humanity, but accepting and melting all into one vast system, which will be a true representative of humanity so far as it is yet developed. We must take broad and liberal views, expect truth and find it in all schools, in all creeds, in all ages, and in all countries. The great mission of our age is to unite the infinite and the finite. Union, harmony, whence proceed peace and love, are the points to be aimed at. We of the nineteenth century appear in the world as mediators. (p. 114)

Although Brownson discussed the problem in terms of European philosophy, the tensions that concerned him had long been a part of the native intellectual scene of New England. This highly dualistic sensibility had been virtually endemic in New England theology from its beginnings, in the efforts of Puritanism to combine Humanism and Calvinism, to see man as an essentially rational and responsible being despite the fact that he was deformed by sin and needed to wait upon God for the special grace that would enable him to perceive the essential reasonableness of all things. To understand Transcendentalism, and thus to understand the Romantic tradition in America, it is necessary to consider the Puritan background from which it grew.

The Puritans posited that a simple and comprehensible divine order permeated the world, an order in which ideas corresponded to objects and were not separate entities of the mind with a logic of their own; there was, in other words, no difference between the laws of thought and the laws of things, but rather a set of immutable essences that existed both within the mind and within the natural order. As Perry Miller explains, for the Puritans, following the logic of Peter Ramus, truth "becomes the clear-eyed perception of immutable essences, beauty becomes correspondence to them, virtue becomes conformity to them. The method of discovering them is inward; they exist not only in nature but in the human intelligence, and though much study and caution are necessary in deriving them from the mind, since the mind is corrupted by sin, and the rules of logic must always preside over the formulating of them, still the soul contains an intuitive knowledge of the eternal truths, which truths also govern the world." [2] Because man's reason is fallible, he needs the direction of God to arrive at truth. This direction is given in the form of grace, or spiritual light, but it is given only to a select few whom God has chosen for salvation. This spiritual light, furthermore, is not an immediate intuition of truth but an elevation of the powers of reason; and man, of course, has no way of knowing for sure whether or not he has received it. However, by toiling to do God's will, by constantly engaging in introspection and self-discipline, examining himself and his behavior, he may at least acquire some idea of his predestined fate. Failure to comprehend the divine order lies, first, in a failure to see the truth within the self, and this failure is an indication of the prospect of spending eternity in hell. Thus, the more insecure man felt, the more he looked within himself, trying to convince himself that he had indeed received the grace necessary to elevate his reason to the proper level. Puritanism placed heavy emphasis on the drama of self, but kept the self at all times totally dependent upon God.

Within Puritan culture there was a strong emphasis on introspection and the attempt to refine and cultivate the self; yet at all times the importance of selfhood was held in check by the overriding commitment to God. As long as the Puritans could maintain the identity between spiritual light and the powers of reason, the innate tension between idealism and sensualism could be controlled; but when this identity collapsed, as it did for a few men in the eighteenth century, their theology was in danger. For then either the spiritual light was an immediate perception of truth, in which case man was liberated from all dependence on the church and the social order, and reason and logical analysis of the world were expendable, or else it was sheer insanity, no longer a necessary adjunct to reason in understanding God's plan; and if reason alone was sufficient, then there was no need for a total and unconditional submission to divine power. It was this split, according to Perry Miller, that began the dissolution of the Old Calvinism and released the full impact of the dilemma of self within Puritanism.[3] This split also released the dualities of the Puritan sensibility from their careful control, so that from innate tensions they became almost rival ways of conceiving reality.

By the early nineteenth century the dilemma had become crucial, and it was not resolved by the Unitarian reinterpretation. Brownson himself was acutely aware of the paradox that existed. In his review of Cousin he wrote:

> Everybody knows that our religion and our philosophy
> are at war. We are religious only at the expense of our
> logic. This accounts for the fact that, on the one hand,
> we disclaim logic, unchurch philosophy, and pronounce
> it a dangerous thing to reason; while, on the other, we
> reject religion, declaim against the clergy, and represent
> it exceedingly foolish to believe. (p. 108)

To Brownson and his colleagues total submission to divine
sovereignty seemed very close to a surrender of the individual reason, and such a denial of self was unthinkable.
Equally unfeasible, however, were the implications of
total divorce represented by Idealism, for in aggrandizing
the self this approach stripped value from everything that
was not self, including, at its extreme solipsistic point,
God. This was a terrifying prospect to the mind of a New
England Christian. Brownson suggested:

> We should re-examine our philosophy, and inquire if
> there be not a philosophy true to human nature, and
> able to explain and verifying, instead of destroying the
> religious belief of mankind? (p. 108)

To find such a philosophy was perhaps the major concern
of the Transcendentalists. Reacting against the cold logic
of the doctrinal formulations of the earlier theologies, the
Transcendentalists rebelled as well against the language of
theology, seeking the warmth of individual responsiveness
in new forms of expression. "Because they desperately
needed forms and concepts in which to embody a passion
that arose out of domestic pressures," Miller writes, "the
Transcendentalists appropriated with avidity the new
literature of 'romanticism' that came to them through
Wordsworth and Coleridge and the new philosophy of

German idealism that came to them at second hand through Cousin and Carlyle." [4]

This new spirit found fertile soil on the American continent, among a people to whom many of the aspects of Romantic expression must have seemed to be simply a confirmation of their own American sense of freedom and newness. The acute observer of American ways, Alexis de Tocqueville, accurately predicted the lines of American poetry when he wrote that "man himself, taken aloof from his age and his country, and standing in the presence of Nature and of God, with his passions, his doubts, his rare prosperities and inconceivable wretchedness—will become the chief, if not the sole theme of poetry among these nations." [5] In the writing of Irving, Cooper, Byrant, and Longfellow, the Romantic sensibility had begun American belles lettres with the triumvirate of the self, nature, and God as their chief subject matter. But their work represented an incomplete commitment to the new sensibility. Too often the self was either flawlessly heroic or melancholy and nostalgic, and nature was conceived without real spiritual power or substance. It was only with the Transcendentalists that the full potential and the full implications of the Romantic spirit were realized in American literature. Although the major dimensions of the movement were religious, in the sense that the Transcendentalists were primarily concerned with rephrasing the ancient religious preoccupations of New England, its outlook was predominantly Romantic, characterized by a new emphasis on individual freedom and aspiration, making literature most valuable as an expression of personal feelings and attitudes, and placing its supreme confidence in nature and in the transcendent power of the human imagination. Thus, the Transcendentalist period, while reflecting a stage in the long, slow dissolution of New England Calvinism, also marks the fulfillment of the potential of the Romantic impulse in American literature.

The combination of Romanticism and New England Protestantism accentuated many of the already innate tensions of American thought, diffusing what had been originally an essentially religious dilemma into virtually all areas of life. With a native emphasis on the drama of the self bolstered by the liberating influence of the Romantic spirit, what Northrop Frye has called the Romantic awareness of man's "fall" into self-consciousness, into "his present subject-object relation to nature," permeated all areas of Transcendental thought.[6] But along with this awareness was an equally strong sense of the necessity of extending this consciousness, the need to reestablish in new ways a sense of man's fundamental relatedness to the natural and supernatural worlds in which he found himself. Somehow a new resolution had to be found that joined the self to the larger whole at all levels of experience without denying the importance of the individual, and this was the central Transcendentalist problem. The tensions involved between self and not self, and within the self between spirit and sense, reach a peak in the writings of Ralph Waldo Emerson. Seeking a reconciliation between these dualities, finding it, losing it, and recreating it again—for such a resolution was almost inherently unstable—was for Emerson a lifelong activity. "Because it was a narrow line," writes Sherman Paul, "Emerson knew that it was hard 'to keep the middle point.' And even though the stupendous antagonisms between spirit and sense created the tensions of his thought and life, still the spanning of the worlds was his aim: in poetry to express

the universal in the particular, the abstract in the concrete; in the total expression of character . . . to remain
at once public and individual." [7]

Emerson began his career as a published writer with an
explicit acceptance of the dualism of the self and everything that is not self. The Introduction to *Nature* makes
this clear:

> Philosophically considered, the universe is composed of
> Nature and the Soul. Strictly speaking, therefore, all
> that is separate from us, all which Philosophy dis-
> tinguishes as the NOT ME, that is, both nature and
> art, all other men and my own body, must be ranked
> under this name, NATURE.[8]

In *Nature* Emerson sketched for the first time the outlines of the basic framework of assumptions that lay
beneath his attempts to reconcile these polarities, a framework that he would retain with remarkable consistency
throughout his life. It was based in the idea of "Correspondence" and may be summarized as follows: "power,"
or the essential creative energy of existence, emanates
from a divine source in two parallel currents, into the
"soul" and into "Nature," and therefore a radical correspondence exists between self and not self, between idea
and object, between "that which intellectually considered
we call Reason" and that which "considered in relation to
nature, we call Spirit" (p. 15). Language is a manifest
example of this correspondence, for "words are signs of
natural facts" (p. 14); but, Emerson continues, "it is not
words only that are emblematic; it is things which are
emblematic. Every natural fact is a symbol of some spiritual fact. Every appearance in nature corresponds to some
state of mind, and that state of mind can only be described

by presenting that natural appearance as its picture"
(p. 15). "And neither can man be understood without
these objects, nor these objects without man" (p. 16). "The
world is emblematic. Parts of speech are metaphors, because the whole of nature is a metaphor of the human
mind" (p. 18).

Emerson's approach required, of course, a supreme confidence in nature, a belief that the natural not self, suffused with the divine power of God, offered an equivalent
response to the expanding and expressive self. He writes
in the Introduction to *Nature:* "We must trust the perfection of the creation so far as to believe that whatever
curiosity the order of things has awakened in our minds,
the order of things can satisfy" (p. 3). A few pages later
he affirms this belief in the equivalent response offered to
man by the natural world:

> Nature stretches out her arms to embrace man, only let
> his thoughts be of equal greatness. Willingly does she
> follow his steps with the rose and the violet, and bend
> her lines of grandeur and grace to the decoration of her
> darling child. Only let his thoughts be of equal scope,
> and the frame will suit the picture. (p. 12)

Such an approach did not deny the duality of the universe,
but simply affirmed that the polarities were reconciled at
their divine source. As Paul has explained, "This dualism
was necessary for a seeker after unity, if God as the un-
conditioned and absolute ground were to be re-instated as
the unifying source who made the laws of nature answer
to the self-evident ideas He planted in the mind of man." [9]

When man can realize the essential unity of these
dual currents of divinity, it is possible for him to experience fully the value of his individual selfhood and at the

same time partake of the divinity immanent in the natural world; and, Emerson writes, because "this relation between mind and matter is not fancied by some poet, but stands in the will of God, [it] is free to be known by all men" (p. 19). Knowledge of this relation is to be achieved through the act of intuitive symbolic perception. This, in its most simple terms, is what the English Romantics called the vision of imagination, which Emerson defines as "the use which the Reason makes of the material world" (p. 29). In *Nature* he describes the process:

> When the eye of Reason opens, to outline and surface are at once added grace and expression. These proceed from imagination and affection, and abate somewhat of the angular distinctness of objects. If the Reason be stimulated to more earnest vision, outlines and surfaces become transparent, and are no longer seen; causes and spirits are seen through them. The best moments of life are these delicious awakenings of the higher powers, and the reverential withdrawing of nature before its God. (pp. 27–28)

This passage is a clear and concise statement of the process that formed the heart of Emerson's visionary thought. Here the meaning of "transcendence" and its relationship to the imagination are clear. In the vision of imagination the natural world becomes "transparent," and Emerson is able to see *through* it to a supernatural realm of divine spirit and power, thus *transcending* the natural world not by dismissing it but by penetrating through and beyond it to a "higher" reality. The imagination uncovers the essential reality that is immanent, but masked, in visible things and to which the ordinary intelligence, the "understanding," is blind. In instances of such vision a perfect balance is achieved between the idealism implicit in the

romantic view of imagination and the romantic insistence
that the imagination be related to an essential truth and
reality that is external to the human mind—what C. M.
Bowra has called Romanticism's "perilous compromise." [10]
For Emerson, however, the "best moments of life" are
just that—moments. In these instances he achieved his
goal of "spanning the worlds"; he reached his diagonal
line, balancing, incorporating, and transcending the polarities of sensual and spiritual, social and private, self and
not self. But Emerson knew that the diagonal line was not
a path that could be followed or maintained without devia-
tion. It was, in fact, no line at all, but rather a point, a
position, a peak of experience that could be achieved only
momentarily and only momentarily retained. The moments when nature seems transparent are evanescent. The
immediacy of these visionary experiences endows them
with a high degree of intensity, but also renders them
fleeting and transient. At other times nature seems opaque,
blank, a world totally unrelated to the thoughts of man.
"This relation between the mind and matter . . . ," Emerson writes in *Nature,* "appears to men, or it does not
appear. When in fortunate hours we ponder this miracle,
the wise man doubts if at all other times he is not blind
and deaf" (p. 19). "Merlin," a poem that comes as close as
any to stating Emerson's bardic ideal, repeats this sense of
the elusive nature of such epiphanic moments:

> There are open hours
> When the God's will sallies free
> And the dull idiot might see
> The flowing fortunes of a thousand years;—
> Sudden, at unawares,
> Self-moved, fly-to the doors,
> Nor sword of angels could reveal
> What they conceal.[11]

Over and over again, in essay after essay, Emerson is drawn to reemphasize the immediate and transient nature of the moments of illumination. A long passage in "The Transcendentalist" best summarizes his attitude:

Mine is a certain brief experience, which surprised me in the highway or in the market, in some place, at some time. . . . Well, in the space of an hour probably, I was let down from this height; I was at my old tricks, the selfish member of a selfish society. My life is superficial, takes no root in the deep world; I ask, When shall I die and be relieved of the responsibility of seeing a Universe I do not use? I wish to exchange this flash-of-lightning faith for continuous daylight, this fever-glow for a benign climate.

These two states of thought diverge every moment, and stand in wild contrast. To him who looks at his life from these moments of illumination, it will seem that he skulks and plays a mean, shiftless and subaltern part in the world. That is to be done which he has not skill to do, or to be said which others can say better, and he lies by, or occupies his hands with some plaything, until his hour comes again. Much of our reading, much of our labor, seems mere waiting; it was not that we were born for. Any other could do it as well or better. So little skill enters into these works, so little do they mix with the divine life, that it really signifies little what we do, whether we turn a grindstone, or ride, or run, or make fortunes, or govern the state. The worst feature of this double consciousness is, that the two lives, of the understanding and of the soul, which we lead, really show very little relation to each other; never meet and measure each other: one prevails now, all buzz and din; and the other prevails then, all infinitude and paradise; and, with the progress of life, the two discover no greater disposition to reconcile themselves. (pp. 99–100)

Here the wide gap betwen the dualities that compose both Emerson's world and his conception of the self is clearly apparent, especially as he views these dualities from the standpoint of "moments of illumination" when they are reconciled and man is aware of the unity within himself and within the whole of creation. The duality that Emerson had established was necessary to his conception of unity, but it tended at all times to pull apart, leaving man with a divided self, in which the understanding and the soul, the senses and the imagination, were at war with each other. At the same time, the polarities of his world view, spirit and matter, pulled apart, and the creation itself became again divided.

Furthermore, the nature of the unifying experience itself is ambiguous. It is never totally clear whether, in the act of intuitive symbolic perception, the imagination actively creates the awareness of the Over-Soul, or whether man simply becomes able to perceive the value in nature that, derived from divinity, has been there all the time, the imagination existing simply as a parallel recipient of divine power. Consequently, when the momentary fusion of self and not self collapses, and between the peaks of experience when it is achieved, Emerson often drifts from his middle point toward the ultimate extremes of either a self-denying pantheism or a solipsistic idealism. Since each half of this duality taken alone negated what was for Emerson an indispensable element, it was necessary to attempt to hold the two halves together in a state of tension, for only in this way could the parallel currents of divinity be joined without denying either God or the self. But the tensions and ambiguities involved in such a union are rarely absent from Emerson's writing.

In the opening section of *Nature,* for example, Emerson is very close to a pantheistic surrender of self, so close that he speaks of himself as a "transparent eyeball; I am nothing; I see all; the currents of Universal Being circulate through me; I am part or parcel of God" (p. 6). As H. D. Gray has pointed out, "The individual who is part or parcel of God is no individual at all; and at certain moments Emerson . . . felt his world of individual things disappearing in an all-absorbing totality." [12] F. O. Matthiessen quotes a letter of Emerson's, written in 1841, that emphasizes his awareness of the dangers of such diffusion: " 'Can you not save me, dip me into ice-water, find me some girding belt, that I glide not away into a stream of infinite diffusion?' " [13] In *Nature* Emerson quickly pulls himself back from this denial and loss of individuality, restoring to the self its central importance; but his very phraseology reflects the uncertainty at the heart of his thought. He asserts: "Yet it is certain that the power to produce this delight does not reside in nature, but in man, or in a harmony of both" (p. 7).

In other essays Emerson is repeatedly drawn close to this self-abandoning position. In his *Divinity School Address,* for example, an affirmation of the divinity within man lapses almost into a standard statement of Christian mysticism:

> If a man is at heart just, then in so far is he God; the safety of God, the immortality of God, the majesty of God do enter into that man with justice. If a man dissemble, deceive, he deceives himself, and goes out of acquaintance with his own being. A man in the view of absolute goodness, adores, with total humility. Every step so downward, is a step upward. The man who renounces himself, comes to himself. (pp. 68–69)

This ambiguity is particularly evident in Emerson's remarks concerning the poet, who is often presented as a mere receptacle or conduit of divine inspiration. Emerson begins his essay "The Poet" by exalting him as the maker of original symbols, the namer of reality; but within a few pages this active role of the imagination has been transformed into a passive state:

> It is a secret which every intellectual man quickly learns, that beyond the energy of his possessed and conscious intellect he is capable of a new energy (as of an intellect doubled on itself), by abandonment to the nature of things; that beside his privacy of power as an individual man, there is a great public power on which he can draw, by unlocking at all risks, his human doors, and suffering the ethereal tides to roll and circulate through him; then he is caught up into the life of the Universe, his speech is thunder, his thought is law, and his words are universally intelligible as the plants and animals. (p. 332)

Equally dangerous to Emerson, however, are the extreme implications of idealism. At the point of extreme idealism, Emerson's thought generally takes one of two forms, leading him either toward the imposition of subjective images and personal value upon external reality, thereby imparting form and order to a chaotic world, or away from external reality in the direction of solipsistic isolation. Imposition is the more common tendency for Emerson. Such a position emerges clearly in *Nature*. Here, in almost direct contrast to "The Poet," he declares that the "namer" must impose his own subjective visions upon nature:

> He unfixes the land and the sea, makes them revolve around the axis of his primary thought, and disposes them anew. Possessed himself by a heroic passion, he uses matter as symbols of it. The sensual man conforms

thoughts to things; the poet conforms things to his thoughts. The one esteems nature as rooted and fast; the other, as fluid, and impresses his being thereon. (pp. 28–29)

"Heroism" grants the same power to the hero, and here Emerson recognizes no middle ground: "There seems to be no interval between greatness and meanness," he writes. "When the spirit is not master of the world, then it is its dupe" (p. 254). The hero is he who imposes his own imagination on the world and "makes his climate genial in the imagination of men, and its air the beloved element of all delicate spirits" (p. 257). In "Spiritual Laws" this tendency is emphatically reiterated: "Not in nature but in man is all the beauty and worth he sees. The world is very empty, and is indebted to this gilding, exalting soul for all its pride" (p. 199). Yet Emerson was aware of the dangers of this position, and if he seemed to accept and portray it without any real hesitation or caution, it was because he believed that at bottom it was not imposition at all, but rather the marriage of two equal and corresponding streams of divinity, the one flowing into nature, the other into man. As long as he is able to retain his faith in this bipolar unity, Emerson is characteristically affirmative and optimistic. But at times the divine value seems absent from nature, and man is left alone with his idealism.

The strongest statement of the dangers of this occurrence is in the essay "Experience." Here Emerson moves very close to a solipsistic dead end:

It is very unhappy, but too late to be helped, the discovery we have made that we exist. That discovery is called the Fall of Man. Ever afterwards we suspect our instruments. We have learned that we do not see di-

rectly, but mediately, and that we have no means of
correcting these colored and distorting lenses which we
are, or of computing the amount of their errors. Perhaps these subject-lenses have a creative power; perhaps
there are no objects. Once we lived in what we saw; now
the rapaciousness of this new power, which threatens to
absorb all things engages us. Nature, art, persons, letters, religions, objects, successively tumble in, and God
is but one of its ideas. (p. 359)

This apocalyptic vision of the imagination encompassing
and absorbing all things leads Emerson to despair of the
possibility of ever reaching a successful, balanced union
with anything that is not self:

Marriage (in what is called the spiritual world) is impossible, because of the inequality between every subject and every object. . . . The soul is not twin-born
but the only begotten, and though revealing itself as a
child in time, child in appearance, is of a fatal and
universal power, admitting no co-life. (pp. 359–60)

Emerson retreats from this extreme, as he must, but he
does so despairingly, acknowledging the real existence of
the external world and the tremendous, seemingly unbridgeable gap between it and the world of thought: "I
know that the world I converse with in the city and in the
farms is not the world I *think*. I observe that difference,
and shall observe it. One day I shall know the value and
law of this discrepance" (pp. 363–64).

Comments such as these have led some critics, such as
Matthiessen, to assert that Emerson "ignored experience
whenever it was in harsh or ugly conflict with his optimism," and that ultimately his vision never escaped his
own subjectivity.[14] But Emerson was fully aware of the

failings and shortcomings of idealism in forcing man into "the splendid labyrinth of [his] perceptions, to wander without end" (*Nature*, p. 35). "Certainly Idealism was a necessity to one of Emerson's nature," writes Gray, "and just as certainly that form of Idealism which swamped the universal in the individual ego was impossible to him." [15] Even in "Self-Reliance," probably the strongest and most affirmative statement of Emerson's idealism, the idealist position is substantially qualified. Self-trust is essential because ultimately it is faith in God, with whom the deepest intuitions of the self have their origin. "Nothing is at last sacred but the integrity of your own mind," Emerson writes. "No law can be sacred to me but that of my own nature" (p. 148). But the reason for this self-reliance, ultimately, must be that "the sense of being which in calm hours rises, we know not how, in the soul, is not diverse from things, from space, from light, from time, from man, but one with them and proceeds obviously from the same source whence their life and being proceed. . . . We lie in the lap of immense intelligence, which makes us receivers of its truth and organs of its activity" (pp. 155–56).

Emerson is quick to affirm the inadequacy of idealism in *Nature,* and his next step is to modify it to make room for divinity without debilitating it to the point where man becomes merely an observer of nature and a passive recipient of divine power. This, of course, is not an easy task; and as Emerson struggles to attain such a balance, his language becomes less precise and more and more figurative:

> But when, following the invisible steps of thoughts, we come to inquire, Whence is matter? and Wherto? many truths arise to us out of the recesses of consciousness.

> We learn that the highest is present to the soul of man;
> that the dread universal essence, which is not wisdom,
> or love, or beauty, or power, but all in one, and each
> entirely, is that for which all things exist, and that by
> which they are; that spirit creates; that behind nature,
> throughout nature, spirit is present; one and not com-
> pound *it does not act upon us from without, that is, in
> space and time, but spiritually, or through ourselves:*
> therefore, that spirit, that is, the Supreme Being, does
> not build up nature around us, but puts it forth through
> us, as the life of the tree puts forth new branches and
> leaves through the pores of the old. As a plant upon
> the earth, so a man rests upon the bosom of God; he is
> nourished by unfailing fountains, and draws at his need
> inexhaustible power. (p. 35, italics added)

Here the extent to which Emerson relies on organic images
and analogies to suggest the linkage of self, God, and
nature, is evident. His profound organicism is not only a
manifestation of his belief in the immanent divinity of
nature but also a stylistic device by which the unification
of the passive and active roles of man may be granted
prime importance without reducing the power of man. A
very fine line exists between the apocalypse of the imagination into the independence of idealism and the renunciation of self to a divine world soul; this was the line to
which Emerson tried to adhere, this the balance that organicism helped him to express. But the instability of the
compromise pushed him now toward one extreme and
now toward the other.

The tensions and ambiguities of the dualities that Emerson tried to hold together could not be explicated logically or reconciled philosophically. Their resolution depended upon imaginative vision. It was an awareness that
had to be felt and known intuitively rather than conveyed

through logical discourse. The world he conceptualized defied systematization and depended, ultimately, on faith. "Every surmise and vatication of the mind," he writes in *Nature*, "is entitled to a certain respect, and we learn to prefer imperfect theories, and sentences which contain glimpses of truth, to digested systems which have no one valuable suggestion" (p. 39). In religion, faith must replace theology, as Emerson makes clear in the *Divinity School Address:*

> Faith makes us, and not we it, and faith makes its own forms. All attempts to contrive a system are as cold as the new worship introduced by the French to the goddess of Reason—today, pasteboard and filigree, and ending tomorrow in madness and murder. Rather let the breath of new life be breathed by you through the forms already existing. For if once you are alive, you shall find they shall become plastic and new. (pp. 83–84)

Such a stance requires the vision not of the philosopher or the theologian but of the artist and poet, whose momentary imaginative perception can realize and express the ultimate relatedness of all things.

The vehicle of expression for the artist with such a vision is the symbol, which enables him to transcend the gap between the world of nature and the world of idea, to blend the Finite and the Infinite in one substance. Emerson comes to the symbol out of the need for a quality of expression that will be true to the fact yet stand for something larger than itself, which will convey his consciousness of the infinite within the moment of experience.[16] But Emerson fully recognizes that the life caught by a symbol flows on beyond the moment of perception, and that therefore any symbol, any one vision, can give only a fragmentary and temporary grasp of ultimate truth, and it is necessary to continually take new positions and sights on reality. He knew, Paul writes, "that he could not rest his perception in a symbol, as [he] believed Swedenborg had, for the life it temporarily caught flowed on and falsified it." [17] Thus, Emerson distinguishes between the poet and the mystic: "The last nails a symbol to one sense, which was a true sense for a moment, but soon becomes old and false. For all symbols are fluxional; all language is vehicular and transitive, and is good, as ferries and horses are, for conveyance" (p. 336). The successive and flowing character of this symbolic vision is stated emphatically in "Art":

> Every object has its roots in central nature, and may of course be so exhibited to us as to represent the world. Therefore each work of genius is the tyrant of the hour and concentrates attention on itself. . . . Presently we pass to some other object, which rounds itself into a whole as did the first. . . . From this succession of excellent objects we learn at last the immensity of the world, the opulence of human nature, which can run out to infinitude in any direction. But I also learn that what astonished and fascinated me in the first work, astonished me in the second work also; that excellence of all things is one. (pp. 307–8)

Emerson's thought is intrinsically and inherently kinetic. Every moment of illumination flows successively on to another, and no single experience can be accepted as final or any one vision of truth taken as absolute. The world itself is ever changing. Divinity is constantly manifesting itself through endless mutations of form, and only by remaining perpetually receptive to new truths and new visions can man stay spiritually alive and in tune with

nature. "I am always insincere," Emerson declares, "as
always knowing there are other moods. . . . I talked yesterday with a pair of philosophers; I endeavored to show
my good men that I liked everything by turns and nothing
long; that I loved the centre, but doated on the superfices"
(pp. 447–48). Man must constantly be changing and growing, and, because the "excellence of all things is one," self-
contradiction is only an illusion. "A foolish consistency is
the hobgoblin of little minds," Emerson writes in "Self-
Reliance":

> Speak what you think now in hard words and to-morrow
> speak what to-morrow thinks in hard words again,
> though it contradict everything you said today. . . .
> There will be an agreement in whatever variety of ac-
> tions, so they be each honest and natural in their hour.
> For of one will, the actions will be harmonious, how-
> ever unlike they seem. (p. 152)

Emerson is at all times insistent about the necessity of
avoiding any kind of stasis. Every thought, every truth, is
a potential prison, which, if taken to be fixed and final,
leads to blindness and stagnation. He writes in "Intellect":

> Truth is our element of life, yet if a man fasten his at-
> tention on a single aspect of truth and apply himself
> to that alone for a long time, the truth becomes dis-
> torted and not itself but falsehood. . . . God offers to
> every mind its choice between truth and repose. Take
> which you please—you can never have both. Between
> these, as a pendulum, man oscillates. He in whom the
> love of repose predominates will accept the first creed,
> the first philosophy, the first political party he meets—
> most likely his father's. He gets rest, commodity and
> reputation; but he shuts the door of truth. He in whom
> the love of truth predominates will keep himself aloof

from all moorings, and afloat. He will abstain from dogmatism, and recognize all the opposite negations between which, as walls, his being is swung. He submits to the inconvenience of suspense and imperfect opinion, but he is a candidate for truth, as the other is not, and respects the highest law of his being. (pp. 299–301)

The chief requirement of poetic vision is that it must refuse to rest in any temporary certainty, but be always alive and open. Without the continuing recreation of the experience of the whole, man is caught in stagnation, as isolated from the ultimate reality of the present as he would be in a solipsistic universe. The continuous employment of proper symbols frees man to participate actively and fully in the dynamic totality of creation. Rather than imposing subjective conceptions upon reality, the ideal poet, through the use of ever new symbols, releases the true nature of reality from the false names and outmoded interpretations men have given it in the past, while at the same time he releases man from the trap of his idealism, the limitations of his individual perception. "The poets are liberating gods," Emerson maintains: "Every thought is a prison; every heaven is also a prison. Therefore, we love the poet, the inventor, who in any form, whether in an ode or in an action or in looks and behavior, has yielded us a new thought. He unlocks our chains and admits us to a new scene" (pp. 334–36).

Emerson's thought is not merely kinetic; it is also experimental and endlessly incomplete. The ineffable fusion of self and not self, the linkage of the dualities that compose his world, can only be expressed through constant experimentation, and every symbol must be considered tentative and left behind when its consciousness-expanding power grows stale. All statements, all positions, must be

considered hypothetical. Even idealism, Emerson writes in
Nature, "is merely a useful introductory hypothesis, serv-
ing to apprize us of the eternal distinction between the
soul and the world" (p. 35). He maintains in "Circles":

> I am only an experimenter. Do not set the least value
> on what I do, or the least discredit on what I do not,
> as if I pretended to settle anything as true or false. I
> unsettle all things. No facts to me are sacred; none are
> profane; I simply experiment, an endless seeker with
> no Past at my back. (p. 288)

Furthermore, the experimentation must always be incomplete, for any cessation of the task of continuing recreation, any acceptance of permanence, means stagnation and
spiritual death. Although Emerson reveals at times a sense
of exhaustion, yet the consequences of stasis remind him
of the need to continue in motion. "People wish to be
settled," he writes; "only as far as they are unsettled is
there any hope for them" (p. 289). "Gladly we would
anchor, but the anchorage is quicksand" (p. 347). Nothing
can be accepted as permanent because everything known
is partial, an awareness of relation rather than a final
answer. Anything less than the whole forms part of the
picture only, and the infinite whole, the "eternal gener-
ator" that "contains all circles," is unknowable except by
living into it. "I know better than to claim any complete-
ness for my picture," writes Emerson in "Experience." "I
am a fragment, and this is a fragment of me" (p. 363).

Emerson, however, distinctly recognizes two very different types of motion. These may be differentiated by calling the first, which involves a sense of the constant presence of divinity and yields continual affirmation, *process,*
and the second *flux,* to denote an aimless, purposeless, un-

achieving drift. Because divinity is endlessly manifesting itself in new and changing forms, Emerson felt that by immersing himself in its flow he could stay within the living present moment of eternity, keep pace with nature in its endless procession. Circles were one of his favorite images for describing this constant expansion of nature and the soul:

> The natural world may be conceived of as a system of concentric circles, and we now and then detect in nature slight dislocations which apprise us that this surface on which we now stand is not fixed, but sliding. . . . Cause and effect are two sides of one fact. . . . The same law of eternal procession ranges all. (p. 286)

It was this "law of eternal procession" that Emerson felt manifesting itself both in the world and in his soul. The continuing task of the poet was to immerse himself in this stream and, by expressing it in the flow of symbolic language, reveal it to men:

> The poet . . . shows us all things in their right series and procession. For through that better perception he stands one step nearer to things, and sees the flowing or metamorphosis; perceives that thought is multiform; that within the form of every creature is a force impelling it to ascend into a higher form; and following with his eyes the life, uses the forms which express that life, and so his speech flows with the flowing of nature. (p. 329)

Although the images of ascension in Emerson's writing at times suggest a movement toward an increasingly intense and pure perception of the Absolute, Emerson is not a mystic, striving laboriously toward God, but rather a visionary who becomes aware of God's presence about him and within him in the successive repetition of epiphanic moments. Emerson's motion is not a journey toward God but the continuous unfolding of God in the unity of the self and nature. The images of soaring, aspiring, and ascending do not seem to me to be a statement of the direction of Emerson's spiritual movement so much as they are an attempt to express the immediate uplifting and expansion of the soul that he feels in these visionary moments. It is this sense of joy and uplift that lends to Emerson's style the qualities of ascension, endless expansion, and infinite possibility that characterize his most impassioned prose, as, for example, in "The Over-Soul," where he describes the effect of cosmic awareness: "It is the *doubling* of the heart itself, nay, the *infinite enlargement* of the heart with a *power of growth* to a new *infinity* on every side" (p. 275, italics added). The very language of this passage breaks all the barriers of a finite and static world.

The force of this affirmation, however, is largely dependent upon the continuous union of man and nature in the Over-Soul. When the sense of this union is lost, the kinetic principle that Emerson observes in all aspects of life becomes a principle of flux rather than process, motion that remains always on the endless circumference of the same circle, without penetrating to the dynamic center whence proceeds the procreation of new and ever expanding circles. It was for this reason, among others, that Emerson rejected society for nature. The natural not self revealed the processes of God to the perceptive eye; the social not self revealed merely an ebb and flow, a frustrated movement, leading man only around in circles. "Traveling is a fool's paradise," Emerson writes in "Self-Reliance." It is a "fool's paradise" because only surface realities will be ob-

served; the deeper Reality, the presence of God pervading
the world, is not to be found by "circumnavigation of the
globe" but by looking inward and communing with
nature. The movement of society is a flux, and the man
caught up in it becomes trapped in the same useless motion:

> Society never advances. It recedes as fast on one side
> as it gains on the other. It undergoes continual
> changes. . . . Society is a wave. The wave moves on-
> ward, but the water of which it is composed does not.
> (pp. 166–68)

Constant change without essential results, with no *processional* dimension, characterizes the flux of society, for it
obscures somehow the essential center of divine spirit that
pulses into man and nature, "that in us which changes not
and which ranks all sensations and states of mind" (p. 357).

At times flux rather than process seems to Emerson to
characterize nature as well as society, but only when he
seems to miss the power of perception that makes him
aware of the essential identity pervading all change. "Motion or change and identity or rest are the first and second
secrets of nature," Emerson writes in the second series of
essays on "Nature" (p. 412). "Rest" is an unfortunate
choice of words, for what he really means is simply the
principle of identity and relatedness. He goes on to explain:

> Things are so strictly related that according to the skill
> of the eye, from any one object the parts and proper-
> ties of any other may be predicted. If we had eyes to
> see it, a bit of stone from the city wall would certify us
> of the necessity that man must exist, as readily as the
> city. That identity makes us all one, and reduces to
> nothing great intervals on our customary scale. (p. 413)

Later in this essay, however, the sense of flux pervading nature becomes very strong, as the intimate awareness of this relatedness is lost. Emerson finds himself in nature without the reinforcement of knowing this metamorphic identity, and his experience truly seems to be one of drift, rather than a process of affirmation. He writes:

In like manner, there is throughout nature something mocking, something that leads us on and on, but arrives nowhere; keeps no faith with us. All promise outruns the performance. We live in a system of approximations. Every end is prospective of some other end, which is also temporary; a round and final success nowhere. (p. 417)

Here the mood of exhaustion, which at times appears in Emerson's writing, is particularly strong. The paradox of endless motion is simply that man must give up all pretense of stability, of permanence, of certainty; and when faith in the value of the journey and the relatedness of its stages diminishes, Emerson is left in flux, alone with fragments. At this point in the essay his experience is characterized almost by despair, a poignant realization of the paradoxical nature of the journey: to be truly alive, one must endlessly experiment; but to endlessly experiment is to sacrifice any final knowledge and any kind of possession of truth:

It is the same among the men and women as among the silent trees; always a referred existence, an absence, never a presence and satisfaction. Is it that beauty can never be grasped? in persons and in landscape is equally inaccessible? (p. 419)

This despondency, however, quickly vanishes with the recovery of faith in the basic principle of unity, and Em-

erson pulls himself out of flux and restores himself to the
eternal procession of the divine spirit. The end of the
essay is fully optimistic and affirmative:

> We are escorted on every hand through life by spiritual
> agents, and a beneficient purpose lies in wait for us.
> We cannot bandy words with Nature, or deal with her
> as we deal with persons. If we measure our individual
> forces against hers we may easily feel as if we were the
> sport of an insuperable destiny. But if, instead of iden-
> tifying ourselves with the work, we feel that the soul of
> the Workman streams through us, we shall find the
> peace of the morning dwelling first in our hearts, and
> the fathomless powers of gravity and chemistry, and,
> over them, of life, pre-existing within us in their high-
> est form. (p. 420)

Despair and exhaustion are not often directly encoun-
tered in Emerson, but they are always present just below
the surface, representing a potentiality that is built in to
the very nature of his experience. "Emerson's unshaken
confidence," Matthiessen writes, "lay in the river's progression onward. . . . Isolation from any coherent community faded away in Emerson's sureness that he could step
immediately out of time into the living moment of eternity. He could therefore delight in the flow, except when
he tried to catch the meaning of the objects and events
that drifted past him, and found himself alone with lonely
fragments." [18] Even in such dark periods, however, Emerson's confidence remained strong. The opening of "The
Over-Soul" best explains the foundation of his continued
affirmation: "Our faith comes in moments; our vice is
habitual. Yet there is a depth in those brief moments
which constrains us to ascribe more reality to them than to
all other experiences" (p. 261).

Self and not self, spirit and matter, idea and object, these are the dualities that comprise Emerson's universe. The Soul and the Understanding represent these dualities psychologically, recreating within man the structural dualism of the cosmos.[19] These dualities form the poles of Emerson's vision, a vision that is always incomplete, kinetic, and experimental. Process and flux are the polar forms that this kinesis takes, and affirmation, exhaustion, and despair characterize the range of Emerson's emotive response to his experience. Except for those occasions when his rhetoric seems to take control of him, as, for example, the "transparent eyeball" passage, Emerson staunchly refuses to drift totally into any one of the dualities he has established; always he pulls himself back to that unstable middle point, to continue the journey and achieve in an endless succession of moments the necessary reconciliation. "I accept the clangor and jangle of contrary tendencies," he writes in "Experience." "Everything good is on the highway" (p. 351). At times he was able to feel and convey the immediate resolution of the various tensions and contradictions of his life. In a sudden flight of imagination or an upsurge of cosmically optimistic faith, the arcs of Emerson's circles were completed, and he achieved the state of being that Paul calls "spheral man." But Emerson's spheres were always dissembling into circles, endlessly promulgating one another and spreading themselves through polarization into rectangles—and Emerson was forced to continue his experiments and try to keep "the diagonal line."

The polarities, tensions, and ambiguities that characterize Emerson's struggle to reconcile the worlds of spirit and sense and to express this reconciliation in language are central to the tradition of Romantic thought in America. The dualities of self and not self that Emerson establishes are the basis of the Romantic vision, and although the ultimate goal is union of "the infinite and the finite," this union is almost inevitably an unstable one, achievable in fleeting instances, but always breaking down or growing stale and demanding to be recreated in a fresh way, in a new place, at another time, following always the kinetic line of the present moment. In the following essays I intend to examine the ways in which this unstable, experimental, and kinetic quality of American Romantic thought shapes the forms and meanings of particular works of art by studying it as it exists in dramatic and mythic form. This involves translating the complex of ideas and tendencies manifest in Emerson's writing into dramatic terms and viewing these ideas and tendencies as patterns of heroic consciousness and behavior. To facilitate such an analysis, I have sketched in the next few pages a framework that presents the various tendencies of Emerson's thought as possible versions of the Romantic world-view. This is a framework of purely ideal types, against which to measure and in terms of which to compare the kinds of self–not self relationship in which a specific hero exists at any given time.

For analytical purposes it is convenient to view the Romantic cosmos as composed of two opposite realms, which are exhaustive and mutually exclusive: self, on the one hand, and everything that is not self on the other, implying everything that is external to the soul or mind. The not self, furthermore, can be separated into two primary divisions: natural, referring—as Emerson says, in the "common" sense—to "essences unchanged by man," and social.

It is also helpful, in terms of the social not self, to distinguish three levels of interaction: societal, communal, and individual. Societal refers simply to the highest level of social abstraction, the whole complex of customs, values, and institutions that characterizes life in a given geographical area at a given time; communal refers to a smaller, more intimate grouping of people, with a larger sense of common bond and a shared identity; the individual dimension refers simply to any other human being. These divisions are helpful because the not self is rarely confronted in monolithic terms. Emerson, for example, responds in a wholly positive manner to the natural not self, finds little value in the societal not self, and is somewhat ambiguous in his attitude toward communal and individual relationships.

Both self and the various aspects of the not self may be conceived in either monistic or dualistic terms, that is, as being composed of a single type of primary substance, or, as in Emerson's view, as being composed of two kinds of substances. For Emerson the dualism of the cosmos was represented by spirit and matter, and the psychological internalization of this dualism was expressed by the Soul and the Understanding; in a more general sense we can speak of two kinds of reality: a surface reality underlaid by a more powerful, spiritual, essential core of Reality. A parallel possibility exists within the self: a surface of personality, formed by sense impressions, social roles, and the various images contributed by other people, and an essential core of inviolable selfhood. This dualism is reflected in Emerson's separation of the faculties of the mind into the Understanding and the Soul. The Understanding is social and wholly practical, formed by, and operating

upon, sense impressions, using nature as "commodity";
the Soul, or Reason, is divine, with a wholly independent
status, and forms the essential core of self.

Furthermore, both self and not self—and the various
divisions of each that I have outlined—may be imbued
with affective connotations. Any or all aspects of the not
self may be perceived as wholly good, wholly evil, or as an
ambiguous mixture of good and evil. The same holds true
for the self. It may be wholly divine and good, as it is for
the Transcendentalists, or it may be a dark abyss of night-
marish psychoses, as it often was for Poe. In addition, the
ultimate source or ground of value in the world may be
seen to be located in any one of these divisions: within the
self, within reality or some vital core of Reality, equally suffused throughout, or not existent at all until created by
man. In cases where the value in the universe is perceived
to be antecedent to human action, we may speak of it as
being *essential;* if it is only consequent to human action,
we may speak of it as *existential.*

It is a relatively simple matter to translate the structural
possibilities of this model into ideal types of heroic action.
The possibilities may perhaps be conceptualized most
clearly in the form of a continuum, ranging from the complete dismissal of concern with all that is not self at one
pole, to the bestowal of individual identity to a larger
whole at the other extreme. These poles represent a dra-
matization of the dualities that the American Romantics
try to mediate and hold together. Rarely is the heroic
experience characterized by these polar responses, but they
express the directions in which the experience tends to
move when the ineffable sense of union collapses and between the peaks of experience when it is achieved.

At the "self" pole of the dichotomy, the heroic experience is characterized by an apocalypse of the imagination, a total abandonment of conventional external reality for private adventures, in effect the creation of a new world patterned solely by the imagination. Such a response has two major forms: retreat into a solipsistic kind of isolation, or the attempt to impose the imaginative vision upon external reality. The solipsistic response involves a recoil from a not self that appears to be valueless into a state in which pure selfhood is cultivated to the fullest extent. All reality is seen to be subjective, all value to be derived from, and grounded within, the self. The hero, as will be suggested in dealing with Poe's *The Narrative of A. Gordon Pym,* creates a world in which the entirety of being ultimately consists of expanded selfhood. Such a world has the potential for positive ideality, but as often as not the solipsistic vision has strong negative overtones and becomes a nightmare of hideous and catastrophic proportions. Unlike the solipsist, the imposing hero—Captain Ahab, for example—does not deny the reality of the not self, only its value. He attempts to bestow his own value upon it making it answer to his own inwardness, and remolding it according to his own specifications. Often the hero has a conception of reality different from the reality in which he finds himself and is able to make his own personal vision manifest only by trying to force the not self to adhere to it. Such is the position toward which Emerson tends to move in his most idealistic moments. Ahab gives us a much darker version of the same tendency.

Response at the opposite pole can also be viewed in two ways, depending upon the manner in which the hero perceives the not self. The surrender of self can be a relinquishment of the personal ego to a greater whole, an absolute divinity or a world soul, which is perceived to be the source of all value and of which the hero may partake only by sacrificing his claim to an individual identity. In this situation the individual soul is submerged into the whole, philosophically implying a pantheistic mysticism. This, too, is a position toward which Emerson tends at those times when he feels himself "part or parcel of God," and is the typical experience of the Christian mystic. In *Moby Dick* it is embodied in the experience of Pip and suggested by several of Ishmael's reveries. However, the gesture of surrender may also have strong negative overtones, as it does to Ishmael in "The Mast-Head," for example. If the not self appears not divine but rather hostile and overbearing, surrender is not relinquishment but renunciation, a surrender to death and defeat rather than to an absolute that offers value and redemption.

At either of these poles of response the Romantic kinesis characteristically takes the hero away from reality, away from the bonds of space and time to a realm where values are chiefly inward or transcendental. Between these poles, in the vast middle range where the Romantic experience generally takes place, the hero's motion is toward or through reality. The mode of the poles is one of estrangement; between them it is one of engagement and continuing encounters with the various social and natural aspects of the not self. If the hero finds in the not self an equivalent response to his own expanding and expressive selfhood, as Emerson found in nature, for example, this endless motion may yield continual affirmation and satisfaction. In this case it appears as a form of what I have designated *process,* and it is the characteristic movement found in Thoreau and Whitman. But if the not self seems hostile or recalcitrant, if the hero fails to achieve any satisfactory type of union, the experience may be laden with despair, and the sense of achievement may degenerate until the hero envisions himself adrift in a world of meaningless *flux*. Such moments can be found in Whitman, and they become dominant in *Moby Dick* and in William Carlos Williams's *Paterson*. In such a situation it is not at all unusual to find the hero moving toward a polar position and seeking death as the only possible release from his exhaustion and despair.

To summarize, then, we can posit six ideal types of response, each dependent upon the particular way in which the universe is perceived at any given time, that may serve as reference points in studying the experience of individual heroes: solipsistic isolation, which may be either dream or nightmare, and imposition—both versions of an apocalyptic imagination; process and flux—the positive and negative aspects of the continuing encounter with reality; merger with a greater whole and surrender to an external force—the positive and negative forms of the relinquishment of self. Rarely do these ideal types actually exist in their pure forms, but they can be seen as strands weaving in and out of the texture of the whole Romantic movement, and the tendencies they represent can be seen not as "deviations" from the optimistic Romantic vision of unity through imagination, but rather as the actualization of potentialities that are inherent in the very nature of the Romantic sensibility.

One

WALDEN

THE EQUIVALENT RESPONSE

Henry David Thoreau, in his life as well as in his art, was preoccupied with the same problem that Emerson grappled with in *Nature* and his other writings. It was the problem, as Perry Miller has put it, "of striking and maintaining the delicate balance between object and reflection, of fact and truth, of minute observation and generalized concept." [1] But as Miller pointed out long ago, Thoreau and Emerson approached this romantic dilemma in different ways. Miller highlights the distinction by juxtaposing Emerson's "transparent eyeball" passage with the following 3 March 1839 entry from Thoreau's journal concerning "the poet":

> He must be something more than natural—even supernatural. Nature will not speak through but along with him. His voice will not proceed from her midst, but, breathing on her, will make her the expression of his thought. He then poetizes when he takes a fact out of nature into spirit. He speaks without reference to time or place. His thought is one world, hers another. He is another Nature,—Nature's brother. Kindly offices do they perform for one another. Each publishes the other's truth. [2]

For Emerson, transcendence implied essentially the ability to view and understand the world of matter, of here-and-now reality, in terms of its relationship to the more essential and immortal Reality of spirit. The vehicle of transcendence for Emerson was the symbol, a means of expression that enabled him to bridge the gap between the world of nature and the world of idea by being true to the fact yet standing for something larger than itself and thus conveying his awareness of the infinite within the moment of experience. Emerson's conception of the symbol—and perhaps, as Joel Porte has suggested, his entire emotional make-up—led him to view nature in a largely *mediate* fashion, as primarily valuable in its capacity to direct the attention beyond itself.[3] Often Emerson found himself so far beyond nature that all concrete particularity vanished. Such was rarely the case with Thoreau. Much more than Emerson, Thoreau emphasized the intrinsic and particular value of nature, and he took a pleasure that Emerson did not in sheer physical contact with the natural world. If the value of nature was *mediate* to Emerson, it was *immediate* to Thoreau, and this difference manifested itself in their styles. As Emerson's imagination operated by perceiving and creating symbols, so Thoreau's imagination constructed metaphors. By viewing both the human object and the natural object *immediately* and investing each with the qualities of the other, Thoreau was able to achieve a balanced union between nature and the self. In Thoreau's metaphors, "each publishes the other's truth."

Thoreau's reasons for going to live in the woods were many and mixed. Probably, as Henry Seidel Canby suggests, it was primarily "the result of economic forethought," a "common-sense expedient." He wanted to sustain himself as cheaply as possible in order to be able to continue his writing.[4] As his own Transcendentalist hero, however, Thoreau in going to Walden is embarking on a quest to create with language a world in which elements of self and not self are held together in delicate balance, a world in which nature and the self are made metaphors of each other and the dualities of the here-and-now reality of the world are transcended by the creation through metaphor of a realm in which they are unified. *Walden* is such a transcendent realm, created by style—"a world elsewhere," to use Richard Poirier's phrase.[5] But it is also a world that contains a record of its own creation, and it is to this record that we must turn to study the heroic experience of Thoreau in dramatic terms.

Thoreau begins his quest with a retreat from society. He makes the reasons for this retreat explicit in his opening chapter, "Economy," which is both a sweeping account of Thoreau's quarrel with the New England society of the 1840s and a prelude to the drama that is to follow. Thoreau's criticism of society has been studied in detail and needs no elaboration here, but among his many motives for leaving society two are especially relevant to the present study: the fact that the superfluities of society keep him from a meaningful encounter with essential Reality, and the fact that life in society is a life of constant and meaningless flux.[6] "My purpose in going to Walden Pond," Thoreau writes, "was not to live cheaply or dearly there, but to transact some private business with the fewest obstacles; to be hindered from accomplishing which for want of a little common sense, a little enterprise and business talent, appeared not so sad as foolish."[7] The idea, as Paul has suggested, is "to reduce the problem of perception to its simplest terms—man and nature."[8] The key

word for Thoreau is "simplification," a purge of superficiality that can only be accomplished by a withdrawal
from society. The primary motive is to free the self from
a life that is necessarily rendered crass and degrading by
society. Thus, Thoreau endeavors to dismiss all but essential elements. Food, clothing, fuel, and shelter are retained
only because they seem to be prerequisites to the encounter he desires: "For not till we have secured these are we
prepared to entertain the true problems of life with freedom and a prospect of success" (p. 32). Beyond these essentials, all products of society are impediments: "Most of
the luxuries, and many of the so-called comforts of life, are
not only not indispensable, but positive hindrances to the
elevation of mankind" (p. 33). Life in society, however,
also debases the individual in another, related way. Not
only do societal superfluities keep man from encountering
the divinity of the natural world but they also operate to
obscure the natural divinity of man. Very early in the
chapter, Thoreau makes this clear by referring to the
example of the teamster:

> Talk of a divinity in man! Look at the teamster on the
> highway, wending to market by day or night; does any
> divinity stir within him? How godlike, how immortal
> is he? (p. 28)

Society for Thoreau means not only men, their artifacts,
and their institutions but also man's inheritance. "I see
young men, my townsmen, whose misfortune it is to have
inherited farms, houses, barns, cattle, and farming tools;
for these are more easily acquired than got rid of. Better
if they had been born in the open pasture and suckled by
a wolf, that they might have seen with clearer eyes what
field they were called to labor in" (p. 26). This inheritance

includes not only physical legacies but also tradition, the entire mass of culture that has been passed down and internalized from previous generations. Outworn tradition must be dismissed before the self can be free. "Old deeds for old people, and new deeds for new," Thoreau declares. "Age is no better, hardly so well, qualified for an instructor of youth, for it has not profited so much as it has lost" (p. 29). Later in the chapter, Thoreau returns to this motif in the famous passage dealing with the deacon's tapeworm, which was to be sold at an auction of his belongings. Thoreau suggests that man would do much better to follow the example of the "primitive tribes," to "cast off slough annually," and rid himself of the effects of his ancestors. Unfortunately, in the case of the deacon, "instead of a *bonfire,* or purifying destruction of them, there was an *auction,* or increasing of them" (p. 71). Thoreau's chapter, "Economy," attempts to remedy this situation by being itself such a "purifying destruction," not only of society, but also of all cumbersome inheritance from the past and all obligation to the future. Thoreau declares:

> In any weather, at any hour of the day or night, I have been anxious to improve the nick of time, and notch it on my stick too; to stand on the meeting of two eternities, the past and the future, which is precisely the present moment; to toe that line. (p. 35)

This emphasis on the eternal present suggests Thoreau's second major reason for rejecting life in society: to escape from endless flux. Nature itself, of course, is characterized by metamorphosis in *Walden,* but the change is one that predominantly aspires to higher forms of being. Paul has examined many of these symbols of gradual transformation, all of which contain a movement to a higher form, for example, the motifs of seed-flower-fruit and grub-chrysalis-butterfly.[9] Even men, Thoreau states, "if they should feel the spring of springs arousing them . . . , would of necessity rise to a higher and more ethereal life" (pp. 52–53). The motions of man in society, however, are circular, reaching not upward but only repeating themselves without reward, so that to Thoreau the inhabitants of Concord appear "to be doing penance in a thousand remarkable ways." He compares their tasks to the labors of Hercules, which he finds "were trifling in comparison with those which my neighbors have undertaken; for they were only twelve and had an end; but I could never see that these men slew or captured any monster or finished any labor" (p. 26). Thoreau's purpose is to escape from the vicious circle of society—to make baskets, but unlike the strolling Indian of his parable, to "avoid the necessity of selling them" (p. 36), and thus to live in debt neither to the past nor to the future. He writes:

> We have built for this world a family mansion, and for the next a family tomb. The best works of art are the expression of man's struggle to free himself from this condition, but the effect of our art is merely to make this low state comfortable and that higher state to be forgotten. There is actually no place in this village for a work of *fine* art. (p. 50)

Only by leaving the village could Thoreau free himself to build the mansion of fine art that *Walden* aspires to be, a work intended not to make life in society comfortable but, by leaving society behind, to escape its endless flux and rise to the "higher state" in which the self and nature become united in the higher reality of the world soul.

Thoreau rejects society not only as a macrocosm but also

in its microcosmic form, the relationship of one man with another. For Thoreau the path to fulfillment must bypass human brotherhood or communication. Thoreau makes this explicit toward the end of "Economy" by relating a "story" that he had "overheard":

> I heard it proposed lately that two young men should travel together over the world, the one without money, earning his means as he went, before the mast and behind the plow, the other carrying a bill of exchange in his pocket. It was easy to see that they could not long be companions or cooperate, since one would not *operate* at all. They would part at the first interesting crisis in their adventure. Above all, as I have implied, the man who goes alone can start to-day; but he who travels with another man must wait till that other is ready, and it may be a long time before they get off. (pp. 74–75)

Here, Thoreau rejects community for the same reason he rejects society; it simply impinges too greatly upon the freedom of the self.

Thoreau elaborates upon his attitudes toward friendship in the chapter "Visitors." He begins by affirming that he is not, by nature, necessarily a recluse: "I think that I love society as much as most, and am ready to fasten myself like a bloodsucker for the time to any full-blooded man that comes in my way. I am naturally no hermit, but might possibly sit out the sturdiest frequenter of the barroom, if my business called me thither" (p. 126). The qualification in the final clause of this passage is extremely important, however, for Thoreau's "business," as he has made clear in "Economy," is *private* business, and it takes him not to the local tavern but to the shores of Walden Pond. A few sentences later, he describes the "ideal" human communication:

> If we would enjoy the most intimate society with that
> in each of us which is without, or above, being spoken
> to, we must not only be silent, but commonly so far
> apart bodily that we cannot hear each other's voice in
> any case. (p. 127)

This, of course, is communication with the self. Thoreau's reasoning here is sensible. By participating in society, or even in the most basic forms of human dialogue,
man must relinquish or at least transform some of his
individuality. Sacrificing any part of the self to a social
role was for Thoreau to sacrifice too much; and only in
silence and solitude could the full nature of selfhood be
realized. Much later in *Walden,* Thoreau again describes
this "ideal" communication, speaking now of "one older
man, an excellent fisher and skilled in all kinds of wood-
craft":

> Once in a while we sat together on the pond, he at one
> end of the boat, and I at the other; but not many words
> passed between us, for he had grown deaf in his later
> years. . . . Our intercourse was thus altogether one of
> unbroken harmony, far more pleasing to remember than
> if it had been carried on by speech. (p. 151)

The perfect communication, then, is no communication at
all, or better yet, communication with the self. Thoreau
continues: "When, as commonly was the case, I had none
to commune with, I used to raise the echoes by striking
with a paddle on the side of my boat, filling the surrounding woods with circling and dilating sound" (p. 152).

It might be argued that, despite the silence, there is
indeed a substantial amount of human *communion,* as
opposed to communication, recorded in these passages.
Transcendental theory would seem to support this asser-

tion. If divinity flows into the self and nature, it obviously flows into the selves of all men; and if the hero is to find fulfillment by uniting the currents of divinity, why not do so by means of communion with other people, any other person being, for the hero, a part of the not self? Indeed, if the Transcendentalists, like Whitman, had accepted the body as well as the intellect as being endowed with divinity, their theory could easily have led to an apotheosis of sexual love as the ultimate means of self-fulfillment— an act in which the self is at once expressing its own creativity and uniting with the essential not self. As it was, however, the Transcendentalists, and perhaps Thoreau more than most, largely repudiated their sexuality in favor of the "higher laws" of the intellect. Thoreau explains that "the generative energy, which, when we are loose, dissipates and makes us unclean, when we are continent invigorates and inspires us. Chastity is the flowering of man; and what are called Genius, Heroism, Holiness, and the like, are but various fruits which succeed it" (p. 184). Perhaps, then, Thoreau has sublimated his desire for sexual communion, locating it on a level at which silent, spiritual intercourse replaces the sexual act and gives the hero the same type of fulfillment that he finds in communion with essential nature.

Such an interpretation is probably possible, but two of the major motifs of *Walden* argue against it. The first is Thoreau's constant allusion to the fact that the great majority of men, unlike nature, have violated their inherent divinity. The example of the teamster has already been mentioned. In "Higher Laws" Thoreau describes the way in which man generically has allowed the body and the animal instincts to spoil the divinity of the intellect. Metaphorically, he is describing the desirable progression

in a man's career as a woodsman: "He goes thither at first
as a hunter and fisher, until at last, if he has the seeds of
a better life in him, he distinguishes his proper objects, as
a poet or naturalist it may be, and leaves the gun and the
fish-pole behind. The mass of men are still and always
young in this respect" (p. 179). The human other, having
spoiled his natural divinity, hardly seems capable of presenting an equivalent response to the pure, unspoiled force
projected by the heroic self.

Second, upon close scrutiny the figures with whom Thoreau portrays this type of communion hardly seem to be
"real" individuals, but rather creations of Thoreau's imagination, projections possibly of Thoreau himself. The
encounters, viewed in this light, seem to be primarily
representations of what we have already seen to be Thoreau's idea of perfect communication—a dialogue with
the self. The "old settler," for example, who "is thought
to be dead" (and whom some critics have associated with
Christ) [10] and the "elderly dame . . . of unequalled fer-
tility . . . , whose memory runs back farther than mythology," (Mary?) are such individuals (p. 124), never definitely described and surrounded by an aura of obscurity
and ambiguity, so that they might easily be objectifications
of the heroic self. Thoreau, in fact, shortly before intro-
ducing the "old settler," describes his ability to achieve
just this sort of objectification:

> I only know myself as a human entity; the scene, so to
> speak, of thoughts and affections; and am sensible of a
> certain doubleness by which I can stand as remote from
> myself as from another. However intense my experience,
> I am conscious of the presence and criticism of a part of
> me which, as it were, is not a part of me, but a specta-
> tor, sharing no experience, but taking note of it, and
> that it is no more I than it is you. (p. 122)

In still other places Thoreau describes explicitly his habit of populating the woods with creations of his own imagination. In winter, for example, he relates that "for human society I was obliged to conjure up the former occupants of these woods" (p. 211). The man with whom Thoreau seems to find communion in his boat is described only as "an old fisher" (Peter?); the conversation in "Brute Neighbors" is between a hermit and a poet—both designations, of course, are applicable to Thoreau himself. Other visitors and acquaintances are described so generically that they have no real sense of individuality. Their names, John Farmer and John Field, for example, define them only as possible variations of Thoreau himself. The one notable exception is the French-Canadian laborer, who exists as a distinct and vivid figure; and with him Thoreau retains a sense of distance and perplexity:

> I sometimes saw in him a man whom I had not seen before, and I did not know whether he was as wise as Shakespeare or as simply ignorant as a child, whether to suspect him of a fine poetic consciousness or of stupidity. (p. 132)

It would seem, then, that Thoreau, though perhaps conceiving of the possibility of this type of rewarding spiritual encounter with men, has never been able to actualize the possibility. Thus, he writes in the latter stages of *Walden:*

> There too, as everywhere, I sometimes expected the Visitor who never comes. The Vishnu Purana says, "The house-holder is to remain at eventide in his court-yard as long as it takes to milk a cow, or longer if he pleases, to await the arrival of a guest." I often performed this duty of hospitality, waited long enough to milk a whole herd of cows, but did not see the man approaching from the town. (p. 221)

Thoreau, consequently, must finally reject human brotherhood as a source of fruitful encounter.

But if Thoreau turns away from society, and even from basic human communication, he does not go so far as to affirm the position of isolated selfhood. His commitment to self outweighs any sense of commitment to society, but it is held in check by a larger commitment to divinity as it manifests itself in nature. The self must be cultivated, but only for the purpose of union with divine nature. Thoreau attaches great importance to the physical senses and takes a real joy in sensual awareness; as Joel Porte observes, he "is alive so long as he can feel himself in contact with the world; and it is just this desire for both specificity and totality of perception that allows him to lump his senses in the only way in which they will not lose their individuality—the unity of synesthesia." [11] Yet, coupled with this sensual joy throughout *Walden,* there is a running undercurrent of revulsion for the body. Thoreau's distaste for the sexual act has already been mentioned, but this repudiation influences other aspects of his thought as well. In the opening pages Thoreau, speaking of inheritance, mentions that "the portionless, who struggle with no such unnecessary inherited encumberances, find it labor enough to subdue and cultivate a few cubic feet of flesh." (p. 26) Thoreau acknowledges the urge toward sensual pleasure, but also recognizes the need to overcome it:

> Perhaps there is none but has cause for shame on account of the inferior and brutish nature to which he is allied. I fear that we are such gods or demi-gods only as fauns and satyrs, the divine allied to beasts, the creatures of appetite, and that, to some extent, our very life is our disgrace. . . . Nature [human and sensual] is hard to overcome, but she must be overcome. (p. 184)

The point to be made here is that though the physical joy of sensual awareness is important and perhaps indispensable to Thoreau, the senses are never to be used self-indulgently and are always to be kept subordinate to the imagination or intellect. The clearest account of this attitude is found, of course, in "Higher Laws," from which examples have already been cited. Thoreau, for instance, explains his diet of bread, rice, and water:

> Like many of my contemporaries, I had rarely for many years used animal food, or tea, or coffee, etc.; not so much because of any ill effects which I had traced to them, as because they were not agreeable to my imagination. The repugnance to animal food is not the effect of experience, but is an instinct. (p. 180)

In contrast to an exoticist, who cultivates sensual experience for the purpose of increasing the intensity of the awareness of self, Thoreau's senses are directed outward and used primarily for an increased awareness of nature; and unlike what Thoreau considered to be the practice of the mass of men, he would not allow the senses to conquer and violate his divinity. His ideal is not to wallow in selfhood but, by utilizing his sensual faculties with careful discipline, to cultivate that portion of the self, the intellect, which is imbued with divine power and to prepare it for the encounter with a similarly divine nature. Although physical sensations are important, the intellect is paramount:

> The intellect is a cleaver; it discerns and rifts its way into the secret of things. I do not wish to be any more busy with my hands than is necessary. My head is hands and feet. I feel all my best faculties concentrated in it . . . , and with it I would mine and burrow my way

through these hills. I think that the richest vein is
somewhere hereabouts; so by the divining rod and
thin rising vapors I judge; and here I will begin to
mine. (p. 95)

There are points in *Walden* where Thoreau seems to
move toward self-indulgence, but he always stops short of
this point and returns to the necessity of the encounter
with nature. Indeed, Thoreau describes at least one occasion when selfhood begins to be almost oppressive and
is redeemed only through contact with external reality:

To be alone was something unpleasant. But I was at the
same time conscious of a slight insanity in my mood, and
seemed to foresee my recovery. In the midst of a gentle
rain, while these thoughts prevailed, I was suddenly
aware of such sweet and beneficent society in Nature, in
the very patterning of the drops, and in every sound and
sight around my house, an infinite and unaccountable
friendliness all at once like an atmosphere sustaining me.
(p. 120)

It is only in communion with nature that the hero can
find the true fulfillment he is seeking. Even with this
premise, however, the task is not simple, for just as the
hero can accept neither life in society nor a position of
pure selfhood, so the encounter with nature must be characterized by neither the surrender nor the imposition of
the self. As the Transcendental duality tends to pull apart,
Thoreau leans now toward one and now toward the other
of these alternatives, but he always attempts to bring himself back to a position of balanced tension and steer a
course that mediates between them. Nature and the self
must meet on equal terms. This balanced encounter is
achieved by populating the world of *Walden* with specific,

detailed, and faithful examinations of both nature and the self, and by making nature and the self metaphors of each other. Through this process *Walden* itself becomes an entirely new world. The manner in which this is accomplished can perhaps best be understood by examining three of the major metaphorical relationships that Thoreau establishes in *Walden:* the house, the bean field, and the pond itself.

Building a house becomes for Thoreau at once an expression of the creative impulse of the self and a means by which the self can be related to nature. As Richard Poirier has explained, the motif of building represents a process by which a man can join forces with the power of nature and make its style his style.[12] As he began *Walden* by rejecting both society and tradition, so Thoreau begins his house by destroying all the elements of the past that might tend to taint it. He begins by insisting that it must be unfurnished:

> At present our houses are cluttered and defiled with it [furniture], and a good housewife would sweep out the greater part into the dust-hole, and not have the morning's work undone. . . . I had three pieces of limestone on my desk, but I was terrified to find that they required to be dusted daily, when the furniture of my mind was all undusted still, and I threw them out the window in disgust. How, then, could I have a furnished house? I would rather sit in the open air, for no dust gathers on the grass, unless where man has broken ground. (p. 49)

To fill in the frame of his house, Thoreau purchases James Collins's shanty, but the shanty must be torn down and the wood purified before Thoreau will use it: "I took down this dwelling the same morning, drawing the nails, and removed it to the pond-side by small cartloads, spreading the boards on the grass there to bleach and warp back again in the sun" (p. 54). The frame itself is to be built of fresh pine timbers, hewn by Thoreau himself, who, in the process, refrains from imposing himself upon them; instead, he attempts to become "intimate" with them. By becoming thoroughly familiar with the pine boughs, Thoreau can draw some of the house inside him and include a part of himself in the frame of the house. Thoreau describes the process at work:

> I usually carried my dinner of bread and butter, and read the newspaper in which it was wrapped, at noon, sitting among the green boughs which I had cut off, and to my bread was imparted some of their fragrance, for my hands were covered with a thick coat of pitch. Before I had done, I was more the friend than the foe of the pine tree, though I had cut down some of them, having become better acquainted with it. (p. 53)

In this fashion, by careful design, the house becomes simultaneously an expression of the self and an expression of nature. The house must first conform to the life of the individual. Regarding ornament, Thoreau maintains: "Let our houses first be lined with beauty, where they come in contact with our lives, like the tenement of the shell-fish, and not overlaid with it" (p. 51). Indeed, the house becomes a major creative expression of the individual:

> It would be worth the while to build still more deliberately than I did, considering, for instance, what foundation a door, a window, a cellar, a garret have in the nature of man, and perchance never raising any superstructure until we found a better reason for it than our temporal necessities even. There is some of the same

fitness in a man's building his own house that there is in a bird's building its own nest. Who knows but if men constructed their dwellings with their own hands . . . , the poetic faculty would be universally developed, as birds universally sing when they are so engaged. (pp. 55–56)

Suffused with the spirit of the individual and constructed from the materials of nature, the house contains an intermixture of self and other. There is no longer a need to maintain the distinction between the two, and Thoreau can state:

> My "best room," however, my withdrawing room, always ready for company, on whose carpet the sun rarely fell, was the pine wood behind my house. Thither in summer days, when distinguished guests came, I took them, and a priceless domestic swept the floor and dusted the furniture and kept the things in order. (p. 127)

The metaphorical as well as physical foundation of the house is the cellar. There is a downward movement, a movement into the soil, present throughout *Walden*, which represents the hero's search for a base of divine Reality in the natural world. In chapter two, Thoreau describes this process:

> Let us settle ourselves, and work and wedge our feet downward through the mud and slush of opinion, and prejudice, and tradition, and delusion, and appearance . . . till we come to a hard bottom and rocks in place, which we can call *reality*, and say, This is, and no mistake; and then begin. (p. 94)

Digging the cellar of his house is such a descent. Thoreau writes of the digging:

It was but two hour's work. I took particular pleasure in this breaking of ground, for in almost all latitudes men dig into the earth for an equable temperature. Under the most splendid house in the city is still to be found the cellar where they store their roots as of old, and long after the superstructure has disappeared posterity remark its dent in the earth. The house is still but a porch at the entrance of a burrow. (p. 55)

Later, Thoreau associates the cellar with the foundation of truth and divinity in man, completing the metaphorical union:

What do we want most to dwell near to? . . . to the perennial source of our life, whence in all our experience we have found that to issue, as the willow stands near the water and sends out its roots in that direction. This will vary with different natures, but this is the place where a wise man will dig his cellar. (p. 121)

The downward movement, however, is only one half of the essential meaning of Thoreau's metaphor. The search for the seat of divinity in man and nature is only a prelude to the aspiration for transcendence. Thus, the metaphors of *Walden* include also a soaring motif, upward, toward God, so that the metaphor itself becomes a tenuous link between self, nature, and divine world soul, a connecting mechanism. In the metaphor of the house this linkage is found in the chimney, which emerges from the earth and rises upward to the heavens. Thoreau devotes only one brief paragraph to the construction of the chimney, but insists that it is "the most vital part of the house" and emphasizes the extremely "deliberate" manner in which it was constructed:

I was pleased to see my work rising so square and solid
by degrees, and reflected that, if it proceeded slowly, it
was calculated to endure a long time. The chimney is
to some extent an independent structure, standing on
the ground, and rising through the house to the heavens; even after the house is burned it still stands sometimes, and its importance and independence are apparent. (pp. 200–201)

The chimney represents the link by which the house is
related to divinity, and through this relation the old world
of dualities is transcended and a totally new world is
created, centered about the hero in communion with
nature and divinity: "Wherever I sat, there I might live,
and the landscape radiated from me accordingly. What is
a house but a *sedes,* a seat" (p. 82)? This new world is one
unaffected by time and unrestricted by space, in which the
hero has total freedom of consciousness:

Both place and time were changed, and I dwelt nearer
to those parts of the universe and to those eras in history
which had most attracted me. Where I lived was as far
off as many a region viewed nightly by astronomers.
We are wont to imagine rare and delectable places
in some remote and celestial corner of the system,
behind the constellation of Cassiopeia's Chair, far from
noise and disturbance. I discovered that my house actually had its sight in such a withdrawn, but forever new
and unprofaned, part of the universe. (p. 87)

The process revealed in the metaphor of the house can
perhaps be summarized in this manner: the hero makes
the house an expression of his own creativity and also an
expression of divine nature, searching downward for the
foundation of divinity in both. Having succeeded in meta-

phorically uniting these dual currents of divinity, the hero
reaches upward toward transcendence of the world of
space and time and realizes the fulfillment of his eternal
vision. The metaphor of the bean field echoes these concerns and repeats this progression, but here Thoreau's
greatest problem is to achieve the fine balance required
between imposition and surrender of the self, either of
which will negate the possibility of the hero's union on
equal terms with nature.

Most farming, Thoreau maintains, makes man a slave to
the land, causing the spoilation of his divinity and the
sacrifice of his individuality to the soil: "Men labor under
a mistake. The better part of the man is soon plowed into
the soil for compost. . . . It is a fool's life, as they will
find when they get to the end of it, if not before" (p. 27).
By approaching nature with a self-centered world-view,
man violates the essential divinity of the natural not self.
Thoreau is conscious of his own tendency toward this
position, struggles against it, and realizes that to some
extent he has failed to avoid it: "We might try our lives
by a thousand simple tests, as, for instance, that the same
sun which ripens my beans illumines at once a system of
earths like ours. If I had remembered this it would have
prevented some mistakes. This was not the light in which
I hoed them" (p. 30). This realization leads him to advocate a complete dismissal of any attempt to impose the self
upon the land: "A man is rich in proportion to the number of things which he can afford to leave alone" (p. 82).
"I knew all the while that it [the land] would yield the
most abundant crop of the kind I wanted, if I could only
afford to let it alone" (p. 84). It seems that only by following this orientation, by refraining from imposing the self

upon the land, can man keep from defiling both himself and nature.

This approach, however, precludes the essential contact that is necessary if the hero is to reach his transcendent goal, and thus, it is highly unsatisfactory. Thoreau, consequently, moves toward the other end of the scale. By relinquishing any claim to individual expression, the self may become a part of nature and, in this indifferent state, allow the land to develop freely, according to its own impulse:

> The gentle rain which waters my beans and keeps me in the house today is not drear and melancholy, but good for me, too. . . . If it should continue so long as to cause the seeds to rot in the ground and destroy the potatoes in the low lands, it would still be good for the grass on the uplands, and, being good for the grass, it would be good for me. (pp. 119–20)

Here the self is seen as an indiscriminate part of nature, but this type of contact has been achieved only by the sacrifice of individual identity. This, too, finally will not do. A resolution must be reached whereby nature is allowed to exist freely and the self is able to engage in the necessary encounter. Thoreau finds this resolution in the metaphor of the "half-cultivated" bean field:

> Mine was, as it were, the connecting link between wild and cultivated fields; as some states are civilized, and others half-civilized, and others savage or barbarous, so my field was, though not in a bad sense, a half-cultivated field. They were beans cheerfully returning to their wild and primitive state that I cultivated, and my hoe played the *Ranz des Vaches* for them. (p. 139)

Half-cultivation is Thoreau's compromise between the extremes of imposition and surrender, tenuously combining self-assertion with relinquishment. As in the building of his house, Thoreau's technique is to first achieve intimacy with nature and then make the expression of the earth identical with the expression of the self. As in building, so in cultivation Thoreau works "deliberately" and alone: "As I had little aid from horses or cattle, or hired men or boys, or improved implements of husbandry, I was much slower, and became much more intimate with my beans than usual" (p. 138). As the metaphor continues, it becomes clear that it is this intimacy, rather than the vegetables themselves, that is being cultivated:

> It was a singular experience, that long acquaintance which I cultivated with beans, what with planting and hoeing, and harvesting, and threshing, and picking over and selling them,—the last was the hardest of all—I might add eating, for I did taste. I was determined to know beans. (p. 141)

Identity of expression grows from this intimacy. Unlike the French-Canadian who innocently imposes his own expression upon nature by writing the name of his parish in the snow, Thoreau allows nature to express itself, asserting his own will by lightly manipulating the natural processes:

> This was my curious labor all summer,—to make this portion of the earth's surface, which had yielded only cinquefoil, blackberries, johnswort, and the like, before, sweet wild fruits and pleasant flowers, produce instead this pulse. (p. 137)

There is no distinct mark of self-expression; rather, "one of the results of my presence and influence is seen in these

beans, corn blades, and potato vines" (p. 138). There is
self-assertion without disruption of natural processes:

> Removing the weeds, putting fresh soil about the bean
> stems, and encouraging this weed which I had sown,
> making the yellow soil express its summer thought in
> bean leaves and blossoms rather than in wormwood and
> pipes and millet grass, making the earth say beans in-
> stead of grass,—this was my daily work. (p. 138)

In the latter part of the chapter Thoreau turns to the
other half of the metaphor and explains clearly the reason
for his labor:

> Not that I wanted beans to eat, for I am by nature a
> Pythagorean, so far as beans are concerned, whether
> they mean porridge or voting, and exchanged them for
> rice; but, perchance, as some must work in the fields if
> only for the sake of tropes and expression, to serve a
> parable-maker one day. (p. 142)

The "parable-maker" is Thoreau himself and *Walden* is
his parable. The product of his labor is not beans but a
new world, which is created by the union of self and other
and in which the reality of both self and other is transcended:

> When my hoe tinkled against the stones, that music
> echoed to the woods and the sky, and was an accom-
> paniment to my labor which yielded an instant and im-
> measurable crop. It was no longer beans that I hoed,
> nor I that hoed beans. (p. 140)

Like Thoreau's chimney, which connects heaven and
earth, his half-cultivated bean field is a transition, a link
that unites him with divinity. The same is true of the

pond itself, the central metaphor of *Walden*. Thoreau begins the metaphor of the pond by offering a detailed record of its physical description and metamorphoses, allowing it to exist in the world of *Walden* in all its uniqueness and individuality, allowing it, as it were, a full range of self-expression. Although there is a continual contrast between the pure, motionless divinity of Walden and the frantic, eccentric movements of men on and around it, Thoreau's main concern, as with the house and the beans, is to create a metaphorical association of the pond and the self. There are innumerable examples of this stylistic process; for example: "A lake is the landscapes's most beautiful and expressive feature. It is earth's eye; looking into which the beholder measures the depth of his own nature" (p. 160). Through metaphor Thoreau renders the self and nature in total interrelationship without slighting either half of the duality. The following passage illustrates this stylistic practice:

> How peaceful the phenomena of the lake! Again the works of man shine as in the spring. Ay, every leaf and twig and stone and cobweb sparkles now at mid-afternoon as when covered with dew in a spring morning. Every motion of an oar, or an insect produces a flash of light; and if an oar falls, how sweet the echo! (p. 162)

Like the carefully disciplined and cultivated intellect of the hero, the pond, by its isolation, has become pure and unspoiled divinity, which must be preserved by continued isolation:

> If by living thus reserved and austere, like a hermit in the woods, so long, it has acquired such wonderful purity, who would not regret that the comparatively

impure waters of Flint's Pond should be mingled with it, or itself should ever go to waste its sweetness in the ocean wave? (p. 166)

As in digging his cellar, Thoreau searches for the essential foundation of the pond and associates this foundation with the seat of divinity in the self. The majority of men angle only for fish, and consequently, "they know nothing about the hook of hooks with which to angle for the pond itself" (p. 179). Thoreau's quest is much different; it is "to recover the long lost bottom of Walden Pond" (p. 232), a source of value that Thoreau relates directly to a similar center in man. Having discovered a means of locating the deepest portion of the pond, Thoreau expands his formula:

> What I have observed of the pond is no less true in ethics. It is the law of average. Such a rule of the two diameters not only guides us toward the sun in the system and the heart in man, but draw lines through the length and breadth of a man's particular daily behaviors and waves of life into his coves and inlets, and where they intersect will be the height or depth of his character. (pp. 235–36)

The pond, too, like the chimney and the bean field, serves as a link between earth and heaven, an intermediary between man and the world soul: "A field of water betrays the spirit that is in the air. It is continually receiving new life and motion from above. It is intermediary in its nature between land and sky" (p. 162). As such, the pond enables the self in communion with it to realize both its own selfhood and natural divinity. Thus, fishing at night, Thoreau relates:

It was very queer, especially in dark nights, when your thoughts had wandered to vast and cosmogonal themes in other spheres, to feel this faint jerk, which came to interrupt your dreams and link you to nature again. It seemed as if I might next cast my line upward into the air, as well as downward into this element, which was scarcely more dense. Thus I caught two fishes as it were with one hook. (pp. 152–53)

To summarize, the metaphors of *Walden* work on three levels. In single paragraphs or groups of sentences, Thoreau establishes metaphorical relationships between self and not self. On a slightly higher level of abstraction, larger entities—the house, the bean field, and the pond—become metaphors of the entire experience: by combining the creativity of the self with the materials of nature, a house is created; by mixing human assertion and manipulation with natural processes, a half-cultivated bean field emerges; by bringing the inherent metaphorical perception of the self to bear on the natural facts of the pond, a new relationship is established and a new experience is realized. Finally, each of these entities is a metaphor of *Walden* itself, a new world created by the self out of its union with nature. This final and most significant level of metaphor is best seen in relation to the pond. Both the pond and the artistic creation bear, of course, the same name, "Walden," and Thoreau is more explicit in establishing the relationship between the book and the pond than is the case with either the house or the bean field.

The pond, Thoreau declares, was "made deep and pure for a symbol" (p. 233). An excellent case has been made by A. B. Hovey, who argues that the pond is a symbol of truth.[13] In two passages written at the same time, Thoreau states: "Of all the characters I have known, perhaps

Walden wears best and best preserves its purity" (p. 165), and "no face which we can give to a matter will stead us so well at last as the truth. This alone wears well" (p. 262). Hovey's association is irresistible, but there is no reason why it should preclude the possibility that the pond is also a symbol of *Walden* itself. "Truth" is a personal concept, and, for Thoreau, belief in the artistic validity of his creation is inevitable and indispensable. *Walden,* too, is truth. Thoreau has created a triple metaphor through the association of pond, art, and truth, or, more abstractly, of nature, man, and divinity; and the association makes *Walden,* like its namesake, immortal, a timeless world in which the self is endlessly recreated through communion with nature.

Early in the second chapter, Thoreau describes the process of renewal through immersion in the pond:

> I got up early and bathed in the pond; that was a religious exercise, and one of the best things which I did. They say that characters were engraven on the bathing tub of King Tching-thang to this effect: "Renew thyself completely each day; do it again, and again, and forever again." I can understand that. (p. 87)

A few pages later, the immortality of the pond, with its extraordinary depth, is contrasted to the "stream of time":

> Time is but the stream I go a-fishing in. I drink at it; but while I drink I see the sandy bottom and detect how shallow it is. Its thin current slides away, but eternity remains. I would drink deeper; fish in the sky, whose bottom is pebbly with stars. (p. 94)

The pond, through which no stream flows, will later be directly associated with the sky:

> In such transparent and seemingly bottomless water,
> reflecting the clouds, I seemed to be floating through
> the air as in a balloon, and their [the fishes] swimming
> impressed me as a kind of flight or hovering, as if they
> were a compact flock of birds passing just beneath my
> level on the right or left. (p. 163)

In "Reading" Thoreau associates truth, and here particularly the truth of the written word, with immortality:

> In accumulating property for ourselves or our posterity,
> in founding a family or a state, or acquiring fame even,
> we are mortal; but in dealing with truth we are im-
> mortal, and need fear no change or accident. The oldest
> Egyptian or Hindoo philosopher raised a corner of the
> veil from the statue of divinity; and still the trembling
> robe remains raised, and I gaze upon as fresh a glory
> as he did, since it was I in him that was then so bold,
> and it is he in me that now reviews the vision. No dust
> has settled on that robe; no time has elapsed since that
> divinity was revealed. That time which we really im-
> prove, or which is improvable is neither past, present,
> nor future. (p. 96)

Thus: the pond is immortal; truth is immortal; the written word is immortal. The association is developed further in "Sounds," where Thoreau describes the language of nature, "which all things and events speak without metaphor," and which provides a similar release from time:

> As the sparrow had its trill, sitting on the hickory be-
> fore my door, so had I my chuckle or suppressed warble
> which he might hear out of my nest. My days were not
> days of the week, bearing the stamp of any heathen
> deity, nor were they minced into hours fretted by the

ticking of a clock; for I lived like the Puri Indians, of whom it is said that "for yesterday, to-day, and tomorrow they have only one word." (p. 106)

Finally, in the "Conclusion," Thoreau transfers these ideas directly to his own work of art, which is based upon natural language, in the parable of the artist of Kouroo, undoubtedly Thoreau himself, who has created a perfect work of art, into which "time does not enter," out of "pure material." His work of art is a "new system . . . , a world of full and fair proportions; in which, though the old cities and dynasties had passed away, fairer and more glorious ones had taken their places" (p. 262). Through the process of uniting the ascetically disciplined self with the equivalent response found in the divine core of the not self, Thoreau, too, is able to transcend the world of space and time and dwell in a new and ethereal realm.

In presenting *Walden* as immortal, Thoreau has two related ideas in mind, both of which are common to the Romantic sensibility: the fact that art gives permanence to fleeting moments and fixes them in unchanging form, and the ability of the creative process, during moments of intensity, to cause the loss of any sense of passing time. The first of these ideas is well expressed in Thoreau's metaphorical use of ice. He writes:

Ice is an interesting subject for contemplation. They told me that they had some in the ice-house at Fresh Pond five years old which was as good as ever. Why is it that a bucket of water soon becomes putrid, but frozen remains sweet forever? (p. 240)

In the "Conclusion" Thoreau directly relates *Walden* to the ice of the pond:

> I do not suppose that I have attained to obscurity, but
> I should be proud if no more fatal fault were found
> with my pages on this score than was found with the
> Walden ice. Southern customers objected to its blue
> color, which is the evidence of its purity, as if it were
> muddy, and preferred the Cambridge ice, which is
> white, but tastes of weeds. The purity men love is like
> the mists which envelop the earth, and not like the
> azure ether beyond. (p. 261)

Walden, like the ice, is a stabilization of a fluid and kinetic
experience, "frozen" into eternal freshness and containing
the articulation of a vision of immortality whose very
purity makes it inaccessible to the mass of men.

If art is a "freezing" of moments of illumination that
preserves them eternally pure and fresh, the moments
themselves have the power to suggest immortality in a
different sense: the fading from consciousness of time
during the intensity of the creative process that produces
them. Each of Thoreau's major metaphors culminates in
an expression of this sense of timelessness, and the sensation is summarized in the parable of the artist of Kouroo:

> His singleness of purpose and resolution, and his ele-
> vated piety, endowed him, without his knowledge, with
> perennial youth. As he made no compromise with Time,
> Time kept out of his way, and only sighed at a distance
> because he could not overcome him. . . . And now he
> saw by the heap of shaving still fresh at his feet, that,
> for him and his work, the former lapse of time had been
> an illusion, and that no more time had elapsed than is
> required for a single scintillation from the brain of
> Brahma to fall on and inflame the tinder of a mortal
> brain. (p. 262)

For Thoreau, the awareness of immortality in no way
precludes the necessity of the endless journey; in fact, it

demands continual experimentation and re-creation, for it
is an awareness that is reached only through process. Although the momentary experience of transcendence af-
fords a glimpse into a world of eternal perfection, and art
transcends time by making these moments last forever, to
the hero himself, as artist, such perfect certainty and
stability are denied by the very nature or terms of his
experience. The awareness of immortality and the ability
to preserve this awareness in art result from a fine responsiveness to the changing forms of burgeoning, organic life;
and without continual receptiveness to this endless re-creation, the power of such moments is quickly lost. "Spring,"
which climaxes the seasonal cycle of *Walden,* also contains
the ultimate expression of Thoreau's deep-seated organicism and comprises the central statement of his theme of continuous renewal in man and nature. Here the only kind
of immortality on Thoreau's mind is that of on-going
process and organic development.

As he stands by the railroad bank, Thoreau begins
describing in concrete, natural language the phenomena
of spring. Gradually he begins to elaborate on his observations, playfully manipulating the images given by the
organic description, moving from the concrete to a sense
of relationship to a virtual explosion of vision, in which,
like Emerson, he perceives a divine force manifesting itself
in endless mutations of form with wider and wider and
ever more complex implications, a metamorphosis that
reaches into every aspect of natural existence:

> I am affected as if in a peculiar sense I stood in the
> laboratory of the Artist who made the world and me,—
> had come to where he was still at work, sporting on
> this bank, and with excess of energy strewing his fresh

designs about. I feel as if I were nearer to the vitals of
the globe, for this sandy overflow is something such a
foliaceous mass as the vitals of the animal body. You
find thus in the very sands an anticipation of the vege-
table leaf. (p. 242)

As he draws out the implications of the form of leaves—
from sand on the railroad bank to man, "a mass of thawing
clay"—Thoreau proclaims, "there is nothing inorganic"
(p. 244). The central significance of the chapter, reinforced
by its position in the overall structure of the book, is its
emphasis on this organic rejuvenation and renewal, a vision of an endlessly re-creative, spiritual nature, which includes man and which Thoreau applies to his own experience, insisting upon the need for the imagination to be
always responsive and attuned to kinetic nature:

> We should be blessed if we lived in the present always,
> and took advantage of every accident that befell us,
> like the grass which confesses the influence of the slight-
> est dew that falls on it; and did not spend our time in
> atoning for the neglect of past opportunities, which we
> call doing our duty. We loiter in winter while it is al-
> ready spring. (p. 249)

Although Thoreau may envision a "perfect summer" in
which the transcendent experience can be preserved eternally pure and fresh, and though he presents *Walden* as a
work of art in which this dream is realized, he knows that
for himself, as artist and man, the transcendent fulfill-
ments of life lie ultimately not in the expansive experience of an endless summer but in the joys and renewals of
recurring springs.

Probably the most often asked question about *Walden*
is why Thoreau went to live in the woods, but equally

important for an appreciation of Thoreau's Romanticism is an understanding of why he decided to leave, and, from an aesthetic point of view, why his return is an essential part of the total dramatic experience of the book. Thoreau does not refrain from making explicit the fact that he returns to society, and he makes the reasons for his return perfectly clear in the "Conclusion":

> I left the woods for as good a reason as I went there. Perhaps it seemed to me that I had several more lives to live, and could not spare any more time for that one. It is remarkable how easily and insensibly we fall into a particular route, and make a beaten track for ourselves. . . . How worn and dusty, then, must be the highways of the world, how deep the ruts of tradition and conformity! I did not wish to take a cabin passage, but rather to go before the mast and on the deck of the world, for there I could best see the moonlight amid the mountains. I do not wish to go below now. (p. 259)

Thoreau retreated to Walden mainly in an attempt to penetrate through the flux and superficiality of society to contact with an essential Reality, to get "off the beaten track" and "on the deck of the world"; to stay "on the deck of the world," in tune with dynamic Reality, he must leave the woods. For the pond is not a sanctuary, and the language of *Walden,* although the vision it reveals may remain eternally valid, is not a "homestead" but a "conveyance," which, once vital, "soon grows old and false." Thoreau recognizes this when he writes: "The volatile truth of our words should continually betray the inadequacy of the residual statement. Their truth is instantly *translated;* its literal monument alone remains" (p. 262). Thoreau could not rest his perceptivity in a hollow monument; like Emerson, he insisted upon staying "aloof from all moorings." He returns from Walden, not to become an integral part of society, but, as he states in his opening paragraph, to be "a sojourner in civilized life," one who lives somewhere temporarily, staying in one place only a little while, a drifter always on the spiritual move. *Walden* is simply a grand experiment, composed of many smaller experiments, and to remain spiritually alive and in touch with flowing and metamorphic life, its hero must continue his experiments in new places and new ways.

Two

WALT WHITMAN

THE PARADOX OF COSMIC SELFHOOD

Along with Emerson and Thoreau, Walt Whitman defines the positive vision of American Romanticism. Like the Transcendentalists, Whitman finds in the not self an equivalent response to his own expanding selfhood, and only an empathetic exercise of the imagination is required for him to perceive the basic unity of self and other. But Whitman goes beyond the Transcendentalists, for although he retains their dualistic conception of reality, he alters it in two significant ways: first, by placing the body firmly on the "self" side of Emerson's dichotomy, and second, by perceiving the entirety of both self and not self to be suffused with the power of divinity. Thus, Whitman's encounters with the essentiality of life involve neither a retreat from society nor a subordination of the senses, but rather a movement through society and a sensual embrace with the whole of the not self. His vision is liberal and inclusive, encompassing the total reality of his age, and *Leaves of Grass* is both a song of himself and a polyphony of the facts and myths of his time. However, Whitman's vision of unity is never totally free of the tensions implicit in his dualistic world-view. The tensions between self and not self, between body and soul, between materiality and spirituality, and in a sociopolitical sense between the separate person and the mass are at the center of his thought, and the attempt to resolve them is the informing principle of his verse. In this chapter I have focused on two poems—"Song of Myself" and "As I Ebb'd with the Ocean of Life"—that seem to me to recapitulate in small the major dimensions and implications of this attempt as it is developed at large in *Leaves of Grass*.

"Song of Myself" is essentially a poem about selfhood as understood through the examination and dramatic presentation of one particular self. The idea of a song about oneself necessarily implies the recognition that the self, in the sense suggested by William James, is divided. It is both subject and object, capacities that James distinguished by calling the former "the I" and the latter "the me." In these terms the "I" presented in "Song of Myself" is really a "me," an aesthetic projection or objectification of the self-image and frame of mind of the self-as-subject, who in this case is the poet Walt Whitman. Thus, analytically, there are two levels of heroic experience in the poem: on one level is the poet engaged in the process of creating the poem; on a second level is the "I" within the poem, who objectifies and dramatizes the poet's thought and experience. To the extent that Whitman invites the reader to take the poem as figuratively being the self, or at least as presenting the self-made-manifest, this distinction is broken down; but it is nevertheless helpful to remember, because it suggests that in reading the poem we are viewing the dramatic representation of a particular self-image, and because in the closing movement of the poem Whitman himself insists upon making it. With this in mind, I propose to study "Song of Myself" primarily in terms of the kind of self-image and the kind of self–not self relationship that it presents at any given time. Viewed from this perspective, a definite progressive movement emerges, leading toward an ever more sublime and affirmative statement about the self.[1]

The first six sections of "Song of Myself" function largely as a prologue to the poem. Here Whitman sets forth his basic tenets and suggests the central movement that is to follow. Throughout these sections the poet's self-image is concrete and personal. Whitman establishes a distinct personal identity in section 1 and elaborates on the joys of this concrete individuality in the catalogue of section 2; section 4 is an explicit statement of an aspect of selfhood that refuses to be identified with its associations or the various influences upon it. However, in these initial sections Whitman also emphasizes the limitations of this kind of personal selfhood and describes the prospects of the cosmic identity that he will assume. After the catalogue of sensations in section 2, the poet pauses and questions the limitations of individual perception:

> Have you reckon'd a thousand acres much? have you
> reckon'd the earth much?
> Have you practis'd so long to learn to read?
> Have you felt so proud to get at the meaning of poems?[2]

In the cosmic stance that Whitman will assume, in which he will "permit to speak at every hazard, / Nature without check with original energy" (p. 29), "the origin of all poems" (p. 30) will be revealed. Because the essential energy of the poem will be cosmic and thus unbound by the limitations of time, space, or personality, the poem will belong to readers of all ages as much as to the poet and will be as much an expression of their individuality as his.

In these opening sections we find the central paradox of the poem and the central tension of Whitman's thought: how the self can be at once both individual and cosmic and how the poem can be the "thoughts of all men in all ages" and at the same time be uniquely personal. As with the Transcendentalists, so with Whitman the resolution to this paradox lay not in logical excursus but in imaginative perception; but both Whitman and the Transcendentalists, though they were not primarily metaphysicians, felt constrained to construct or suggest a particular world-view in which the imaginative vision of unity might be based. In "Song of Myself" this world-view is centered in the relationship that Whitman establishes between the "I" and the "soul" and in the conception of endlessness that he sets forth in section 3.

Throughout the poem, and especially in the early sections, Whitman maintains a strict distinction between the "I" and the "soul." "I cannot understand the Mystery," he wrote in an early notebook, "but I am always conscious of myself as two—my soul and I; and I reckon it is the same with all men and women." [3] At first this seems to be but a restatement of Emerson's psychological division of the Understanding and the Intellect, or in a larger sense of the characteristic Romantic distinction between the ordinary intelligence and the divine imagination. Although this interpretation has some validity regarding Whitman, the matter is not quite that simple.[4] Often, as for example in the case of Emerson, this division led the Romantics to a deprecation of the non-soul element of selfhood, a feeling that the essential element of the self was spiritual while the material aspect of selfhood was only a shell or, as in Emerson's initial statement of the dichotomy, not strictly self at all. Walt Whitman could have no sympathy with a conclusion such as this. To Whitman, as he repeatedly emphasized, the body and the soul had equal validity and were equally divine. In fact, as is apparent in the above notebook entry and in the opening section of "Song of Myself," Whitman's essential individuality is that which is somehow *distinct* from the soul, a conception that is the reverse of Emerson's.

In unearthing just what Whitman would convey by this distinction, the phraseology of the opening lines of "Song of Myself" is important and revealing:

> I celebrate myself and sing myself,
> And what I assume you shall assume,
> For every atom belonging to me as good belongs to you.
>
> I loafe and invite my soul. . . .

(p. 28)

In line four there is certainly distinction, but it is a distinction that implies relationship. At this point in the poem the "I" is strictly individual, whereas the "soul" is both individual, in the sense that it is "my soul," and something apart, in the sense that it can be "invited"; and both are somehow subsumed under the larger, more encompassing concept of self, which is also something more than individual, since "every atom belonging to me as good belongs to you." Thus, it seems reasonable to assume that in making the distinction Whitman means by the "I" that aspect of selfhood which is individual, whereas the "soul" is that aspect of selfhood which is both individual and cosmic, part of the Absolute and containing the essential spiritual energy of all souls and all things.

The nature of this relationship becomes clearer in sec-

tion 3. Here Whitman presents an image of infinite procreation at work throughout the universe:

> Urge and urge and urge,
> Always the procreant urge of the world.
>
> Out of the dimness opposite equals advance, always
>   substance and increase, always sex,
> Always a knit of identity, always distinction, always
>   a breed of life.
>
> (p. 31)

The sexual imagery is of great importance here. As Gay
Allen writes, "At 'birth' each object in nature becomes
individualized momentarily (*i.e.* receives its 'identity'
through form or 'body') and represents some portion of
the soul-stuff which pervades the universe . . . it is by
means of sex that the soul receives its identity and perpetually fulfills the cosmic plan. . . ." [5] Selfhood, in other
words, has individual identity only as it exists in material
form. Thus, the body, for the moment out of eternity that
it exists, is visible spirit, an individual manifestation of
the soul of the world. But the individual manifestation is
only one aspect of Whitman's larger concept of selfhood,
for inseparable from the individual "I" is the cosmic
"soul" that gives it life; and between the "I" and the
"soul" in any self there is "always a knit of identity, always distinction." In the moment of individual identity
the self is dualistic, composed of the individual, material
"I" and the cosmic, spiritual "soul," and this same dualism
exists in every aspect of creation at a given time, each
object being cosmic at the same time that it is individual.
Both elements are equally divine and equally essential to
existence:

Clear and sweet is my soul, and clear and sweet is all
that is not my soul.
Lack one lacks both, and the unseen is proved by the seen,
Till that becomes unseen and receives proof in its turn.

(p. 31)

Of course, Whitman's faith in this world-view derives
neither from empirical demonstration nor from its logical
inevitability, but from an intense awareness of the unity
within himself of that spirit which presently manifests itself in material form as the electric, individual "I" and
that spirit which presently exists as part of the cosmic
"soul." Section 5 is a dramatic representation of this
awareness, culminating in the hero's first vision of his
cosmic selfhood:

Swiftly arose and spread around me the peace and knowledge
that pass all the argument of the earth,
And I know that the hand of God is the promise of my own,
And I know that the spirit of God is the brother of my own,
And that all the men ever born are also my brothers, and
the women my sisters and lovers,
And that a kelson of the creation is love. . . .

(p. 33)

With this knowledge Whitman realizes the fundamental
unity of all creation, from God to "mossy scabs of the
worm fence, heap'd stones, elder mullein, and poke-
weed." [6]
It is clearly apparent, however, that the dualism that
allows the "soul" and "the other I am" to exist on equal
terms is highly unstable. Ultimately, since any given individual identity is mortal and transient, this dualism is an

illusion, for that which appears as matter is essentially spiritual in nature, manifesting itself in material form for but an instant. Thus, Whitman's thought could easily lead to a spiritual pantheism, in which objective reality is essentially unreal and in which individuality is totally surrendered to the Absolute. On the other hand, if Whitman were to insist that the cosmic soul could not exist without manifesting itself in individuals, that spirit has no existence whatever outside of its incarnation in material form, then his thought could easily become a materialistic monism, asserting that for all practical purposes matter is the only reality and that selfhood is thus purely individual. Whitman, like Emerson, has to tread a diagonal line; and to do this, he must extend the dualism of the moment in which selfhood is both material and spiritual, individual and cosmic, into eternity. The result is Whitman's vision of a universe that is thoroughly processional and metamorphic, composed of endless manifestations of spirit in an infinite variety of material forms.[7] The idea of endlessness is absolutely essential to Whitman's world-view, for to set a limit of any kind or at any point to the metamorphosis is, in effect, to deny the bipolar unity of cosmic and individual identity, body and soul, spirit and matter. For only in the infinite processional motion of the universe are these dualities held together and kept from becoming distinct polarities of experience.

Aside from the sexual act, grass is the symbol that Whitman most often calls upon to represent and express this endlessly procreative metamorphosis of spirit and matter. From the beginning of the poem grass is intimately associated with the hero's "invitation" to his soul:

> I loafe and invite my soul,
> I lean and loafe at my ease observing a spear of
>   summer grass.

Here Whitman is certainly viewing the grass through his imagination, in the manner that Emerson views organic nature, seeing in it the fundamental unity of the I and the soul, a manifestation of the unity of man and nature in a larger scheme. In section 5 this relationship is developed further in the dramatic portrayal of the union of the I and the soul that takes place quite literally in the grass. Finally, in section 6 the association is made explicit, rounding out and completing the prologue to the poem. The poet cannot answer the question that the child asks, for the grass, representing the presence of the infinite in the moment of experience, is all things. Whitman offers a few "guesses" and then dismisses the question, for the grass is not to be defined, but rather to be used: "Tenderly will I use you curling grass . . ." (p. 34). The grass provides "hints about the dead young men and women," which the poet declares, "I wish I could translate" (p. 34). In the final lines of the section he realizes that the grass cannot be translated, but also that to the perceptive eye it does not need translation; it speaks for itself, revealing by the very nature of its existence the endlessness of nature and the self. Whitman's vision culminates in a suggestion of the infinite expansion of all life:

> They are alive and well somewhere,
> The smallest sprout shows there is really no death,
> And if ever there was it led forward life, and does not
>   wait at the end to arrest it,
> And ceas'd the moment life appear'd.

> All goes onward and outward, nothing collapses,
> And to die is different from what any one supposed,
>   and luckier.
>
> (pp. 34–35)

The actual dramatic expansion of the self within the poem begins in section 7 with a bold statement of the ubiquitousness of the heroic self:

> I pass death with the dying and birth with the new-wash'd
>   babe, and am not contain'd between my hat and boots . . . ,
> And am around, tenacious, acquisitive, tireless, and
>   cannot be shaken away.
>
> (p. 35)

In sections 7 and 8 Whitman retains the strongly individual self-image established in the prologue. He declares:

> I am not an earth nor an adjunct of an earth,
> I am the mate and companion of people, all just as
>   immortal and fathomless as myself. . . .
>
> (p. 35)

The hero exists in section 8 as an observer, drawing the things he sees into himself. As each thing is observed, realized or created in language, and brought into the song, it becomes figuratively a part of the self. In these sections the movement is inward; the scope of individual selfhood is enlarged by a process of "absorption," which Whitman summarizes in section 13:

> In me the caresser of life wherever moving, backward as
>   well as forward sluing,
> To niches aside and junior bending, not a person or object
>   missing,
> Absorbing all to myself and for this song.
>
> (p. 40)

Beginning in section 9 a subtly different type of movement emerges, one that is actually the opposite of the first.
Here the hero appears not simply as an observer, absorbing whatever he sees into himself, but rather as an active
participant in the life of various times and places. The
sense of a distinct, separate identity fades and is replaced
by a metamorphic self-image. Through a process of imaginative projection the self is extended into diverse identities: a farm-worker, a solitary hunter, a seaman, a clam-
digger, and a frontiersman. This process is explained metaphorically in section 11, by the image of the woman who,
while remaining "stock still" in her room, becomes at the
same time the "twenty-ninth bather," wandering along
the shore, caressing the men, feeling the salt spray. In
these projections the movement is not of external reality
inward but of the self outward. Selfhood is enlarged by a
process of identification and diffusion, rather than absorption. As Whitman writes at the end of section 14:

> What is commonest, cheapest, nearest, easiest, is Me,
> Me going in for my chances, spending for vast returns,
> Adorning myself to bestow myself on the first that will
>   take me,
> Not asking the sky to come down to my good will,
> Scattering it freely forever.
>
> (p. 41)

The two kinds of movement revealed in these early sections form a clearly dialectical process, which characterizes
the initial stage of the poem's development. On the one
hand, there is an absorption of things observed into the
self; on the other hand there is a diffusion of the self into
things observed or imagined. The polar forms of this

dialectic are the same as the poles between which Emerson tried to draw his diagonal line and the same as the forms of monism toward which Whitman's vision at times tends to move: a rapacious idealism that engulfs the entire not self in the individual ego, and an "infinite diffusion" of individuality into the Absolute, the tendency that D. H. Lawrence recognized so clearly when he described Whitman's "private soul leaking out of him all the time. All his privacy leaking out in a sort of dribble, oozing into the universe." [8] However, Whitman lacks Emerson's metaphysical awareness of the dangers of these poles; and in the sheer expansiveness and power of his vision the poles are transcended, and the logically opposite processes of absorption and diffusion become a single process of merger. Paradoxically, by the projection of the self into other people, places, and objects, these are at the same time absorbed into the self, and the unity of cosmic selfhood emerges from the dialectic. Whitman summarizes this process at the end of the long catalogue of characters in section 15:

> And these tend inward to me, and I tend outward to them,
> And such as it is to be of these more or less I am,
> And of these one and all I weave the song of myself.
>
> (p. 44)

The dialectic is not logically resolved or synthesized here so much as it is simply dissolved in the sweep of Whitman's vision, for in his conception of reality no dialectic can be maintained for long. Like the ideas of "beginning" and "end," or "best" and "worst," which are rejected at the opening of the poem (section 3), the very concept of opposition implies limitation and is possible only in a finite universe. In Whitman's infinite universe all is relative and relational. One of his favorite techniques is to set out a scheme of opposites usually considered irreconcilable, embrace them all, and move beyond them to a position where the whole concept of opposition fades away in the vigor of his acceptance. Section 16 is a clear example and functions almost as an exclamation point to the first 15 sections. Whitman begins with a characteristic catalogue in which the self envelops contradictions:

> I am of old and young, of the foolish as much as the wise,
> Regardless of others, ever regardful of others,
> Maternal as well as paternal, a child as well as a man. . . .
>
> (p. 44)

In the middle of the paragraph this careful, parallel opposition begins to fade into a mere list, and by the end of the section it has vanished entirely into the poet's inclusiveness:

> Of every hue and caste am I, of every rank and religion,
> A farmer, mechanic, artist, gentleman, sailor, quaker,
> Prisoner, fancy-man, rowdy, lawyer, physician, priest.
>
> I resist any thing better than my own diversity,
> Breathe the air but leave plenty after me,
> And am not stuck up, and am in my place.
>
> (p. 45)

With section 17 there is a shift in the tone and movement of the poem. Whitman pauses abruptly and directs what seems to be almost an aside to the reader:

These are really the thoughts of all men in all ages and
   lands, they are not original with me,
If they are not yours as much as mine they are nothing,
   or next to nothing.

(p. 45)

In sections 7–16 the essential energy of selfhood was projected into some of its possible manifestations as the hero
assumed various potential identities and made these potentialities visible and concrete in poetry. Now Whitman
turns his attention from this dramatic process of expansion to a more reflective discussion of the meaning and
significance of the poem and an examination of the fundamental qualities of cosmic selfhood. The rationale behind
this shift is explained parenthetically in section 22, as
Whitman asks: "Shall I make my list of things in the house
and skip the house that supports them?" (p. 50). Through
these reflections and meditations Whitman takes his experience into a wider dimension and is able to make an
even stronger statement of the limitlessness of the self.
When he emerges from this phase of the poem in section
33, the self-image projected in the "I" is not that of an
individual enlarging himself, nor of a metamorphic being
assuming his various identities, but of a truly inclusive
and pervasive cosmic being delighting in the joys of his
own infinite, divine nature.

In sections 17–19 the object of Whitman's meditation
is the poem itself. Through a series of metaphors "Song
of Myself" is likened to grass, air, music, a "meal equally
set"—all comparisons that emphasize its democratic, timeless, and inclusive nature. But Whitman also affirms in
section 19 that the poem has an "intricate purpose," the
same purpose that "the Fourth-month showers have, and

the mica on the side of a rock has" (p. 46). This purpose is simply to reveal, as the grass and the air and all of nature reveal, the presence of infinity in each object and in each moment of experience. The reader is to use the poem just as Whitman previously used the grass, to realize the endlessness of his own nature. Whitman makes this function of the poem explicit in section 23. Here he points to the technique of "indirection" as a means of approaching transcendent reality through language:

> Less the reminders of properties told my words,
> And more the reminders they of life untold, and of
>   freedom and extrication. . . .
>
> (p. 51)

For Whitman, as for Emerson, words express spiritual facts, "life untold," at the same time that they are signs of concrete reality, "properties told." The specific, material reality denoted by a word is transient, but the abstract spirituality of the world which it suggests is infinite and immortal. Thus, the words and the poem that they comprise are less important for the concrete facts that they embody at any given time ("my list of things in the house") than for the unseen truth that the dynamic process of language itself continually reveals. Whitman returns to this theme in section 25, asserting:

> My voice goes after what my eyes cannot reach,
> With the twirl of my tongue I encompass worlds and
>   volumes of worlds.
>
> Speech is the twin of my vision, it is unequal to
>   measure itself. . . .
>
> (p. 55).

Like Whitman's vision, which transcends all finite limits, his speech is cosmic, the voice of original energy, "the pass-word primeval," which includes and encompasses all the voices of all ages.

But despite the prime importance and transcending power of words, the hero's cosmic selfhood cannot be fully conveyed by language. Whitman recognizes, at times with a genuine sense of frustration, the limitations of speech. He writes in section 14, for example:

> The press of my foot to the earth springs a hundred
>   affections,
> They scorn the best I can do to relate them.
>
> (p. 41)

In section 25 he reaffirms that there is more within his cosmic nature than can be suggested by words, even in their symbolic capacity:

> My final merit I refuse you, I refuse putting from me
>   what I really am,
> Encompass worlds, but never try to encompass me . . .
> Writing and talk do not prove me,
> I carry the plenum of proof and every thing else in my
>   face. . . .
>
> (p. 55)

These assertions grow directly from the meditations on selfhood in the immediately preceding sections, in which Whitman expands his self-image into truly cosmic proportions. Beginning in section 20, Whitman develops the same hypothesis about the self that he has stated with regard to language: it is less important for the various individual manifestations it assumes than for the ultimate truths represented by the very fact of its existence. His poem will have value only as the reader recognizes that the poet's cosmic selfhood implies his own, indeed implies the cosmic nature of all creation. Whitman asserts that cosmic selfhood is not a mystical state of being to be achieved through laborious exercise, but an "elementary law," which is to be perceived in all things:

> I do not trouble my spirit to vindicate itself or be
> understood,
> I see that the elementary laws never apologize,
> (I reckon I behave no prouder than the level I plant
> my house by, after all.)
>
> (p. 48)

The statements about the self in sections 20 and 21 culminate in dramatic portrayals of the fusion of the poet with the earth and the sea, moments similar to the one portrayed in section 5. These lead almost directly to the wider vision of sections 24 and 25 in which the self-image becomes totally pervasive and divine:

> Divine am I inside and out, and I make holy whatever I
> touch or am touch'd from,
>
> .   .   .   .
>
> Dazzling and tremendous how quick the sun-rise would
> kill me,
> If I could not now and always send sun-rise out of me.
>
> We also ascend dazzling and tremendous as the sun,
> We found our own O my soul in the calm and cool of the
> day-break.
>
> (pp. 53–54)

Realizing his own divine inclusiveness, Whitman can now scoff at the question posed by speech: *"Walt you*

contain enough, why don't you let it out then?" (p. 55).
The nature of his being denies the very terms of this question, for the self does not merely contain all things, but
fundamentally *is* all things, and the essential energy of
which it is composed is manifest throughout all creation.
The hero does not have to "let it out," for it is already
suffused throughout the world. Section 27 is almost a
direct refutation of the terms of the question:

> To be in any form, what is that?
> (Round and round we go, all of us, and ever come back
>   thither,)
> If nothing lay more develop'd the quahaug in its callous
>   shell were enough.
>
> Mine is no callous shell,
> I have instant conductors all over me whether I pass or
>   stop,
> They seize every object and lead it harmlessly through
>   me.
>
> > (p. 57)

The image here is of an instantaneous and continuous
metamorphosis of spiritual energy, which denies the implications that anything can be trapped within the self
or that the self can be kept isolated and distinct from any
thing. As Whitman makes clear in sections 26–29, hearing
and touch are also "twins of his vision" and come no
nearer than speech to containing him or being contained
by him. All senses lead him to the larger fact of *being*
and the simple conclusion of section 30:

> All truths wait in all things,
> They neither hasten their own delivery nor resist it,

> They do not need the obstetric forceps of the surgeon,
> The insignificant is as big to me as any,
> (What is less or more than a touch?)
>
> Logics and sermons never convince,
> The damp of the night drives deeper into my soul.
>
> (p. 58)

Sections 30 and 31 affirm Whitman's belief in this truth, a belief that enables him to present his experience on a much more inclusive and more powerful plane than before. The vast catalogue of section 33, beginning with a declaration of the poet's freedom from space and time, releases the full power of his cosmic energy:

> Space and Time! now I see it is true, what I guess'd at,
> What I guess'd when I loaf'd on the grass,
> What I guess'd while I lay alone in my bed,
> And again as I walk'd the beach under the paling stars
>   of the morning.
>
> (p. 61)

The scenes mentioned here certainly refer to the epiphanic moments, such as those described in sections 5, 21, and 22, in which Whitman becomes intensely aware of the unity of his individual I and the cosmic soul; and "what he guess'd" is certainly the fundamental relatedness of all things and the limitlessness of the self. The result of this conviction is a sense of total freedom:

> My ties and ballasts leave me, my elbows rest in sea-gaps,
> I skirt sierras, my palms cover continents,
> I am afoot with my vision.
>
> (p. 61)

Here the dramatic movement of the poem reaches a peak, as the self-image of the poet becomes completely unlimited, present in every facet of experience and every aspect of creation.

Toward the end of section 33 Whitman moves toward facing the full implications of his cosmic nature by including the harsh, unpleasant aspects of experience. He begins with an incorporation of evil and suffering, through an identification with suffering heroes: "The disdain and calmness of martyrs, / The mother of old, condemn'd for a witch, burnt with dry wood, her children gazing on, / The hounded slave . . . , the mash'd fireman with breast-bone broken . . . , an old artillerist" (pp. 66–67). Sections 34, 35, and 36 continue this account of heroic suffering. In section 37 the poet's vision expands to include the pure victim, the non-heroic sufferer, whose lot is "dull unintermitted pain" (p. 71), an image that culminates in identification with the abject misery and poverty of a beggar: "I project my hat, sit shame-faced, and beg" (p. 72).

With section 38, however, there is an important pause and a change of direction:

> Enough! enough! enough!
> Somehow I have been stunn'd. Stand back!
> Give me a little time beyond my cuff'd head, slumbers,
>   dreams, gaping
> I discover myself on the verge of a usual mistake.
>
>   (p. 72)

The "usual mistake" is to have dwelt too long on isolated, individual suffering, to have lost sight of the totality of the cosmic self by allowing his attention to rest too long in some of its various individual manifestations. In a larger sense this is the same mistake that Whitman had fallen into in sections 7–16 and that was corrected in the meditations of 17–32: the tendency to identify the self with its metamorphic potentialities, "the things in the house," while forgetting the nature of cosmic selfhood, "the house that supports them." Remembering now that he is cosmic and divine, the hero realizes that he contains within himself the endless cycle of death and recreation, that he is redeemer and savior as well as sufferer, that, in fact, within the cosmic self the sufferer and the redeemer of suffering are one. The image of Christ is ideal to express this paradox:

> That I could forget the mockers and insults!
> That I could forget the trickling tears and the blows
>   of the bludgeons and hammers!
> That I could look with a separate look on my own
>   crucifixion and bloody crowning.
>
> I remember now,
> I resume the overstaid fraction,
> The grave of rock multiplies what has been confided to
>   it, or to any graves,
> Corpses rise, gashes heal, fastenings roll from me.
>
> (p. 72)

Although the imagery here is definitely Christian, Whitman is not identifying with Christ so much as he is affirming that the principle illustrated in Christ's death and resurrection is constantly operative in the world, in himself, in all selves. In sections 39–41 the hero "troop(s) forth replenish'd with supreme power, one of an average un-

ending procession" (p. 72); he reverses his role and becomes the savior, the helper of the sick, the divine principle wherever and whenever manifest.

In sections 42 and 43 Whitman brings this redeeming
principle into the context of his role as a poet, the leader
and teacher of mankind. Like Emerson, Whitman envisions the poet as an illumined seer, whose imaginative
perception reveals truths to which the ordinary intelligence is blind. In these sections the dichotomy between
the sufferer and the redeemer is transformed into a dichotomy between the mass of "doubters and sullen mopers"
and those who are awakened, represented in the cata-
logues of God-figures in sections 41 and 43. On the one
hand are the insensitive masses who go through life as
living dead:

> Here and there with dimes on the eyes walking,
> To feed the greed of the belly the brains liberally
>   spooning,
> Tickets buying, taking, selling, but in to the feast
>   never once going,
> Many sweating, ploughing, thrashing, and then the chaff
>   for payment receiving,
> A few idly owning, and they the wheat continually
>   claiming.
>
> (p. 77)

It is perhaps more difficult for Whitman to include this
attitude within himself than it is to include suffering,
which reveals at least a sensitivity to life. Yet he identifies
with these people too, taking them also as "duplicates of
myself":

> The little plentiful manikins skipping around in
>   collars and tail'd coats,

> I am aware who they are, (they are positively not
>   worms or fleas,)
> I acknowledge the duplicates of myself, the weakest and
>   shallowest is deathless with me,
> What I do and say the same waits for them. . . .
>
> (p. 77)

In this passage the tenacity with which Whitman holds to the paradoxical dualism of his vision is clear. Although he insists that all things share a fundamental unity, he refuses to allow this unity to obscure the fully individual nature of objects and people. This insistence increases the significance of his acceptance, for he includes the "weak and shallow" not only as parts of the cosmic whole but also as they exist as individuals: "I am aware who they are, (they are positively not worms or fleas)." However, although he identifies with these individuals, Whitman at this point does not make his "usual mistake." He never loses sight of the cosmic self's equally redemptive nature, which is represented here through his own role as a poet. As the following lines and section 43 make clear, the poet reveals the essential, living Reality that is immanent in the world, but which the mass of men never see because of the limitations of their own perception:

> Not words of routine this song of mine,
> But abruptly to question, to leap beyond yet
>   nearer bring. . . .
>
> (p. 77)

By breaking through the limiting categories of routine existence, his words make all men aware of their cosmic limitlessness, or, as Roy Harvey Pearce writes, he makes them "poets in spite of themselves." [9] As Whitman describes it in the Preface to the 1855 edition of *Leaves of Grass,* the role of the poet is to be "complete in himself . . . the others are as good as he, only he sees it and they do not" (p. 713).

In the final sections of "Song of Myself" (44–52), Whitman "turn[s] and talk[s] like a man leaving charges before a journey" (p. 79). In effect, this is precisely what he is doing. The poem itself becomes a "charge," a fragment of the cosmic self left behind as an invitation to the reader to take up his own journey as the poet leaves to continue his. The distinction between the poet and the poem, which had previously been collapsed, is reestablished in these closing sections, for the poet cannot be contained within his poem, not even by a cosmic self-image. The final paradox of cosmic selfhood is that the hero's identity can never be complete, despite the fact that it is "perfect" at any given moment. Whitman must "refuse putting from me what I really am," for "what he really is" will be constantly in a process of becoming and will always be unfinished and finally unknowable. Sections 44–46 are assertions of the total impossibility of limiting the self, the total impossibility of ever completing the journey through the metamorphoses of cosmic identity. The discussion centers about the question posed early in section 44: "The clock indicates the moment—but what does eternity indicate?" (p. 80). Whitman answers with an image of himself poised on the present moment, encompassing the infinities of past and future, the perfection of a continuous development from the distant recesses of time, yet containing the promise of infinite expansion:

I am an acme of things accomplish'd, and I am encloser of things to be.

My feet strike an apex of the apices of the stairs,
On every step bunches of ages, and larger bunches between
    the steps,
All below duly travel'd, and still I mount and mount.

                                                    (pp. 80–81)

The self revealed in the poem is but the manifestation of
a single moment in a journey that culminates each instant,
but has no completion.

In section 45 Whitman continues the theme of limitlessness by contrasting the life cycle of youth, manhood,
and old age with the infinite spiraling of the universe.
Just as each stage of human life in the very instant that it
rounds itself into its own perfection promises another, so
each life cycle proclaims the existence of one that is wider
and more encompassing than itself:

Every condition promulges not only itself, it
    promulges what grows after and out of itself,
And the dark hush [death] promulges as much as any.

I open my scuttle at night and see the far-sprinkled
    systems,
And all I see multiplied as high as I can cipher edge
    but the rim of the farther systems.

Wider and wider they spread, expanding, always
    expanding,
Outward and outward and forever outward.

                                                    (p. 82)

With all this the cosmic self is integral; it, too, is limitless:
"I know I have the best of time and space, and was never
measured and never will be measured" (p. 83). The poet
"tramps[s] a perpetual journey," continuously realizing
more and more of his infinite nature, but finding no prospect of final completion:

This day before dawn I ascended a hill and look'd
   at the crowded heaven,
And I said to my spirt *When we become the enfolders*
   of those orbs, and the pleasure and knowledge of every thing
   in them, shall we be fill'd and satisfied then?
And my spirit said, *No, we but level that lift to pass*
   and continue beyond.

                                        (pp. 83–84)

Beginning in section 46, Whitman also redirects himself
to the reader, reconsidering his poetic role and the difficulty of communicating the truths about the nature of
God and death and the endlessness of all creation that
have been revealed to him through his cosmic awareness.
The problem of communication is crucial for Whitman,
for how do you convey a vision whose magnitude virtually
defies expression? In sections 44 and 45 Whitman seems to
take language almost to the breaking point, and still he is
not satisfied. Indirection, the use of the symbolic power
of language to convey the spirituality of the world, is
Whitman's most characteristic approach, but in the last
analysis he realizes that even this is not enough, that ultimately the cosmic self, like the universe, is "untranslat-
able":

   I hear you whispering there O stars of heaven,
   O suns—O grass of graves—O perpetual transfers
      and promotions,
   If you do not say any thing how can I say any thing?
                                        (p. 87)

As Roger Asselineau demonstrates, Whitman was haunted
by "the problem of the inexpressible." [10] Section 50 is a
clear example of his struggle to achieve articulation, a

struggle that eventually ends in a plea to the common faculty of sight: "Do you see O my brothers and sisters?" (p. 88). Whitman's vision cannot be explained; it must be vividly felt and realized in each element of creation, and for this it is enough that his poem, like the grass of section 6, simply exists. Ultimately, Whitman places his faith in sheer *being*. The great achievement of the poem is its total organicism, in which the ultimate truth of the universe becomes immanent and available to all who can see, to all who will embark on their own journeys:

If you would understand me go to the heights or water-shore,
The nearest gnat is an explanation, and a drop or motion
   of waves a key,
The maul, the oar, the hand-saw, second my words.

(p. 85)

Finally it is to simple, pervasive *being*, represented characteristically by grass, that Whitman "bequeaths" himself and his song. In the final lines of the poem the self-image of the poet is presented in the very process of metamorphosis, withdrawing from visible reality and launching into the infinite unknown beyond:

   I depart as air, I shake my white locks at the runaway
     sun,
   I effuse my flesh in eddies, and drift it in lacy jags.

   I bequeath myself to the dirt to grow from the grass I
     love,
     If you want me again look for me under your boot-
      soles.

(p. 89)

As Richard Chase has written, "Song of Myself" "has to do not with the self searching for a final identity, but with the self escaping a series of identities which threaten to destroy its lively and various spontaneity." [11] In this respect, at least, the poem represents the dramatic fulfillment of Emerson's concept of art and life as a series of endless experiments, in which any single thought or conclusion becomes a "prison" if held too rigidly or assumed to be the revelation of an unchanging truth. The Whitman of "Song of Myself" is the poet heralded by Emerson as a "liberating god," through whom "men have got a new sense, and found within their world another world, or nest of worlds; for the metamorphosis once seen, we divine that it does not stop" (Selected Writings, p. 334). Whitman's sense of the unity of self and not self in his cosmic consciousness is totally inseparable from on-going process, for in his vision the metamorphoses of the universe and the process in which he is engaged have neither climax nor completion. "Song of Myself" is not a "freezing" of experiences of unity, but a "flowing" accumulation and accretion of such moments in endless succession, and Whitman's dynamic vision makes it impossible for him to be satisfied with any single experience, statement, or form. With Emerson, he realizes that something "which was a true sense for a moment . . . soon becomes old and false." But though the heroic journey of "Song of Myself" must necessarily be endless, because it is a process that yields the affirmation and satisfaction of a continuous sense of the unity of divine self and divine not self, this very endlessness becomes its most positive quality.

The optimism and the confident affirmation of "Song of Myself" are the dominant notes of Leaves of Grass, as they were to be a sort of personal trademark of Walt Whitman's life and career. But beneath the buoyant ex-

terior there was always an undercurrent of doubt and in-
security. In the years between 1857 and 1860, in particular, Whitman was a troubled man for a variety of reasons,
not the least of which were the financial difficulties he
experienced subsequent to the relative failure of the
second (1856) edition of his poems.[12] Gay Allen speculates a correlation between the crises in Whitman's personal life during these years and the instances of loneli-
ness and depression that began to appear for the first time
in the 1860 edition of *Leaves of Grass*.[13] Certainly these
darker moments reflect the poet's personal depression,
but they also suggest a less affirmative version of the central mythical experience of his poetry. Often they convey
a much more negative attitude toward the prospect of an
endless journey than does the bulk of Whitman's verse.
Within the "Children of Adam" cluster, for example,
there is often a strong sense of exhaustion and frustration, centered about the facts that in a journey without
end there can be no final goal or objective, and that in
Whitman's vision of infinite, processional, metamorphosis
there can be nothing that is complete and certain. In the
second poem of the cluster, "From Pent-up Aching Rivers,"
the poet, in the midst of a typical catalogue, introduces
this somber note:

> From the hungry gnaw that eats me night and day,
> From native moments, from bashful pains, singing them,
> Seeking something yet unfound though I have diligently
>   sought it many a long year,
> Singing the true song of the soul fitful at random. . . .
>   (p. 91)

Characteristically, the end envisioned here is only an
indefinite "something yet unfound," but Whitman ex-

presses, as he does not in "Song of Myself," a desire for
some kind of final goal, and his soul appears not as an integral part of the cosmic procession but as an individual
spirit that is only "fitful at random."

In other poems of "Children of Adam" there is a feeling of regret at the fact that the fulfillment of the way-
faring individual hero can be only fleeting and transitory,
a longing for the kind of lasting relationship with a single
person that is denied by the very terms of Whitman's
vision. In "Out of the Rolling Ocean the Crowd," for example, Whitman's confidence in the cosmic unity of all
things is undercut by a sense of sadness at the necessity of
parting from a loved one. He begins optimistically:

> Now we have met, we have look'd, we are safe,
> Return in peace to the ocean my love,
> I too am part of that ocean my love, we are not so
>   much separated,
> Behold the great rondure, the cohesion of all, how
>   perfect!
>
> (p. 107)

But note the melancholy introduced at this point in the
poem:

> But as for me, for you, the irresistible sea is to
>   separate us,
> As for an hour carrying us diverse, yet cannot carry
>   us diverse forever;
> Be not impatient—a little space—know you I salute
>   the air, the ocean and the land,
> Every day at sundown for your dear sake my love.
>
> (p. 107)

In a later poem within the cluster, "Once I Pass'd Through a Populous City," this balance is upset, and sadness and nostalgia, unredeemed by cosmic faith, become the poet's sole emotions:

> Once I pass'd through a populous city imprinting my
>   brain for future use with its shows, architecture,
>   customs, traditions,
> Yet now of all that city I remember only a woman I
>   casually met there who detain'd me for love of
>   me,
> Day by day and night by night we were together—all
>   else has long been forgotten by me,
> I remember I say only that woman who passionately clung
>   to me,
> Again we wander, we love, we separate again,
> Again she holds me by the hand, I must not go,
> I see her close beside me with silent lips sad and
>   tremulous.
>
> (pp. 109–10)

"Facing West from California's Shores" expresses at greater length, in the form of an unanswered question, the feeling of exhaustion and unsatisfied searching that is intimated in "From Pent-up Aching Rivers":

> Long having wander'd since, round the earth having
>   wander'd,
> Now I face home again, very pleas'd and joyous,
> (But where is what I started for so long ago?
> And why is it yet unfound?)
>
> (p. 111)

In this poem the exaltation of ever-expanding procession has become the frustrated circularity, not of cyclical renewal, but of a longing that must be ever unsatisfied. This undercurrent of exhaustion and frustration finds probably its most complete expression in "As I Ebb'd with the Ocean of Life," another poem that first appeared in the 1860 edition of *Leaves of Grass*. In this poem, as the title indicates, the sense of procession is lost entirely, and Whitman envisions himself as a particle adrift in a world of flux. The central metaphor of the poem compares the poet to a bit of debris washed up from the ocean onto the land of Paumanok for a brief moment, depositing on the land shreds of his being, the poems, and returning eventually, and always in the process of returning, to the ocean. As in "Song of Myself," Whitman conceives of his individual identity as a momentary manifestation in material form of cosmic, spiritual energy; but here the sense of vital unity between the dual elements of the self is lost. He exists in an unstable, mediatory position between the dualities of concrete reality, represented by the land, and cosmic spirituality, represented by the ocean. Also similar to "Song of Myself" is the identification of self and poem, the conception of the poems as revelations or symbols of the poet's being. Here, associated with the rim of sediment that forms from the meeting and blending of land and sea, they represent a manifestation of the earthly and spiritual elements of the self. The poem, appropriately, was originally titled "Bardic Symbols." The metaphor, implicit throughout, is explicitly stated in the third section:

> I too Paumanok,
> I too have bubbled up, floated the measureless float,
>   and been wash'd on your shores,
> I too am but a trail of drift and debris,

> I too leave little wrecks upon you, you fish-shaped
> island.
>
> (p. 255)

Section one, in the past tense, is a reminiscence of a
time, such as that presented in "Song of Myself," when
the poet felt he had achieved a meaningful, organic union
of self and not self in his poetry. The first stanza presents
the urge of the electric, spiritual self reaching out toward
the land:

> Held by this electric self out of the pride of which
>   I utter poems,
> [I] Was seiz'd by the spirit that trails in the lines
>   underfoot,
> The rim, the sediment that stands for all the water and
>   all the land of the globe.
>
> (pp. 253–54)

The second stanza records the equivalent response of the
land to the expanding spirituality of the poet. At this
point the journey is perceived in the processional terms
of "Song of Myself," the poet seeking a response from the
not self and finding there the concrete "likenesses" to his
selfhood for which he is searching:

> Paumanok there and then as I thought the old thought
>   of likenesses,
> These you presented to me you fish-shaped island,
> As I wended the shores I know,
> As I walk'd with that electric self seeking types.
>
> (p. 254)

Section 2 counters this remembrance with the poet's
present feeling that his achievement has been insignifi-

cant, that he has revealed in his poems not the cosmic unity of all creation but "at the utmost a little wash'd up drift," and that the poems themselves represent only a false unity, for they contain nothing of either the "real me" or the essential not self. They no longer appear as living "grass," revealing the truths that are immanent in all organic life, but only as "dead leaves." This feeling provokes a cry of despair and disillusionment, in which Whitman repudiates his poetic journey:

O baffled, balk'd, bent to the very earth,
Oppress'd with myself that I have dared to open my mouth,
Aware now that amid all that blab whose echoes recoil upon
    me I have not once had the least idea who or what I am,
But that before all my arrogant poems the real Me stands
    yet untouch'd, untold, altogether unreach'd.

(p. 254)

Here Whitman reflects on the central paradox of his conception of cosmic selfhood: that finding or revealing "what I really am" is impossible. In "Song of Myself" Whitman meets this paradox with arrogant optimism and confidence: "Encompass worlds, but never try to encompass me." Here, however, he perceives the elusiveness of certain, essential identity more as a curse than as a cosmic blessing.

Section 3 opens with a new, but vastly different and more negative, vision of the commonality of self and not self, for both now seem to be only the victims of a cosmic meaninglessness; their unity rests only in a mutual insignificance, which manifests itself in the poems:

You oceans both, I close with you,
We murmur alike reproachfully rolling sands and drift,
    knowing not why,

> These little shreds indeed standing for you and me and
>   all.
>
> (p. 255)

As in section 1, the poems, "little shreds," "stand" for both self and not self, but in section 1 they contained positive spirituality; here, without the sense of equivalent response, they represent merely a cosmic confusion, the "reproachful murmur" of man, concrete reality, and the spiritual absolute. Section 3 builds to the emotional climax of the poem, as the poet desperately throws himself on the land, yearning now for some kind of positive response, some hint of meaning and value:

> I throw myself upon your breast my father,
> I cling to you so that you cannot unloose me,
> I hold you so firm till you answer me something.
>
> Kiss me my father,
> Touch me with your lips as I touch those I love,
> Breathe to me while I hold you close the secret of the
>   murmuring I envy.
>
> (p. 255)

The secret, however, is not revealed.

In section 4, the emotional pitch of the poem is much lower and much more level. The hero has not found the total response he is seeking, or the "secret of the murmuring," but the failure now does not occasion a despairing plea. Instead the last stanza contains the poet's melancholy, almost tragic, resignation to his instability. He begins with an acceptance of endless motion and metamorphosis: "Ebb, ocean of life, (the flow will return,)"; and he rededicates himself to his poetic journey: "I gather for myself and for this phantom looking down where we

lead, and following me and mine" (p. 255). If all sense of
a reinforcing process is gone, so too is the utter desperation
of section 3. What remains is a more balanced vision in
which some value can be achieved in the midst of instability, a "limp blossom or two" within the insignificant
drift washed up on the shore, redeeming moments within
an encompassing and baffling flux. At the end of the
poem, as at the end of "Song of Myself," Whitman writes
from the perspective of one already reabsorbed into the
absolute, but leaving behind a part of himself in his
poems:

Me and mine, loose windrows, little corpses,
Froth, snowy white, and bubbles,
(See, from my dead lips the ooze exuding at last,
See, the prismatic colors glistening and rolling,)
Tufts of straw, sands, fragments,
Buoy'd hither from many moods, one contradicting another,
From the storm, the long calm, the darkness, the swell,
Musing, pondering, a breath, a briny tear, a dab of
    liquid or soil,
Up just as much out of fathomless workings fermented and
    thrown,
A limp blossom or two, torn, just as much over waves
    floating, drifted at random.

(p. 256)

These images of a prismatic and glistening life oozing
from the midst of death, of the limp and torn blossom
washed up among the other sediment, suggest positive
value achieved in fleeting instances, at random, within a
lifetime of ultimate decay, the redeeming moments in
the ebb and flow of human existence.

The vision of "As I Ebb'd with the Ocean of Life" is, of course, hardly characteristic of Whitman. It presents a dark, poignant mood that is not often found in his published poetry and is virtually absent from everything before 1860.[14] The typical self-image of Whitman's poetry is an affirming, optimistic hero, for whom life is not a meaningless flux that terminates only in death but an eternal procession, constantly reinforced by the union of self and not self within his cosmic consciousness. Like Emerson and Thoreau, Whitman perceives an essential value inherent in the self and the not self, and he finds in the world an equivalent response to his own outreaching selfhood, a response that gives the romantic hero a strong, if not unequivocal, sense of stability, and allows an equally strong affirmation of life and the endless journey through and beyond it.

Three

ISHMAEL

THE HERO IN FLUX

The Transcendentalist movement, which in our literary
heritage serves as a focal point for the spirit of the early
nineteenth century, represented both the full-fledged ar-
rival of serious Romanticism in American writing and a
stage in the long, slow dissolution of New England Calvinism. By the 1820s Unitarianism had done a good deal to
soften the pessimism of Massachusetts Puritanism and prepare the ground for the growth of Romanticism, rolling
away, as Perry Miller put it, "the heavy stone of dogma
that had sealed up the mystical springs in the New England
character," and thus opening the way for a religion of
passion and enthusiasm at the same time, paradoxically,
that it attempted to replace the enthusiasm implicit in
Puritanism with a religion based on cold, sober rationality.[1] Consequently, for young men such as Emerson and
Thoreau the ogres of original sin, determinism, and the
awesome transcendence of God were of less concern than
the sense of emotional and spiritual starvation fostered by
their own religious environment and to which the currents of Romanticism offered an attractive alternative.
Whitman, too, had only a minimal exposure to the darker
moods of his American background, hardly enough to

hinder in any significant way his receptivity to the positive new spirit of the age.

Such was not the case with Herman Melville. Although his father was nominally a Unitarian, it was in the orthodox Calvinism of the Dutch Reformed church that Melville's sense of man and the universe were molded, and he brought to Romanticism a tough intellectual skepticism and a tragic sense of human limitations that stayed with him throughout his life.[2] Yet Romanticism, just as much as his Calvinist background, became one of the deep and abiding currents of Melville's mature thought, and though he rejected much of it as being naïvely affirmative and optimistic, his best work was produced within the context of the Romantic tradition.

In a letter to Nathaniel Hawthorne written in 1851 while he was working on *Moby Dick,* Melville expressed a certain degree of ambivalence regarding the Romantic vision of the transcendent unity of all things and insisted on the necessity of viewing each individual experience in its own integrity:

> In reading some of Goethe's sayings, so worshipped by his votaries, I came across this, *"Live in the All."* That is to say, your separate identity is but a wretched one, —good; but get out of yourself, spread and expand yourself, and bring to yourself the tinglings of life that are felt in the flowers and the woods, that are felt in the planets Saturn and Venus, and the Fixed Stars. What nonsense! Here is a fellow with a raging toothache. "My dear boy," Goethe says to him, " you are sorely afflicted with that tooth; but you must *live in the all,* and then you will be happy!" As with all great genius, there is an immense deal of flummery in Goethe, and in proportion to my own contact with him, a monstrous deal of it in me. . . .

> N. B. This "all" feeling, though, there is some truth
> in. You must often have felt it, lying on the grass on a
> warm summer's day. Your legs seem to send out shoots
> into the earth. Your hair feels like leaves upon your
> head. This is the *all* feeling. But what plays the mischief
> with the truth is that men will insist upon the universal
> application of a temporary feeling or opinion.[3]

It is in this reluctance to accept any single vision or experience as final, which is central to the thought of Emerson, Thoreau, and Whitman, that Melville was most fully
involved in the central drama of American Romanticism.
Although the results of his encounters were often vastly
different from those of Whitman and the Transcendentalists, Melville, too, was an endless experimenter.

This aspect of his thought finds its clearest expression
in the heroic drama of Ishmael, his persona in *Moby
Dick*. "I promise nothing complete," Ishmael says, "because any human thing supposed to be complete must for
that reason infallibly be faulty." [4] "God keep me from
ever completing anything" (p. 195). "I try all things. I
achieve what I can" (p. 446). Ishmael's vision is one of
endless movement, in which no single encounter can ever
be final and no single truth absolute. Like Walt Whitman, he must sing "hoping to cease not till death," but his
tune sounds more like the poignant notes of "As I Ebb'd
with the Ocean of Life" than the barbaric yawp of "Song
of Myself." Ishmael's consciousness is not cosmic like
Whitman's but highly personal, a vision in which selfhood
is distinct from all other objects and beings in the universe, in which a "raging toothache" remains a raging
toothache, and his endless journey is not one of cosmic
procession, but one which must be undertaken alone. Like
Melville's Pierre, he fights "a duel in which all seconds

are forbid." [5] In describing his part in "the grand pro-
gramme of Providence," Ishmael maintains that "it came
in as a sort of brief interlude and solo between more extensive performances" (p. 29).

Moreover, failing to find an equivalent response in
either man or nature, except possibly in his momentary
communion with Queequeg, Ishmael can derive little affirmation or satisfaction from his continual motion. In contrasting "Song of Myself" with "As I Ebb'd with the
Ocean of Life," it becomes clear that Whitman's affirmation is largely contingent upon a sense of the constant re-
creation of the union of self and other. Since Ishmael cannot achieve this union, the Romantic kinesis of *Moby
Dick* becomes not a process of affirmation but rather a
state of flux, in which the hero appears truly as the no-
madic figure suggested by his name, wandering alone
through his world, seeking full realization of self and
searching for possibilities of a fruitful encounter in society,
in man, and in nature, trying to mediate between the
human and the absolute, accumulating and weighing ideas
and beliefs, but unable to hold fixedly to any unvarying
truth. Hawthorne's observation of Melville is as appropriate to Ishmael as to his creator: "He can neither believe
nor be comfortable in his unbelief; and he is too honest
and courageous not to try to do one or the other." [6] To
find certainty is to be removed from the world of space
and time and to relinquish all possibility for further
growth and development; but to live in constant uncertainty is to suffer the curse of isolation and continual frustration. Faced with this paradox, Ishmael exists in a state
of flux, and the exhaustion and despair that are only
minor themes of the Transcendentalists and Whitman
gradually become the dominant motifs of *Moby Dick*.

Technically, of course, there are two Ishmaels: a narrator and a character. With this fact in mind, *Moby Dick*
can be read profitably as the narrator's log, a day-to-day,
in some cases moment-to-moment, record of the progress
and performance of the hero in his journey. Ishmael the
character is an objectified self, a projection of the self-
image and frame of mind of the narrator hero. In effect,
the book itself becomes identical with the journey, as the
exploring consciousness of the hero observes and investigates his self and his world through the medium of the
written word. Such an orientation makes it possible to see
that Ishmael the character, when he appears as a projection of the narrator, remains a distinct figure, essentially
passive, since uncommitted, egocentric and self-consciously
introspective, always aware, sometimes passionately and
sometimes morbidly, of his own identity in an amorphous
world. It is also possible to see that many of the other
characters represent not extensions of his selfhood but
rather alternate approaches to the not self. These alternatives are primarily three: the way of the landsman, who
rejects the journey entirely; the way of Pip, who loses
himself into a pantheistic world soul; and the way of
Ahab, who imposes his own vision upon a shapeless absolute. These are alternatives against which Ishmael the
narrator defines his own identity and the nature of his
own quest, alternatives that he observes and investigates,
but must finally reject. By following the changing moods
of Ishmael's consciousness, it is possible to examine not
only his journey, but also his sometimes hopeful and
sometimes despairing meditations about it and about the
alternative approaches to the not self that are available to
him.

    Moby Dick begins with a declaration of the necessity

for voyage, and in going to sea, Ishmael is rejecting life in society in a fashion typical of the early nineteenth-century American hero. As with Thoreau, the first clue to understanding Ishmael's experience lies in an awareness of the reasons for his retreat. The retreat is a natural concomitant of Ishmael's basic attitude toward external reality. Ishmael's vision is not holistic; the not self does not appear completely hostile and without value, but neither does it appear to be a mere transformation of the essential spiritual energy of his own selfhood, and thus wholly receptive, as it does to the Whitman of "Song of Myself." Ishmael shares the basic Transcendentalist world-view of a surface reality underlaid by a deeper spiritual, essential Reality that the hero must seek out. Like Thoreau, Ishmael must leave society to confront this essential not self. Land and sea stand in much the same relationship for Ishmael as society and the woods for Thoreau: the former represents an artificial, surface reality, and the hero must retreat to the latter for an encounter with the meaningful, spiritual core.

Beyond this basic cosmology, however, the attitudes of Thoreau and Ishmael have very little in common. The society that Thoreau rejects in *Walden* positively stifles individuality; it not only keeps the hero from an encounter with the divine not self but also corrupts the divinity within him. The core, on the other hand, consists of divine goodness. Ishmael's view is more balanced; he looks at both with "an equal eye," and he sees that both are highly ambiguous. "Ambergris," for example, suggests a core of goodness, but at the same time it is closely related to a vague and ambiguous corruption:

Now that incorruption of this most fragrant ambergris should be found in the heart of such decay; is this noth-

ing? Bethink thee of that saying of St. Paul in Corin-
thians, about corruption and incorruption; how that we
are sown in dishonor, but raised in glory. . . . Also for-
get not the strange fact that of all things of ill-savor,
Cologne-water, in its rudimentary stages, is the worst.
(p. 524)

And at its worst, the essential sea is clearly treacherous
and deceitful:

> But not only is the sea such a foe to man who is an alien
> to it, but it is also a fiend to his own offspring; worse
> than the Persian host who murdered his own guests;
> sparing not the creatures itself hath spawned. Like a
> savage tigress that tossing in the jungle overlays her own
> cubs, so the sea dashes even the mightiest whales against
> the rocks, and leaves them there side by side with the
> split wrecks of ships. No mercy, no power but its own
> controls it. Panting and snorting like a mad battle steed
> that has lost its rider, the masterless ocean overruns the
> globe.
>   Consider the subtleness of the sea; how its most dreaded
> creatures glide under water, unapparent for the most
> part, and treacherously hidden beneath the loveliest tints
> of azure. Consider also the devlish brilliance and beauty
> of many of its most remorseless tribes, as the dainty em-
> bellished shape of many species of sharks. Consider, once
> more, the universal cannibalism of the sea; all whose
> creatures prey upon each other, carrying on eternal war
> since the world began. (p. 364)

In *Walden* society is evil because it corrupts the hero's
divinity. In *Moby Dick* society, if not beneficient, is at
least bland and mild, easily understood and coped with
when viewed with equanimity. Yet life in society is still
"evil" in Ishmael's terms, because he associates it with an
avoidance of true intellectual activity and a renunciation
of the quest for a meaningful encounter with the essential
not self. He makes this association perfectly clear in

"Loomings," presenting land and water in direct opposition and concluding that "as every one knows, meditation
and water are wedded for ever" (p. 25). When this relationship is extended, life on land becomes equated not
only with non-questing but with spiritual non-being. From
the beginning, the land is related to stasis and death, as
Ishmael finds himself "involuntarily pausing before coffin
warehouses and bringing up the rear of every funeral I
meet" (p. 23). The sea journey is his "substitute for pistol
and ball," the only way of avoiding stasis and stagnation.

For Ishmael, land and society must be forsaken not so
much because of what they are as because of what they
are not. "What we have in the opening chapter," writes
Henry Nash Smith, "is a hostility toward all social institutions rather than a specific indictment of American society." [7] This position is just the reverse of that of Thoreau, who does not deny the concept of life in society, but
rather the specific society in which he finds himself. Positing a divine energy flowing into the souls of all men, it
was possible for the Transcendentalists to envision an
ideal society (one such as Brook Farm, perhaps) in which
the self, regenerate and pure, could unite with divinity
within a community of similarly unspoiled and regenerate
men. Thus, for example, Thoreau writes in the "Conclusion" to *Walden:*

> It is not for a man to put himself in such an attitude to
> society, but to maintain himself in whatever attitude he
> finds himself through obedience to the laws of his own
> being, which will never be one of opposition to a just
> government, if he should chance to meet with such.
> (p. 259)

Ishmael, on the other hand, does not specifically condemn
American society so much as he rejects the very idea of

life in any society on land, and his retreat is occasioned
not so much by a belief that life in society will cause positive harm as by the necessity to avoid stagnation by undertaking the voyage toward whatever meaningful realities
might exist.

That Ishmael's rejection of nineteenth-century American society in particular is not as emphatic as that of
Thoreau is symptomatic of Ishmael's particular paradox;
for though there is perhaps nothing that he completely
denies, there is also nothing that he can completely and
finally accept. His journey includes an examination of all
things. His attitude toward society is a guarded, somewhat pessimistic pragmatism.[8] This orientation is made
explicit in "Loomings":

> Not ignoring what is good, I am quick to perceive a
> horror, and could still be social with it—would they let
> me—since it is but well to be on friendly terms with all
> the inmates of the place one lodges in. (p. 30)

In the first section of *Moby Dick* (that is, up to the point
where the *Pequod* sails) Ishmael records his travels through
society from New York through New Bedford to Nantucket, at each stage leaving behind more of society and
approaching nearer the ocean. Through these pages
Ishmael's skeptical pragmatism is evident. He accepts the
facts of society, but maintains a certain distance, preserving his own separate nature and finding nothing to which
he can comfortably join himself. Thus, at the Spouter Inn,
"supper over, the company went back to the bar-room,
when, knowing not what else to do with myself, I resolved
to spend the rest of the evening as a looker on" (p. 40).
Ishmael's pragmatic attitude toward institutions, whether

they are ordained by society, divinity, or both, is particularly evident with regard to the church. The Negro re-
vival is described as "The Trap," and although Ishmael
listens carefully to Father Mapple's sermon, the teachings
contained therein are later molded to fit the demands of
the occasion in Ishmael's relationship with Queequeg:

> I was a good Christian; born and bred in the bosom of
> the infallible Presbyterian Church. How then could I
> unite with this wild idolator in worshipping his piece of
> wood? But what is worship? thought I. Do you suppose
> now, Ishmael, that the magnanimous God of heaven and
> earth—pagans and all included—can possibly be jealous
> of an insignificant bit of black wood? Impossible! But
> what is worship?—to do the will of God—*that* is wor-
> ship. And what is the will of God?—to do to my fellow
> man what I would have my fellow man to do to me—
> *that* is the will of God. Now Queequeg is my fellow
> man. And what do I wish that this Queequeg would do
> to me? Why, unite with me in my particular Presby-
> terian form of worship. Consequently, I must then unite
> with him in his; ergo, I must turn idolator. (p. 85)

Later, religion is completely subordinated to practicality:

> Now, as I before hinted, I have no objection to any per-
> son's religion, be it what it may, so long as that person
> does not kill or insult any other person, because that
> other person don't believe it also. But when a man's
> religion becomes really frantic; when it is a positive
> torment to him; and, in fine, makes this earth of ours
> an uncomfortable inn to lodge in; then I think it high
> time to take that individual aside and argue the point
> with him. (p. 125)

If Ishmael does not completely reject society, however,
it is clear that he can never be an integral member of

even the whaling community toward which he gravitates, for this requires an allegiance that Ishmael is unwilling to give. He is only a wanderer through New Bedford and Nantucket, and even on the *Pequod,* with the exception of the sperm-squeezing incident, he never takes part in any substantial group life. Ishmael's first commitment is to the self. This, of course, is implicit in the structure of the novel, in the narrator hero observing and exploring a projected self-image, and Ishmael makes it explicit at the very beginning, by referring to

> that story of Narcissus, who because he could not grasp the tormenting, mild image he saw in the fountain, plunged into it and was drowned. But that same image, we ourselves see in all rivers and oceans. It is the image of the ungraspable phantom of life; and this is the key to it all. (p. 26)

Ishmael's commitment to self supercedes any commitment to the community of men. Thus, he always goes to sea before the mast: "It is quite as much as I can do to take care of myself, without taking care of ships, barques, brigs, schooners, and what not" (p. 26). In this respect, Ishmael is a "true whale-hunter":

> Long exile from Christendom and civilization inevitably restores a man to that condition in which God had placed him, *i.e.* what is called savagery. Your true whale-hunter is as much a savage as an Iroquois. I myself am a savage, owning no allegiance but to the King of Cannibals; and ready at any moment to rebel against him. (p. 358)

Ishmael's attitude toward human brotherhood and personal communion, even with another "savage," is characterized by this same guarded pragmatism and dominated by a reluctance to accept any single experience as a final truth. A close analysis of Ishmael's friendship with Quee-queg, and of his attitudes toward human brotherhood in general, suggest that although Ishmael does undeniably find a momentary communion with the primitive, both he and Queequeg feel bound to withhold themselves from the responsibilities of a lasting, close friendship in order to maintain their individuality and preserve the freedom to continue their own highly personal voyages.

When Ishmael first hears of Queequeg, his reaction is one of aversion to sharing a bed, an aversion based not so much on the character of his potential mate as on a prin-ciple of individual privacy: "No man prefers to sleep two in a bed. In fact, you would a good deal rather not sleep with your own brother. I don't know how it is, but people like to be private when they are sleeping" (p. 40). Sailors, Ishmael declares, may sleep together in the same compart-ment, "but you have your own hammock, and cover your-self with your own blanket, and sleep in your own skin" (p. 40). When he awakes and finds Queequeg's arm about him, he accepts the gesture as one of friendship; but at the same time, recalling a memory from childhood, he cannot help associating it with something vaguely hostile to his mind: "Now, take away the awful fear, and my sensations at feeling the supernatural hand in mine were very simi-lar, in their strangeness, to those which I experienced on waking up and seeing Queequeg's pagan arm thrown around me" (p. 54).[9]

The highest point of communion between Ishmael and Queequeg occurs in "A Bosom Friend." Here Ishmael re-lates: "I felt a melting in me. No more my splintered heart and maddened hand were turned against the wolfish

world. This soothing savage had redeemed it" (p. 83).
Ishmael's part in the friendship, however, remains pragmatic, and his attitude is largely exploratory and tentative: "I'll try a pagan friend, thought I, since Christian
kindness has proved but hollow courtesy" (p. 84). Finally,
as they retire, their "marriage" seems complete: "Thus,
then, in our hearts' honeymoon lay I and Queequeg—a
cozy, loving pair" (p. 86). Immediately following this
"consummation," however, Ishmael strives for a reasser-
tion of his individual identity, and he emerges from this
experience feeling a certain revulsion:

> I have a way of always keeping my eyes shut, in order to
> concentrate the snugness of being in bed. Because no
> man can ever feel his own identity aright except his
> eyes be closed; as if darkness were indeed the proper
> element of our essences, though light be more congenial
> to our clayey part. Upon opening my eyes then, and
> coming out of my own pleasant and self-created dark-
> ness into the imposed and coarse outer gloom of the
> unilluminated twelve-o'clock-at-night, I experienced a
> disagreeable revulsion. (p. 87)

Finally, Ishmael's friendship with Queequeg and his deci-
sion to ship with him are as much a consequence of
Ishmael's pragmatism as of any type of real communion:

> For besides the affection I now felt for Queequeg, he
> was an experienced harpooner, and as such, could not
> fail to be of great usefulness to one, who, like me, was
> wholly ignorant of the mysteries of whaling, though
> well acquainted with the sea, as known to merchant
> seamen. (p. 90)

Once the voyage begins, very little mention is made of
the friendship between the two. Ishmael, of course, is con-

stantly present, at least as narrator, and Queequeg appears
more than occasionally, often in the role of a savior; but
the two are no longer seen in terms of a communal relationship. Coupled with this fact, many of Ishmael's comments on human brotherhood indicate that although he
did accept communion with Queequeg, he has subse-
quently rejected the finality of this close friendship; and
both he and Queequeg have retreated into their individual selves, becoming, like the entire crew, "federated
Isolatoes":

> They were nearly all Islanders in the *Pequod, Isolatoes,*
> too, I call such, not acknowledging the common con-
> tinent of men, but each *Isolato* living on a separate
> continent of his own. (p. 166)

Ishmael himself, in several places, reaffirms his own individual identity and exhorts man to be similarly detached
from the world of both men and objects. Most notable,
perhaps, is this passage from "The Blanket":

> It does seem to me that herein we see the rare virtue of
> a strong individual identity, and the rare virtue of thick
> walls, and the rare virtue of interior spaciousness. Oh,
> man! Admire and model thyself after the whale! Do
> thou, too, remain warm among ice. Do thou, too, live
> in this world without being of it. (p. 401)

These attitudes strongly suggest that Ishmael would be
unwilling to continue his brotherhood with Queequeg or
to accept human communion itself as a final truth. Even
more convincing is the portrayal of Ishmael and Queequeg
in "The Monkey Rope." This is the only concrete relationship between them following the embarkation of the

Pequod, and here the association appears as a liability and a sacrifice of free will:

> Queequeg was my own inseparable twin brother, nor could I any way get rid of the dangerous liabilities which the hempen bond entailed.
> So strongly and metaphysically did I conceive of my situation then, that while earnestly watching his motions, I seemed distinctly to perceive that my own individuality was now merged in a joint stock company of two; that my free will had received a mortal wound; and that another's mistake or misfortune might plunge innocent me into unmerited disaster and death. (p. 416)

Ishmael's commitment to self and to motion must render this type of "liability" finally unacceptable.

The ambivalence with which Ishmael reacts to both society and human brotherhood is his dominant characteristic. It is no wonder that critics arguing for completely opposite interpretations of Ishmael have been able to develop equally convincing presentations, for Ishmael, like Whitman, envelops contradictions.[10] But where Whitman could accept and affirm all things, Ishmael can only investigate them. Ishmael apprehends reality in all of its ambiguity and complexity, and, perceiving the dark as well as the light in all things, he cannot find the perfect and equivalent response in anything. His primary commitment is to self-realization, but this must be a process that leads outward rather than inward, toward a confrontation with the essential not self. Thus, for Ishmael, the solipsistic approach is out of the question, "for unless you own the whale, you are but a provincial and a sentimentalist in truth" (p. 438). Nor can Ishmael tolerate imposition upon a hostile not self or surrender to a benign nature, for both of these orientations imply finality, and to Ishmael finality means stasis and stagnation.

Positing an ambiguous and complex reality, Ishmael's approach is an attempt to acquire total knowledge of it and reveal it through the powers of his artistic perception. The whale is, of course, the focus of the essential not self in *Moby Dick,* and Ishmael's own approach toward it is most clearly illustrated in the cetological chapters. In these chapters Ishmael attempts to reveal the whale through language, to draw out the latent truth and value of reality rather than impose himself upon it in the manner of Ahab or relinquish himself to it in the manner of Pip. Again and again he restates his purpose with regard to the whale. In "Cetology," for example, he writes: "It is some systematized exhibition of the whale in his broad genera, that I would now fain put before you" (p. 179); in "Of the Monstrous Pictures of Whales":

> I shall ere long paint to you as well as one can without canvas, something like the true form of the whale as he actually appears to the eye of the whaleman when in his own absolute body the whale is moored alongside the whale ship so that he can be fairly stepped upon there. (p. 346)

The cetological chapters are Ishmael's way of trying to find some sort of stable order in the world to which he can relate himself. Ishmael is constantly aware of the difficulties involved, but he insists upon the necessity of the attempt. In "Cetology," for example, he acknowledges the enormity of his undertaking: "Yet it is no easy task. The classification of the constituents of chaos, nothing less is here assayed" (p. 179). In "The Prairie" he writes: "Though I am but ill-qualified for a pioneer, in the application of these two semi-sciences [physiognomy and phrenology] to the whale, I will do my endeavor. I try all things; I achieve what I can" (p. 446). The importance that Ishmael attributes to his task is most clearly revealed in "The Whiteness of the Whale": "But how can I hope to explain myself here; and yet, in some dim, random way explain myself I must, else all these chapters might be naught" (p. 253). In "Cetology," he describes the essential confrontation and the possible sufferings that are required of him:

> But it is a ponderous task; no ordinary lettersorter in the Post-office is equal to it. To grope down into the bottom of the sea after them; to have one's hands among the unspeakable foundations, ribs, and the very pelvis of the world; this is a fearful thing. What am I that I should assay to hood the nose of this leviathan! The awful tauntings in Job might well appal me. "Will he [the leviathan] make a covenant with thee? Behold the hope of him is in vain!" But I have swam through libraries and sailed through oceans; I have had to do with whales with these visible hands; I am in earnest; and I will try. (p. 182)

In this chapter Ishmael develops an analytical classificatory scheme for the whale. This system, however, leads him only to a realization of the ultimate inscrutability of the whale and the endless nature of his quest, although at this point he remains optimistic:

> I now leave my cetological System standing thus unfinished, even as the great Cathedral of Cologne was left, with the crane still standing upon the top of the uncompleted tower. For small erections may be finished by their first architects; grand ones, ever leave the copestone to posterity. God keep me from ever complet-

ing anything. This whole book is but a draught—nay, but the draught of a draught. Oh, Time, Strength, Cash, and Patience! (pp. 195–96)

Ishmael here is using the scientific method, but as J. A. Ward observes, the system he develops, with its Folio, Octavo, and Duodecimo whales, each "Book" divisible into "Chapters," seems to be more a mockery than an honest utilization of the method of objective observation, measurement, and classification.[11] The same tone characterizes Ishmael's other experiments with science, particularly in "A Bower in the Arsicades" and "Measurement of the Whale's Skeleton." Thus, for example, Ishmael humorously describes his investigation:

> Cutting me a green measuring-rod, I once more dived within the skeleton. From their arrow slit in the skull, the priests perceived me taking the altitude of the final rib. "How now!" they shouted; "Dar'st thou measure our god! That's for us." "Aye, priests—well, how long do ye make him, then?" But hereupon a fierce contest rose among them, concerning feet and inches; they cracked each other's sconces with their yardsticks—and seizing that lucky chance, I quickly concluded my own admeasurements. (p. 575)

Here, as in "Cetology," empirical science, whether it be classification or measurement, appears inadequate as a method for fully comprehending the whale, for getting at essential reality: "I saw no living thing within; naught was there but bones" (p. 575); "In considering these ribs, I could not but be struck anew with the circumstance, so variously repeated in this book, that the skeleton of the whale is by no means the mould of his invested form" (p. 578).

Science is unsatisfactory, however, not merely because it is inadequate to reach the essential living Reality of the whale but because this particular type of science is self-denying, for it requires a total faithfulness to the object and refutes the role of the imagination in forming reality. Classification and measurement are not creations of man, but only the transference of natural fact from one form to another. The mind, from this Lockean point of view, becomes a "tabula rasa," upon which the forms of matter are imprinted, and the self is denied an essential freedom. Ishmael is fully aware of this: "I am not free to utter any fancied measurements I please. Because there are skeleton authorities you can refer to, to test my accuracy" (p. 575). Furthermore, such a method denies the interaction of mind and matter:

> How vain and foolish then, thought I, for timid un-travelled man to try to comprehend aright this won-drous whale, by merely poring over his dead attenuated skeleton, stretched in this peaceful wood. No, only in the heart of quickest perils; only when within the eddy-ings of his angry flukes; only on the profound un-bounded sea, can the fully invested whale be truly and livingly found out. (p. 578)

Thus, something more than the method of science is required in the quest for the whale. Ishmael, consequently, also investigates the antithetical approach, the method of pure subjective perception. His exploration of the possi-bilities of both science and imagination—as well as other unnamed areas—is made clear as he records the measure-ments of the whale:

> The skeleton dimensions I shall now proceed to set down are copied verbatim from my right arm, where I

had them tattooed; as in my wild wanderings at that
period, there was no other secure way of preserving such
valuable statistics. But as I was crowded for space, and
wished the other parts of my body to remain a blank
page for a poem I was composing—at least, what un-
tattooed parts might remain—I did not trouble myself
with odd inches. (p. 576)

Pure subjectivism, however, proves equally inadequate,
for it, too, denies the essential confrontation of mind and
object. Ishmael begins his discussion of imaginative render-
ings of the whale by announcing his intention of correcting
the erroneous impressions created by such portrayals.

It may be worth while, therefore, previously to advert
to those curious imaginary portraits of him which even
down to the present confidently challenge the faith of
the landsman. It is time to set the world right in this
matter, by proving such pictures of the whale all wrong.
(p. 346)

The deceptiveness of the approaches of both science and
subjectivism clearly lies in their evasion of the encounter;
Ishmael again affirms the necessity of his quest and its
inherent dangers:

So there is no earthly way of finding out precisely what
the whale really looks like. And the only mode in which
you can derive even a tolerable idea of his living con-
tour, is by going a whaling yourself; but by so doing,
you run no small risk of being eternally stove and sunk
by him. (p. 352)

Neither empirical science nor subjective imagination,
which are the epistemological versions of the poles of the
Romantic duality, can fully reveal the whale, for the

former denies too much of the self and the latter too much
of the object:

> So, when on one side you hoist in Locke's head, you go
> over that way; but now, on the other side, hoist in Kant's
> and you come back again; but in very poor plight. Thus
> some minds forever keep trimming boat. Oh, ye foolish!
> throw all these thunderheads overboard, and then you
> will float light and right. (p. 426)

However, Ishmael here is admonishing in the aftermath
of his own experience, as he often does. For though
neither empiricism nor idealism are satisfactory in themselves, Ishmael does make use of both. His own method is
centered in the continuing encounter of self and not self,
but he brings the facilities of science and subjective perception to bear on these encounters. Ishmael in a very real
sense is "shoring up fragments against his ruin," calling
upon the aid of all approaches to knowledge in his attempt to know and reveal the whale and achieve a union
of object and personal imagination.

In this regard, Ishmael's use of history becomes clear.
History itself is a further aid to understanding, and the
fragments of historical references collected in the "Ex-
tracts" and referred to throughout the novel function as an
integral part of Ishmael's quest. By ignoring the rationality
and chronology of history, by blending fact and legend,
Ishmael attempts to provide a total illumination of the
whale. The historical ingredients themselves are significant only to the degree that they can be made meaningful
to Ishmael's particular intelligence, in the same way that
science and subjective perception are valuable only as they
can be brought to bear on the encounter itself. For this
reason Ishmael's total method is neither that of the empiri-

cist nor of the idealist, but a blending of both in a typically Romantic compromise: the symbolic perception and imagination of the artist.

Nowhere is this technique more apparent than in "The Whiteness of the Whale." Here Ishmael brings the vision of imagination to bear on the objective reality of the whale, seeing the whale symbolically in an attempt to find "some chance clue to conduct us to the hidden cause we seek" (p. 259). The result, however, is a gross parody of the Transcendentalists' confidence in imaginative perception; for instead of revealing an essential truth that is immanent but masked in visible reality, and which yields an awareness of the fundamental, divine unity of man and nature in a larger scheme, all symbolic extension and associations lead Ishmael only to the facts of ambiguity and complexity, so that having established an indefinite plurality of possible meanings, he can only declare with frustration: "And of all these things the Albino whale was the symbol. Wonder ye then at the fiery hunt?" (p. 264). For Emerson, symbolism is the vehicle for finding spiritual possibilities; here the fact of a symbolic universe is seen in negative terms, and symbolic extension is seen as potentially denying, rather than affirming, any real meaning, the very image of whiteness suggesting total absence. Ishmael begins, perhaps, with Transcendentalist premises, but his results lead him in an opposite direction. Many of Ishmael's other symbolic extensions are self-evident; in the words of Ward, "there is hardly a detail in the cetological chapters that does not have meaning that extends beyond itself." [12] A complete examination of the extensions is not really necessary, however, for although Ishmael relates the whale and whaling to virtually every field of human endeavor, he never succeeds in establishing a final and fixed pattern of unity between self and other. All Ishmael's attempts ultimately lead him only to the center of the whale, where he finds not an equivalent response but complexity, ambiguity, and a final inscrutability.

Again and again, Ishmael is faced with the impossibility of successfully completing his task. In "Cetology," for example, he states: "It was stated at the outset that this system would not be here, and at once, perfected. You cannot but plainly see that I have kept my word" (p. 195); in regard to "painting the whale": "For all these reasons, then, you must needs conclude that the great Leviathan is that one creature in the world which must remain unpainted to the very last" (p. 352). The whale's head is a riddle, comparable to "The Sphynx," and Ishmael later asserts:

> Dissect him how I may, then, I but go skin deep; I know him not, and never will. But if I know not even the tail of this whale, how comprehend his face, when face he has none? Thou shalt see my back parts, my tail, he seems to say, but my face shall not be seen. But I cannot completely make out his back parts; and hint what he will about his face, I say again he has no face. (p. 486)

Similarly, with regard to "The Fountain," he states:

> And as for this whale spout, you might almost stand in it, and yet be undecided as to what it is precisely. (p. 478)

Ishmael's position in the face of this inscrutability is the same "armed neutrality" associated with his response to society and human brotherhood. He can neither fully comprehend nor fully dismiss the not self, and thus he must remain always in motion, moving from one possibility to another in endless succession, committed, as it were, to uncommitment, involved in a journey that has no achievable end.

Initially, Ishmael is completely optimistic about this endless journey, affirming both the motion and the endless uncertainty associated with it. As has already been mentioned, the land is associated with stasis and stagnation, with spiritual non-being. When Ishmael affirms the essentiality of the spiritual life and motion that derive from voyaging, even physical death seems preferable to life on land:

> Yes, there is death in this business of whaling—a speechlessly quick chaotic bundling of a man into Eternity. But what then? Methinks we have hugely mistaken this matter of Life and Death. Methinks that what they call my shadow here on earth is my true substance. Methinks that in looking at things spiritual, we are too much like oysters observing the sun through the water, and thinking that thick water the thinnest of air. Methinks my body is but the less of my better being. In fact take my body who will, take it I say, it is not for me. And therefore three cheers for Nantucket; and come a stove boat and stove body when they will, for stave my soul, Jove himself cannot. (p. 66)

If Ishmael has any intimations of foreboding about the voyage, these are based only in the fear that he may in some way be forced into a commitment, and he easily manages to ignore them:

> If I had been downright honest with myself, I would have seen very plainly in my heart that I did but half fancy being committed this way to so long a voyage, without once laying my eyes on the man who was to

be the absolute dictator of it, so soon as the ship sailed out upon the sea. But when a man suspects any wrong, it sometimes happens that if he be already involved in the matter, he insensibly strives to cover up his suspicions even from himself. And much this way it was with me. I said nothing, and tried to think nothing. (p. 138)

Ishmael's early optimism reaches its peak in the apotheosis of Bulkington, the figure in eternal movement, unable to rest on land:

But as in landlessness alone resides the highest truth, shoreless, indefinite as God—so better it is to perish in that howling infinite, than be ingloriously dashed upon the lee, even if that were safety. (p. 149)

As early as "The Lee Shore," Ishmael senses the impossibility of achieving success in his quest, but here the questing nature overshadows inevitable failure and realizes a significant victory. Like Bulkington, Ishmael is bound to keeping the "open independence of his sea." In regard to his inability to define the nature of the whale's spout, for example, he declares:

For d'ye see, rainbows do not visit the clear air; they only irradiate vapor. And so, through all the thick mists of the dim doubts in my mind, divine intuitions now and then shoot, enkindling my fog with a heavenly ray. And for this I thank God; for all have doubts; many deny; but doubts or denials, few along with them have intuitions. Doubts of all things earthly and intuitions of some things heavenly; this combination makes neither believer nor infidel, but makes a man who regards them both with equal eye. (p. 480)

The redeeming moments of illumination that pierce through a fog of uncertainty, the unique equilibrium achieved through instability, these are the rewards of Ishmael's position, rewards similar to Whitman's "oozing life" and "limp blossoms." But Ishmael does not always describe his position in such positive terms. Much more frequently, he perceives his constant motion and uncertainty in a more ambivalent manner than the figure of Bulkington would suggest. For example, as he and Queequeg ferry to Nantucket, the first time they take to water in the novel, Ishmael stands at the rail, watching New Bedford float by, and he observes

> that one most perilous and long voyage ended, only begins a second; and a second ended, only begins a third, and so on, for ever and aye. Such is the endlessness, yea, the intolerableness of all earthly effort. (p. 93)

Yet the observation does not at this point preclude an affirmation of the quest, for Ishmael adds:

> Gaining the more open water, the bracing breeze waxed fresh; the little Moss tossed the quick foam from her bows, as a young colt his snortings. How I snuffed that Tartar air!—how I spurned that turnpike earth!—that common highway all over dented with the marks of slavish heels and hoofs; and turned me to admire the magnanimity of the sea which will permit no records. (p. 93)

The circularity suggested in the first part of this passage is central to Ishmael's image of his own quest, a sea voyage never to be completed but that must constantly and endlessly be renewed. The same ambivalent attitude toward the quest is present when Ishmael goes aboard the *Pequod* for the first time and, at Peleg's command, looks out at sea: "The prospect was unlimited, but exceedingly monotonous and foreboding; not the slightest variety that I could see" (p. 110).

At times, and increasingly as the journey proceeds, this ambivalent attitude leans more toward a renunciation of the value of the quest, a feeling provoked by the fact of its impossible nature. The gam with the *Albatross* puts Ishmael in such a mood:

> Round the world! There is much in that to inspire proud feelings; but whereto does all that circumnavigation conduct? Only through numberless perils to the very point whence we started, where those that we left behind secure were all the time before us.
>
> Were this world an endless plain, and by sailing eastward we could forever reach new distances, and discover sights more sweet and strange than any Cyclades or Islands of King Solomon, then were there promise in the voyage. But in pursuit of those far mysteries we dream of, or in tormented chase of that demon phantom that, some time or other, swims before all human hearts; while chasing such over this round globe, they either lead us on in barren mazes or midway leave us whelmed. (p. 316)

This sense of exhaustion and despair drives Ishmael so far as to advise entirely against the quest and to advocate the alternative of the landsman who repudiates the effort:

> Consider all this [the hostility of the not self]; and then turn to this green, gentle, and most docile earth; consider them both, the sea and the land; and do you not find a strange analogy to something in yourself? For as this appalling ocean surrounds the verdant land, so in the soul of man there lies one insular Tahiti, full of peace and joy, but encompassed by all the horrors of the half known life. God keep thee! Push not off from that isle, thou canst never return! (p. 364)

To voyage is to bring the self into confrontation with the
essential not self; Ishmael is firmly committed to this experience, but here he exhorts against it. Squeezing sperm
produces a similar reaction:

> For now, since by many prolonged, repeated experi-
> ences, I have perceived that in all cases man must even-
> tually lower, or at least shift, his conceit of attainable
> felicity; not placing it anywhere in the intellect or fancy;
> but in the wife, the heart, the bed, the table, the saddle,
> the fire-side, the country; now that I have perceived all
> this, I am ready to squeeze case eternally. (p. 533)

Ishmael, however, does not "squeeze case eternally"; nor
is there convincing evidence that he has "lowered his conceit of attainable felicity." Again, Ishmael is speaking in
the aftermath of his own irrevocable experience and giving
advice that he is unable to accept for himself. Having already "pushed off from that isle," the truth of his own
statement guarantees that he can never return. These feelings arise from his sense of exhaustion with the endlessness of his quest and the despair that grows from frustration and failure. To borrow a phrase from *Pierre* via
Harry Levin, Ishmael at this point is dreaming "the avenging dream":

> Weary with the invariable earth, the restless sailor
> breaks from every enfolding arm, and puts to sea in
> height of tempest that blows off shore. But in long
> night-watches at the antipodes, how heavily that ocean
> gloom lies in vast bales upon the deck; thinking that
> that very moment in his deserted hamlet-home the
> household sun is high, and many a sun-eyed maiden
> meridian as the sun. He curses Fate; himself he curses,

his senseless madness, which is himself. For whoso once
has known this sweet knowledge, and then fled it; in
absence, to him the avenging dream will come.[13]

"The "avenging dream" suggests that Ishmael's despair
is of a dual nature. The circularity and uncertainty of the
quest produce an initial feeling of exhaustion, but once
Ishmael begins to doubt the validity of his commitment
to it, the sense of despair is compounded, arising not
merely from the nature of the quest but also from the
hero's attitude toward it. At this point it is profitable to
recall Father Mapple's sermon, for the "two-stranded
lesson" developed there prefigures Ishmael's present situation. Like Jonah, Ishmael has become a fugitive from any
abstraction that may be posited as a final truth (the Puritan God, for Father Mapple). This is the "first strand,"
the despair arising from the quest itself. The second strand
applies potentially to "Pilots [preachers]," and becomes
applicable to Ishmael when he begins to exhort man to
denounce the quest that he himself has already undertaken. Now, added to the despair that arises from the
quest itself is the curse of the false preacher, he who
"while preaching to others is himself a castaway." As
Father Mapple declares:

"Woe to him who seeks to please rather than to Appal!
Woe to him whose good name is more to him than
goodness! Woe to him who, in this world, courts not
dishonor! Woe to him who would not be true, even
though to be false were salvation! Yea, woe to him who,
as the great Pilot Paul has it, while preaching to others
is himself a castaway." (p. 80)

Thus, Ishmael's preachments advocating a position that he
himself has rejected do not lighten his burden, but rather

increase the agony of the "avenging dream" and compound his despair, for while he can be drawn to, and praise the way of, the unquesting landsman, he realizes that his acceptance of the quest is irrevocable and that he himself can never actualize his preachments.

Furthermore, he remains continually aware of the landsman's utter vulnerability to the deeper, spiritual forces of the not self. To as great an extent as is possible aboard ship, Starbuck represents the non-questing landsman. Although he has left the land, he continues to accept society and personal relationships as the final truth; his "conceit of attainable felicity" is indeed placed in "the hearth, the wife, and the bed." This is evident throughout, and Starbuck makes it clear in his final conversation with Ahab:

> "Oh, my captain! my captain! noble soul! grand old heart, after all! why should any one give chase to that hated fish! Away with me! Let us fly these deadly waters! Let us home! Wife and child, too, are Starbuck's—wife and child of his brotherly, sisterly, play-fellow youth; even as thine, sir, are the wife and child of thy loving, longing, paternal old age! Away! let us away!—this instant let me alter the course! How cheerily, how hilariously, O my Captain, would we bowl on our way to see old Nantucket again! I think, sir, they have some such mild blue days, even as this, in Nantucket." (p. 684)

Starbuck is a man of strong individuality, but his individuality is like a shell that guards him against a confrontation with the essential not self:

> His pure tight skin was an excellent fit; and closely wrapped up in it, and enbalmed with inner health and strength, like a revivified Egyptian, this Starbuck seemed prepared to endure for long ages to come, and

to endure always, as now; for be it Polar snow or torrid
sun, like a patent chronometer, his interior vitality was
warranted to do well in all climates. (p. 158)

Starbuck endures primarily because he is able to withhold
himself from an encounter with essential reality. He is
involved in the voyage, but for him whaling is not an end
but merely the means to a more comfortable life on land,
and as a non-quester he is unaware of the deeper implications of voyaging:

Starbuck was no crusader after perils; in him courage
was not a sentiment; but a thing simply useful to him,
and always at hand upon all mortally practical occasions. Besides, he thought, perhaps, that in this business
of whaling, courage was one of the great staple outfits of
the ship, like her beef and her bread, and not to be
foolishly wasted. Wherefore he had no fancy for lower-
ing for whales after sun-down; nor for persisting in fighting a fish that too much persisted in fighting him. For,
thought Starbuck, I am here in this critical ocean to kill
whales for my living, and not to be killed by them for
theirs. (p. 159)

Starbuck can deal successfully only with those aspects of
the not self that are somewhat receptive and easily perceived, aspects that Ishmael associates primarily with life
on land. Confrontation with the hidden, more complex,
and more powerful forces at the core of reality inevitably
leads to his downfall, which is foreshadowed early in the
novel:

And brave as he might be, it was that sort of bravery
chiefly, visible in some intrepid men, which, while generally abiding firm in the conflict with seas, or winds,
or whales, or any of the ordinary irrational horrors of

the world, yet cannot withstand those more terrific because more spiritual terrors, which sometimes menace
you from the concentrating brow of an enraged and
mighty man. (p. 159)

Ishmael, with his devastating insight into Starbuck's spiritual limitations, knows that he cannot accept the way of
the landsman, and all his preachments advocating it yield
him only the greater despair of this knowledge. It is from
the depths of this despair that he is forcefully drawn to
the alternative approaches to the not self that are finite in
nature and do not require the endless encounters of his
own quest. These, as suggested, are the way of relinquishment, represented by Pip, and the way of imposition, represented by Ahab.

Pip's experience is typically mystical. Cast into the
ocean, he realizes an "intense concentration of self in the
middle of such a heartless immensity" (p. 529), and his
mind is driven inward until he realizes "heaven's sense,"
the spirituality of a divine world soul existing within him;
having come to this awareness, he achieves a transcendence
of earthly reality, projecting himself outside the visible
world to a transcendent atmosphere where he unites with
divinity. Pip relinquishes his personal ego to the greater
whole, the source of all value of which he may partake
only by sacrificing his claim to human reason and individual identity. In Pip's experience the Romantic duality
is broken and replaced with a pantheistic monism, in
which selfhood is submerged into the Absolute. "Pip,"
Paul Zweig writes, "maddened and made wise by his
glimpse through the veil, rises into himself; he abandons
the world which has abandoned him." [14] Pip successfully
bridges the gap between human and Absolute, but he

manages to do so only at the cost of his sanity and his humanity.

Like Pip, Ahab replaces the dualism of Ishmael's world-view with a monistic conception of reality, but Ahab's monism is the opposite of Pip's. Whereas Pip by looking inward achieves a total abandonment of self, fusing with the not self into a world soul, Ahab, also looking inward, seeks not the loss but the fullest possible development of self and the imposition of that self upon the not self. An "ungodly God-like man," Ahab is fiercely and fatedly committed to closing the gap between human and Absolute, and his approach is to substitute the self for God. As Zweig has observed, he is obsessed with molding "the chaotic waters into his own image"; he cannot rest until he has made the not self "answer to his own inwardness." [15] Ahab's objective throughout is conceptualized as a vision of apocalyptic stasis, a final destruction of a dualistic reality and its replacement with a new order in which the self has total freedom and power. For this end, all his energies have been directed into an intense concentration of self, centered about a single goal. His human "mind," or intelligence, has become so large and powerful that it completely dominates all other features of his being, including his "eternal soul," which is free from this control and able to assert its own sovereignty only while Ahab sleeps:

> The latter [i.e., the sleepwalking Ahab] was the eternal, living principle or soul in him; and in sleep, being for the time dissociated from the characterizing mind, which at other times employed it for its outer vehicle or agent, it spontaneously sought escape from the scorching contiguity of the frantic thing, of which, for the time, it was no longer an integral. (p. 272)

As Feidelson explains, in Ahab the traditional Christian
and Transcendentalist view of the relation between the
mind and the soul is reversed. "Normally, the mind gives
individual character to the soul and depends upon the
soul for its own existence; but in Ahab's case the mind,
through the intensity of its will, has created out of itself,
and then has been superseded by, an independent being:
Ahab's 'purpose.' " [16] Ahab's monomania, in other words,
now controls his divine soul:

> But as the mind does not exist unless leagued with the
> soul, therefore it must have been that, in Ahab's case,
> yielding up all his thoughts and fancies to his one
> supreme purpose; that purpose, by its own sheer in-
> veteracy of will, forced itself against gods and devils
> into a kind of self-assumed, independent being of its
> own. (p. 272)

Ahab represents a fulfillment of the dark possibilities inherent in the Romantic belief in the individual self. Unlike the Transcendentalists and Whitman, Melville had a
powerful sense of the sinister potentialities of human
beings, a real awareness of the possibility that deep inside
man there lay not a core of divinity but a malignant,
frightening evil, which could destroy the self if given free
reign. In Ahab the Romantic imagination becomes divorced from both God and nature, determined to make
its own laws and impose them on the common world.
Ahab's imagination creates a monster that feeds upon
itself, as Ishmael recognizes:

> God help thee, old man, thy thoughts have created a
> creature in thee; and he whose intense thinking thus
> makes him a Prometheus; a vulture feeds upon that

heart forever; that vulture the very creature he creates. (p. 272)

Ahab's stature and vigor are admirable, but they have been achieved only by a concentration of all his energy into a single objective and a single strategy. Ishmael tells us that upon first seeing him he was "struck with the singular posture he maintained. . . . There was an infinity of firmest fortitude, a determinate, unsurrenderable willfulness, in the fixed and fearless, forward dedication of that glance" (p. 170). Ahab's approach to the not self is purely finite; the single act of encounter and imposition is the crucial and final moment, at which time self and other will be forged into a violent and apocalyptic monism.

Ahab conceives of alternatives as existing only in the past and cannot imagine continuing beyond the encounter with Moby Dick. Ahab's rejection of alternatives becomes clear in his final encounter with Starbuck. Here he momentarily relents to think of pleasant days in Nantucket, but as Starbuck hopefully encourages him, "Ahab's glance was averted; like a blighted fruit tree he shook and cast his last cindered apple to the soil" (p. 685). Only once does Ahab mention the possibility of surviving in time, and here he does so cynically, suggesting it is to be an impossibility. Fedallah has interpreted the prophecy contained in Ahab's dream, and Ahab replies:

"I am immortal then, on land and on sea," cried Ahab, with a laugh of derision;—"immortal on land and on sea!" (p. 632)

And earlier, when Starbuck suggests the small economic value of Ahab's quest, Ahab disregards all practical results,

indeed, all consequences of any kind. Invoking Starbuck
to hark to the "little lower layer," he smites his chest and
exclaims, "My vengeance will fetch a great premium
here!" (p. 220).

Ahab says "NO! in thunder" to all things but the self,
and, as has often been observed, he admirably fulfills
Melville's conception of the tragic hero, "the man who,
like Russia or the British Empire, declares himself a
sovereign nature (in himself) amid the powers of heaven,
hell, and earth. He may perish; but so long as he exists he
insists upon treating with all Powers on an equal basis." [17]
Ahab's sovereignty is such that he can easily manipulate
the other individuals about him and use them to help him
in achieving his goal, so great that he acknowledges no
superior force. "Talk not to me of blasphemy, man,"
Ahab cries, "I'd strike the sun if it insulted me" (p. 221).
Furthermore, as Melville suggests earlier in *Moby Dick*,
Ahab's tragic greatness is closely related to the "half wil-
ful overruling morbidness at the bottom of his nature. For
all men tragically great are made so through a certain
morbidness. Be sure of this, O young ambition, all mortal
greatness is but disease" (pp. 111–12). In a larger sense
Ahab represents the full tragic potential of the dark
Romantic questing hero, who refuses to accept the distance
between self and not self. Ahab believes in the supremacy
of his own will and power and asserts himself through the
distinction of his own spirit; but he does not live in a
universe equivalent to his own spirit, and he is unable
to exist without making a relentless attempt to bridge
that gap. Although he is defeated in his attempt at final
imposition, he achieves a tragic affirmation from his effort,
for he realizes his "topmost greatness" in his "topmost
grief."

Although the approaches of Ahab and Pip represent opposite poles of the Romantic response, the final result in each case is largely the same: a single, final vision, culminating in one climactic experience, in which the gap between self and not self is erased and the dualism of the Romantic world-view is collapsed by a denial of one of the essential terms of the duality: self, in Pip's case, and not self in Ahab's. Thus the two share a peculiar affinity in the latter stages of the book. In "The Cabin," for example, Ahab remarks to Pip:

> There is that in thee, poor lad, which I feel too curing to my malady. Like cures like, and for this hunt, my malady becomes my most desired health. (p. 672)

Obviously Ahab is talking, in Shakespearean fashion, about madness, but the meaning of this passage lends itself readily to extension. Ahab's malady is his expanded concept of self and his firm belief that the self must be imposed upon a hostile not self. That in Pip which is "too curing" is the total lack of selfhood and antithetical perception of the not self. The two are similar in their denial of a compromising or mediating position, and Ahab realizes that a blending of the two would produce a balanced individual. Ishmael is such a balanced individual, but his mediating position has produced its own kind of despair.

Ishmael explicitly rejects Pip's pantheistic vision during his own experience at "The Mast-Head." Ishmael has been drawn into that type of pantheistic reverie that he describes in several places throughout the novel, in which the not self seems totally receptive:

> (He) at last loses his identity; takes the mystic ocean at his feet for the visible image of that deep, blue, bottom-

less soul, pervading mankind and nature; and every
strange, half-seen, gliding, beautiful thing that eludes
him. (p. 214)

But Ishmael realizes that:

Move your foot or hand an inch; slip your hold at all;
and your identity comes back in horror. Over Descartian
vortices you hover. And perhaps, at midday, in the fair-
est weather, with one half-throttled shriek you drop
through the transparent air into the summer sea, no
more to rise forever. Heed it well, ye Pantheists! (pp.
214–15)

Later, however, when Ishmael's own despair has height-
ened, he sees a certain positive value in such an experience:

Pip saw the multitudinous, God-omnipresent, coral in-
sects, that out of the firmament of waters heaved the
colossal orbs. He saw God's foot upon the treadle of
the loom, and spoke it; and therefore his shipmates
called him mad. So man's insanity is heaven's sense; and
wandering from all mortal reason, man comes at last
to that celestial thought, which, to reason, is absurd and
frantic; and weal or woe, feels then uncompromised,
indifferent as his God. (p. 530)

Yet Ishmael, who at this point compares his own subsequent experience to Pip's, must ultimately reject this
approach, a fact to which the continuing quest embodied
in the novel stands as confirming proof. For Ishmael's
quest is not only one of mediation and reconciliation but
one directed equally toward self-realization and definition.
Because of this concern with self, the way of Ahab represents finally a more feasible alternative to Ishmael than the
way of Pip. This is the reason, perhaps, why Ishmael de-

votes the bulk of his meditation to an examination of the story of Ahab.

Ishmael's attraction toward the way of Ahab is made explicit in "Moby Dick":

> I, Ishmael, was one of that crew; my shouts had gone up with the rest; my oath and been welded with theirs; and stronger I shouted, and more did I hammer and clinch my oath, because of the dread in my soul. A wild, mystical, sympathetical feeling was in me; Ahab's quenchless feud seemed mine. (p. 239)

Paul Brodtkorb has suggested that alleviation of the "dread" mentioned here is the primary motive behind Ishmael's journey, and, to the extent that this emotion is associated with the boredom and restlessness displayed toward life on land in the opening chapter, this is quite true.[18] However, Ishmael's emotions at this point seem quite different from the feelings that made it impossible for him to be at ease on land. In the opening chapters Ishmael's attitude and tone were sardonic and somewhat flippant; here he is desperate. The intensity of this emotion suggests that it is quite distinct from that initial discontent, that it is, rather, a manifestation of the darker despair that grows on Ishmael during the course of his voyage. As Ishmael becomes disenchanted with his own paradoxical and circular situation, the linear view of Ahab seems to present the most satisfactory and heroic escape from the uncertainty and instability of the endless journey. At times Ishmael yearns for finality and stasis. Death itself even appears to be the only solution to the *Weltschmerz* produced by the unbridgeable gap between human and Absolute. Viewing Queequeg in his coffin, Ishmael verbalizes this feeling:

For whatever is truly wondrous and fearful in man,
never yet was put into words or books. And the drawing
near of Death, which alike levels all, alike impresses all
with a last revelation, which only an author from the
dead could adequately tell. So that—let us say it again
—no dying Chaldee or Greek had higher and holier
thoughts than those, whose mysterious shades you saw
creeping over the face of poor Queequeg, as he quietly
lay in his swaying hammock, and the rolling sea seemed
gently rocking him to his final rest, and the ocean's in-
visible flood-tide lifted him higher and higher towards
his destined heaven. (pp. 607–8)

Queequeg, however, decides that he is not ready to die.
Here the parallel nature of Ishmael and Queequeg, and
the reason why neither could accept their friendship as
final, becomes clear. Both have a larger commitment,
Queequeg to unraveling the key to the universe that has
been cryptically tatooed on his body by a prophet in his
native land, and Ishmael to the endless attempt to find a
satisfactory relationship with the not self through an understanding and artistic revelation of the whale. At this
point both Queequeg and Ishmael sense that the final
truth they are seeking lies only in death. Ishmael describes
this intuition as he views the apparently dying Queequeg,
and the savage illustrates its symbolically by transferring
his "secret" from his living body to a more appropriate
location—his coffin. But Ishmael and Queequeg also realize that everything certain, absolute, and eternal is also
lifeless and cold. Therefore, just as Queequeg decides that
he is not ready to die, so Ishmael, though recognizing the
inevitable failure of his own quest, continues it and remains true to its kinetic requirements. The crucial scene
in this regard is "The Try-Works," for here Ishmael himself "tries out" each of the three major alternatives, under-

goes his own ordeal by fire, and emerges tempered, to engage his own quest with renewed vigor.

In the overall structure of the novel "The Try-Works" stands as the climax of a five-chapter configuration beginning with "The Castaway," which presents the way of Pip. This is followed by "A Squeeze of the Hand", embodying the alternative of the unquesting landsman. Each of these chapters has already been discussed and needs no further explanation here. The next chapter, "The Cassock," presents the way of Ahab. Like Ahab in "The Quarter-Deck" and "The Candles," the mincer is portrayed as a priestly figure in charge of an inverted worship, whose foreskin cloak itself represents an idol to be worshipped, an exaltation of masculinity and self. Also like Ahab, the mincer's task is one of imposition upon, and destruction of, the whale, chopping it into "bible-leaf" slices, shielded by the expanded concept of self symbolized by his cloak: "Immemorial to all his order, this investiture alone will adequately protect him, while employed in the peculiar functions of his office" (p. 536). "All his order" includes all men who defiantly impose themselves upon either God or the not self; the "investiture" is the concentrated and exalted self that is essential to such an approach.

All three of these approaches are brought together in the pots and fire of the try-works. Ishmael begins by identifying the pots with the human communication he has previously associated with the land: "While employed in polishing them—one man in each pot, side by side—many confidential communications are carried on, over the iron lips" (p. 538). The kiln itself is something of a hearth, an object that Ishmael associates with land and home: "The hatch, removed from the top of the works, now afforded

a wide hearth in front of them" (p. 539). The windlass is
described as a "sea-sofa" (p. 540), and, like the traditional
hearth, the setting becomes a place for fraternization and
sociability.

But Ishmael also identifies the scene with Ahab's monomania:

> The burning ship drove on, as if remorsely commis-
> sioned to some vengeful deed . . . and the *Pequod,*
> freighted with savages, and laden with fire, and burning
> a corpse, and plunging into that blackness of darkness
> seemed the material counterpart of her monomaniac
> commander's soul. (pp. 539, 540)

Finally, the loss of self appears in the self-consuming
whale, associated with the pantheistic ritual burning of
eastern religion, in whose smoke the self is enveloped:

> Like a plethoric burning martyr, or a self-consuming
> misanthrope, once ignited, the whale supplies his own
> fuel and burns by his own body. Would that he con-
> sumed his own smoke! for his smoke is horrible to in-
> hale, and inhale it you must, and not only that, but you
> must live in it for the time. It has an unspeakable, wild,
> Hindoo odor about it, such as may lurk in the vicinity
> of funeral pyres. (p. 539)

As Ishmael looks on and examines these three visions,
all distorted into nightmare form, they creep inside of
him and become his own: "These at last begat kindred
visions in my soul, so soon as I began to yield to that unaccountable drowsiness which would ever come over me
at a midnight helm" (p. 541). The "midnight helm" is, of
course, also the setting of Pierre's "avenging dream."
Yielding to this dream, Ishmael accepts these alternatives,

an acceptance that necessarily includes a denial of his own quest. As soon as this happens, however, Ishmael is "conscious of something fatally wrong" (p. 541); he has been turned around, spiritually as well as physically, and he realizes that these alternatives, which seek only stasis or avoidance of the quest, have no valid direction, but only offer an artificial escape from the earthly predicament:

> Uppermost was the impression, that whatever swift, rushing thing I stood on was not so much bound to any haven ahead as rushing from all havens astern. A stark, bewildered feeling, as of death, came over me. (p. 541)

Death and stasis now appear as a "jet gloom," not only invalid goals but goals that can be reached only by sacrificing the possibilities for self-development and reconciliation with objective reality. These possibilities, however, few and far between they may be, can be found only through endless motion. Death here represents not a release from *Weltschmerz* but only a greater bewilderment. It is not attractive, but something to be avoided, and Ishmael struggles fitfully against it, barely managing to avoid the catastrophe.

This experience leads him to a firm affirmation of the validity of his own quest:

> Look not too long in the face of the fire, O man! Never dream with thy hand on the helm! Turn not thy back to the compass; accept the first hint of the hitching tiller; believe not the artificial fire, when its redness makes all things look ghastly. (pp. 541–42)

At this point Ishmael has achieved his highest degree of sophistication, for though his attitude is one of optimistic renewal, his optimism is balanced, as it is not, for example, in "The Lee Shore," by a full acknowledgement of the negative aspects of the quest. The natural sun, symbolic of space and time, is bright and clear, but "hides not . . . the dark side of this earth. . . . So, therefore, that mortal man who hath more of joy than sorrow in him, that mortal man cannot be true—not true, or undeveloped" (p. 542). But despite these negative elements, he realizes that following the urges of the despair that tempt him toward the solutions of stasis can lead only to inversion and deadness of spirit:

> But even Solomon, he says, "the man that wandereth out of the way of understanding shall remain" (*i.e.* even while living) "in the congregation of the dead." Give not thyself up, then, to fire, lest it invert thee, deaden thee; as for the time it did me. (p. 543)

Ishmael realizes that "there is a wisdom that is woe, but there is a woe that is madness" (p. 543). Knowledge of the necessity for an endless journey produces "woe," but Ishmael realizes that this woe must not be allowed to force him into the "madness" typified by Ahab and Pip. His balanced affirmation is symbolized by the Catskill eagle, a more mature and less innocent Bulkington figure, who "can alike dive down in the blackest gorges, and soar out of them into the sunny spaces. And even if he forever flies within the gorge, that gorge is in the mountains; so that even in his lowest swoop the mountain eagle is still higher than other birds upon the plain, even though they soar" (p. 543). This description is similar to Ishmael's position with regard to the whale's spout: "And so through all the thick mists of the dim doubts in my mind, divine intuitions now and then shoot, enkindling my fog with a heavenly ray" (p. 480). Such moments of inspiration can be achieved only in the midst of uncertainty, instability, and flux.

This affirmation is continued in the following chapter, "The Lamp," which serves as a brief postscript to the experience of the four previous chapters. Here the quest is again seen as the sole source of value:

> But the whaleman, as he seeks the food of light, so he lives in light. . . . He goes and hunts for his oil, so as to be sure of its freshness and genuineness, even as the traveller on the prairie hunts up his own supper of game. (p. 544)

Only in endless movement can the hero remain alive; stasis means darkness and death.

But the redeeming moments of light are too often overshadowed by a sense of exhaustion and despair. As "The Try-Works" stands as the climax of these five chapters, so in a sense it is the climax of the story of Ishmael as it is recorded in *Moby Dick*. It represents a commitment that Ishmael will never revoke, but it is also the high point of his affirmation. From here on, his attitude becomes more and more negative. Immediately following this point, the circularity of the quest begins again to impinge upon him, for even when light is found, it is only temporary. The decks must be "stowed down and cleared up" and the "whole weary thing" must be repeated:

> Oh! my friends, but this is man-killing! Yet this is life. For hardly have we mortals by long toilings extracted from this world's vast bulk its small but valuable sperm; and then, with weary patience cleansed ourselves, from its defilements, and learned to live here in clean tabernacles of the soul; hardly is this done when—*There she blows!*—the ghost is spouted up, and away we sail

to fight some other world and go through young life's
old routine again. (p. 548)

Furthermore, Ishmael begins to perceive that there is
an inherent danger in the nature of this approach. Constant and endless motion requires that the self exist in a
state of almost constant metamorphosis, and the protean
character demanded by this endless motion may reduce
the self to nothingness.[19] This danger is dramatized late
in the novel by the introduction of a new, low-comic
character, the carpenter, a creator like Ishmael, and also a
protean figure who exists as a living corpse. Ishmael's own
protean nature emerges in several places. In the opening
chapter he tells us that he has been a schoolmaster, and
later we learn that he has been, as well as a sailor, a
traveler, a scientist, an artist, and a historian, a "stone-
mason, and also a great digger of ditches, canals, and wells,
wine-vaults, cellars, and cisterns of all sorts" (p. 580). The
carpenter, too, is a jack-of-all-trades, "prepared at all
points and alike indifferent and without respect in all.
Teeth he accounted bits of ivory; heads he deemed but
top-blocks; men themselves he lightly held for capstans"
(p. 594). "Faith," for him, has become "just an expression" (p. 666). "Was it," Ishmael asks, "that this old carpenter had been a life-long wanderer, whose much rolling, to and fro, not only had gathered no moss; but what
is more, had rubbed off whatever small outward clingings
might have originally pertained to him? He was a stript
abstract; an unfractioned integral; living without pre-
meditated reference to this world or the next" (p. 595).
    This is the third time of note that Ishmael has described
this state of utter indifference. With regard to Bulkington (p. 149) it is totally positive, representing "the highest

truth." Pertaining to Pip (p. 530) it is still desirable, but
primarily as compensation for an otherwise ambiguous
experience. Here it seems to be a completely negative attitude. This change suggests the direction that Ishmael's
view of his own quest has taken, from an early optimism,
through ambivalence, to solid pessimism. Lacking individuality or personality, the carpenter exists only by the
"unaccountable, cunning, life-principle." Ishmael brings
him closest to his own identity when he describes him "a
great part of the time soliloquizing; but only like an unreasoning wheel, which also hummingly soliloquizes"
(p. 596). Ishmael fears that in his quest, his own soliloquy,
he, too, may become only as an "unreasoning wheel,"
stripped of all components of vital selfhood. In the figure
of the carpenter Ishmael recognizes the darkest, most pessimistic reflection of his own nature.

Perth, the blacksmith, another low-comic character, offers a similar commentary on Ahab and Pip. Ruined on
land, alienated from his work, his friends, and his family,
Perth has gone to sea seeking a release from his despair in
stasis and death: "To the death-longing eyes of such men,
who still have left in them some interior compunctions
against suicide, does the all-contributed and all-receptive
ocean alluringly spread forth his whole plain" (p. 617).
Unlike Pip, he does not see the not self as fully receptive,
yet he still yearns for personal extinction in the universal
life.[20] Unlike Ahab, he has no great conception of self or
any desire for imposition. His character is as equally indifferent as that of the carpenter, and as a result he longs
for death and stasis. Ahab, perhaps, sees his own reflection
in the blacksmith and realizes that only his monumental
madness keeps him from degenerating into a similar
figure. Ahab says:

"Thy shrunk voice sounds too calmly, sanely woeful
to me. In no paradise myself, I am impatient of all other
misery in others that is not mad. Thou should'st go
mad, blacksmith; say, why dost thou not go mad? How
can'st thou endure without being mad? Do the heavens
yet hate thee, that thou can'st not go mad? (p. 619)

Ishmael might ask himself a similar question, for in his
despair the "madness" of static finality continues to tempt
and beckon him.

The next chapter, "The Gilder," presents the most
comprehensive description of Ishmael's despair. Initially
he reaches out toward pantheism, but realizing that the
not self is rarely totally receptive, and that the redeeming
moments are few, he turns immediately toward death as
the only possible release. Like the blacksmith, he seems
here almost to yearn for death:

Oh, grassy glades! oh, ever vernal endless landscapes in
the soul; in ye, men yet may roll, like young horses in
new morning clover; and for some few fleeting moments,
feel the cool dew of the life immortal on them. Would
to God these blessed calms would last. But the mingled,
mingling threads of life are woven by warp and woof:
calms crossed by storms, a storm for every calm. There is
no steady unretracing progress in this life; we do not
advance through fixed gradations, and at the last one
pause:—through infancy's unconscious spell, boyhood's
thoughtless faith, adolescence' doubt (the common
doom), then skepticism, then disbelief, resting at last in
manhood's pondering repose of If. But once gone
through, we trace the round again; and are infants, boys,
and men, and Ifs eternally. Where lies the final harbor,
whence we unmoor no more? In what rapt ether sails the
world, of which the weariest will never weary? Where
is the foundling's father hidden? Our souls are like those
orphans whose unwedded mothers die in bearing them:

the secret of our paternity lies in their grave, and we
must there to learn it. (pp. 623–24)

Here the romantic kinesis is clearly mere flux rather than
a process of affirmation. Motion is perceived in the circular
terms that are characteristic of Ishmael, and instead of
producing satisfaction and affirmation, it leads to despair.

If "The Gilder" is the most complete statement of the
nature of Ishmael's despair, the "Epilogue" is the most
conclusive statement of his firm commitment to his quest
as it has been and will continue to be. When *Moby Dick*
is seen as Ishmael's "log," the circular motion embodied
in the structure of the book becomes clear, for it is precisely at the point where the adventure ends that the
quest, the writing of the book, begins. Ishmael the character, after the "Epilogue," becomes Ishmael the narrator,
who then projects back a self-image in the creation of the
novel. Thus, within the work of art Ishmael is endlessly
recreated; and so is the narrator's quest.

This basic circularity is reflected in the imagery of the
"Epilogue." Ishmael describes himself, as he has been
throughout, as a passive, uncommitted figure, "floating on
the margin of the ensuing scene," but bound like Ixion to
an ever revolving wheel:

> Round and round, then, and ever contracting towards
> the button-like black bubble at the axis of that slowly
> wheeling circle, like another Ixion I did revolve. (p. 724)

When the circular motion ceases, Queequeg's coffin
emerges from the "black bubble." The end of motion
means death. The coffin functions naturally as a significant
memento mori, but its meaning is extended by its con-
tents, for upon it Queequeg has transcribed from his body

"a complete theory of the heavens and the earth, and a mystical treatise on the art of attaining truth" (p. 612). The location of these secrets merely stresses what Ishmael already knows: that the certainty they promise can be found only in death.

The coffin, however, is also strongly associated with life. In the immediate moment it is a "life-preserver," but more importantly, it exists as evidence of artistic achievement, the life of the imagination, for it was built by the carpenter and inscribed by Queequeg, both of whom are parallel figures to Ishmael. The intimate mixture of life and death contained in the symbol of the coffin and implicit in the "Epilogue" itself reinforces the paradox of the endless journey. Despite the fact that certainty and stability lie only in death and stasis, that death itself *is,* perhaps, the only final truth, the only value that exists is to be found in the instability of motion and life, in the continuing encounters of self and not self.

The "Epilogue" affirms the value of the endless circularity involved in Ishmael's quest, but undercuts this affirmation with a reminder of the fact that it can yield no certainty and reveal no final truth, and is much more conducive to despair and frustration than to satisfaction. There is no reason to assume that Ishmael's survival is in any way representative of any moral or spiritual "salvation." [21] On a literal level Ishmael lives through the wreck of the *Pequod* only because, by chance, he happened to be thrown out of the whale boat, where he was placed by chance in the first place, as a result of the death of Fedallah and the switched position of Ahab's bowsman. On a doctrinal level his survival does not grow out of the novel so much as it precedes it. *Moby Dick* is the record of a hero involved in an endless quest, who will accept no static alternatives—the type of quest recorded here presupposes the hero's continuity. The "Epilogue" simply reemphasizes the fact of Ishmael's endless journey; it represents neither curse nor blessing, but a mixture of both. Ishmael affirms the life-through-motion of the flowing, rather than freezing, imagination, and he accepts the uncertainty associated with such a resolution. His success lies in the illuminating moments that flare up within his instability. But these redeeming moments are few and far between, and the figure riding Queequeg's coffin, although not as negative as the image of the carpenter, is neither the tragically heroic Bulkington nor the soaring, balanced Catskill Eagle. As he was at the beginning and as he describes his soul in "The Gilder," he is only another orphan, "fitful at random," who, like the lost children of Rachel, must wander until death in the wilderness of flux that is his life.

Four

THE APOCALYPTIC
IMAGINATION OF
A. GORDON PYM

The Romantic attempt to unify through imaginative perception the polarities of a world conceived in dualistic terms contains within itself a critical ambiguity: it is never totally clear whether the self discovers a vision of transcendent unity that is immanent in the not self, or whether the imagination actively creates this vision and projects it onto nature. Consequently, the Romantic sensibility is always in danger of embracing either a pantheism that denies individual identity, as illustrated by Pip in *Moby Dick,* or an idealism that in its extreme form can become solipsistic. These dangers are present—for example, in the Transcendentalists and Whitman—even when the not self appears receptive and offers an equivalent response to the imaginative vision; but when the not self appears hostile or ambiguous, as it does, for example, in *Moby Dick,* the tendency to allow the imagination to assert its own sovereignty and freedom from external reality is inevitably increased. When this happens, the imagination becomes apocalyptic, destroying the old reality and replacing it with a new and more felicitous vision. Ahab represents one form of the apocalyptic Romantic imagination, the sensibility that makes its own laws and values and relentlessly insists on imposing them on the common world. But the apocalyptic imagination, rather than imposing itself on reality, may also totally dismiss reality and retreat into its own solipsistic isolation, with no concern at all for the common world. In this case the direction of the heroic journey is inward, toward the development of pure selfhood and toward estrangement from, rather than engagement with, the not self; and such is the heroic journey portrayed in Poe's *The Narrative of A. Gordon Pym.*

Certain critics, such as Killis Campbell, have demonstrated that Poe was, to a much greater extent than is commonly assumed, a child of his times.[1] These critics emphasize Poe's high degree of involvement and concern with the social and intellectual issues of his age and the manner in which this concern finds its way into his art. This critical approach is important, for it must not be forgotten that Poe did face the New World. He demanded a confrontation with his locale, demanded something from his locale; but he found nothing out of which to forge his art. The not self appeared barren, artificial and deceptive, irrelevant, or what is worse, detrimental to the search for self-realization. Poe's artistic movement into selfhood was largely a response to this environment. As William Carlos Williams puts it in *In The American Grain:*

> Either the New World must be mine as I will have it, or it is a worthless bog. There can be no concession. . . . It was a gesture to be CLEAN. It was a wish to HAVE the world or leave it. It was the truest instinct in America demanding to be satisfied, and an end to makeshifts, self-deceptions, and grotesque excuses. And yet the grotesque inappropriateness of the life about him forced itself in among his words.[2]

Poe could not "have" the world on his own terms and therefore, as an artist, he left it. Unable to find satisfaction in the reality around him, Poe created another world through his imagination, a world in which the self was absolute and sufficient and external reality was destroyed. Poe, undeniably, was a product and a part of his environment, but as Harry Levin maintains, he "is never more the child of his century than when he is denouncing it or else, with all of his mechanical ingenuity, busily devising the means to transcend it." [3] Nowhere did Poe devise these means more effectively than in *The Narrative of A. Gordon Pym.*

The critic assumes several risks in attempting to deal thematically with *The Narrative.* Whether one accepts Poe's own statement that it is a "silly book," [4] or holds with Edward H. Davidson that "it forms the most complete statement Poe ever made of his artistic practice," [5] the immense textual problems associated with the writing of the book cannot be ignored. J. V. Ridgely and Iola Haverstick present convincing biographical and stylistic evidence that the book was written in five distinct stages, each with a new plot, a new central character, and a new purpose, and they maintain that the tale as a whole has at most only a spurious unity.[6] The relatively few critics who have taken *The Narrative* seriously seem to be as unsure in their interpretation as Ridgely and Haverstick suggest that Poe was in his writing. The only firm point of agreement seems to be on Poe's sources, and even here there are conflicting interpretations regarding his use of them.[7] Yet if it is difficult to view the work in terms of structural or thematic unity, it is equally difficult to accept as a logical necessity Ridgely and Haverstick's conclusion that "the story lacks a controlling theme and has no uncontroverti-

ble serious meaning." [8] There does seem to be at least one
"controlling theme," and it is a theme that is present not
only in the many fragmentary voyages of A. Gordon Pym
but also throughout most of the remainder of Poe's artistic
world: the retreat from social and natural reality, from a
world of endless metamorphosis, flux, and illusion, to an
experience that is fixed and eternal, a world constituted
purely of the expanded and interminate imagination,
existing "out of space—out of time."

The Narrative, however, is not a direct and steady
movement toward this or any other goal. Rather, it is com-
prised of a number of repeated encounters with the not
self, encounters which become the major incidents in the
narrative structure of the tale. Each of these encounters
consists of the repetition of a basic motif: the exploration,
rejection, and subsequent destruction of some facet of the
not self, followed by a movement into a state of isolation
in which Pym asserts the superior validity of the supernal
vision of his imagination. Although, as the textual evidence indicates, these encounters are largely self-contained,
they are not unrelated. There is a halting progression evident in the tale as a whole, for each encounter begins on
a more primitive level of the not self than its predecessor,
and each ends with a slightly stronger assertion of the
independent validity of the imagination. Rejecting society,
Pym turns first toward primitive nature and human community or brotherhood. However, he finds there not
divinity or other value but hostility. His initial retreats
into selfhood, moreover, yield more horror than ecstasy,
and he scrambles frantically for a renewal of contact with
the not self, for reentry into the world, seeking for possibilities there on an ever more primitive level, each time
stripping away more and more of the superfluities imposed

by the environment of nineteenth-century America, and each time finding no possibility, until at last, having exhausted all the possibilities of even the ultimate in primitivism, he accepts completely the state of pure solipsistic selfhood, the world of the apocalyptic imagination, be it nightmare or dream, heaven or hell. It is as if each time Poe resumed work on *The Narrative* he did so with a vengeance, embodying an increasingly negative verdict on the world around him.

The Narrative begins with Poe's almost ceremonial, scornful slap at the American public, a slap that, as much as anything else, is the purpose of the preface. Mr. Poe, Pym relates,

> advised me, among others, to prepare at once a full account of what I had seen and undergone, and trust to the shrewdness and common sense of the public—insisting, with great plausibility, that however roughly, as regards mere authorship, my book should be got up, its very uncouthness, if there were any, would give it all the better chance of being received as truth.[9]

Pym goes on to explain how the "shrewd" public refused to be taken in by the "ruse" that presented the account as fictional, and how he came to realize that he thus had "little to fear on the score of popular incredulity" (2:725). This same attitude is implicit throughout Poe's artistic world. In the stories of ratiocination it is illustrated by M. Dupin, the alienated intellectual who takes his stand on the fringes of society and condescendingly waits for the masses to come to him when they are unable to resolve their own dilemmas; in the poetry, by Israfel, who dwells out of space and time and can for that reason alone "sing so wildly well"; in the letters it is found in wry comments

such as the one that Poe directs to his fellow poet, B—:
"I would be as much ashamed of the world's good opinion
as proud of your own" (2:855).

The Narrative itself, however, begins in the full reality
of the not self. Pym opens with a brief autobiographical
sketch, placing himself firmly within the context of New
England society, to the extent that even his own identity
and his own values seem to be socially derived:

> My name is Arthur Gordon Pym. My father was a re-
> spectable trader in sea-stores at Nantucket, where I was
> born. My maternal grandfather was an attorney in good
> practice. He was fortunate in everything, and had specu-
> lated very successfully in stocks of the Edgarton New-
> Bank, as it was formerly called. By these and other
> means he had managed to lay by a tolerable sum of
> money. He was more attached to myself, I believe, than
> to any other person in the world, and I expected to in-
> herit most of his property at his death. He sent me, at
> six years of age, to the school of old Mr. Ricketts, a
> gentleman with only one arm, and of eccentric manners
> —he is well known to almost every person who has
> visited New Bedford. I stayed at his school until I was
> sixteen, when I left him for Mr. E. Ronald's academy
> on the hill. Here I became intimate with the son of
> Mr. Barnard, a sea captain, who generally sailed in the
> employ of Lloyd and Vredenburgh—Mr. Barnard is
> also very well known in New Bedford, and has many
> relations, I am certain, in Edgarton. (2:725)

The *Ariel* adventure in chapter one represents Pym's
first encounter with a not self other than the society to
which he has been accustomed. Leaving behind the society
of the Barnards' house and the land, Pym, accompanied
by his friend Augustus, ventures into an encounter with
the elemental sea. Pym's "intimate" relationship with

Augustus Barnard is one of brotherhood. The two share a bed and escape together in a state of mutual intoxication; and Pym's first disillusioning realization is that this human brotherhood is illusory and deceptive. "At this period," Pym relates, "I knew little about the management of a boat, and was now depending entirely upon the nautical skill of my friend" (2:726). His dependence is betrayed, for Augustus has deceived him, and Pym realizes that "his conduct in bed had been the result of a highly concentrated state of intoxication—a state which, like madness, frequently enables the victim to imitate the outward demeanor of one in perfect possession of his senses" (2:727). Left alone in confrontation with the sea, Pym relates that it was "hardly possible to conceive the extremity of my terror" (2:727). Nature is hostile and destructive:

> A fierce wind and strong ebb tide were hurrying us to destruction. A storm was evidently gathering behind us; we had neither compass nor provisions; and it was clear that, if we held our present course, we should be out of sight of land before daybreak. (2:727)

Faced with such a situation, Pym resolves to recommend himself to God, but:

> Hardly had I come to this resolution, when suddenly, a loud and long scream or yell, as if from the throats of a thousand demons, seemed to pervade the whole atmosphere around and above the boat. (2:728)

At this point Pym has experimented with human brotherhood and elemental nature, and he has found both to be deceptive and painful. Yet it is this very pain that becomes the principle tactic in his strategy of self-realization.

The physical senses are most active and most fully alive
when stimulated by suffering; the mind is keenest and
most acute when confronted with the strange and un-
familiar. The bizzare shipwreck that brings to a peak the
physical and mental agony that has been mounting
throughout the *Ariel* affair climaxes Pym's self-awareness
and enables him to raise his consciousness of self to an
apocalyptic pitch, totally erasing all consciousness of a
not self: "I tumbled headlong and insensible upon the
body of my fallen companion" (2:728). As Geoffrey Hart-
man writes concerning the apocalyptic imagination, it
describes "a mind which actively desires the inauguration
of a totally new epoch . . . and since what stands between
us and the end of the [old] world is the world . . . [it
may also] characterize any strong desire to cast out nature
and to achieve an unmediated contact with the principle
of things." [10] For Pym, the "principle of things" is the
imaginative vision of a world elsewhere that can be at-
tained only by a total withdrawal into the personal ego, a
complete lack of consciousness of any objective reality. In
The Narrative this withdrawal is represented by uncon-
sciousness and expressed by total silence. As C. M. Bowra
writes, "By setting its strongest hopes on some supernal
order of things, in the end it [Poe's Romanticism] broke
the bonds which kept the poet to earth, and by doing this
made poetry itself unnecessary. If all that matters is the
final vision, and if this world is an ugly sham, there is no
need for the poet to put his experience into words." [11] In
essence, the opening chapter of *The Narrative* contains a
microcosm of the total movement of the tale.

When Pym again becomes conscious, he finds himself in
the midst of a less complex and more primitive social
reality—not society, but rather the smaller and more

simple community of a whaling vessel. Paradoxically, it is
only because this community, like the apparent brotherhood of Pym and Augustus, is deceptive and illusory, that
Pym is rescued; for immediately upon crashing into the
Ariel, the social order of the whaler is destroyed by the
mutiny of Henderson the mate, who "told the Captain he
considered him a fit subject for the gallows, and that he
would disobey his orders if he were hanged for it the moment he set his foot on shore" (2:729). The rejection of
human brotherhood, however, cannot at this point be
complete, for Henderson, in disrupting the community of
the ship, is acting out of motives of genuine human concern for the castaways. Throughout the *Ariel* adventure
the mood is one of illusion and constant metamorphosis.
Intoxication and sobriety, destruction and salvation, social
disregard and human concern become intimately mixed
and unidentifiable, opposites merging into each other and
emerging only in an unclear and deceptive form.

When Pym returns to land, he is no longer the integral
member of society that he was before the night's adventure. He now stands apart from society, his identity conceived in opposition to the Barnards. At the breakfast
table Pym himself becomes an agent of deception against
society:

> Schoolboys, however, can accomplish wonders in the
> way of deception, and I verily believe not one of our
> friends in Nantucket had the slightest suspicion that
> the terrible story told by some sailors in town of their
> having run down a vessel at sea and drowned some
> thirty or forty poor devils, had reference either to the
> Ariel, my companion, or myself. (2:731)

At this point in the tale it seems that Pym's rejection of
society has already been decided. Before it can become

complete, however, the initial deception must be expanded, with the help of Augustus, into an intricate scheme to hoodwink his family. This scheme climaxes when Pym, disguised as a sailor, denies his identity to his grandfather, thus, as Harry Levin suggests, making himself an orphan.[12] Pym's identity is derived now neither from society nor from ancestry, but from within.

Pym's rejection of society is obvious, but the motives behind his retreat are not as clear. In fact, with the prospect of a substantial inheritance from his grandfather, he seems to occupy quite a comfortable niche, and he evinces no apparent discontent with his situation. Pym's attitude toward his journey, however, provides the answer:

> It might be supposed that a catastrophe such as I have just related would have effectually cooled my incipient passion for the sea. On the contrary, I never experienced a more ardent longing for the wild adventures incident to the life of a navigator than within a week after our miraculous deliverance. This short period proved amply long enough to erase from my memory the shadows, and bring out in vivid light all the pleasurably exciting points of color, all the picturesqueness, of the late perilous accident. My conversations with Augustus grew daily more frequent and more intensely full of interest. . . . It is strange, too, that he most strongly enlisted my feelings in behalf of the life of a seaman, when he depicted his more terrible moments of suffering and despair. For the bright side of the painting I had a limited sympathy. My visions were of shipwreck and famine; of death or captivity among barbarian hordes; of a lifetime dragged out in sorrow and tears, upon some gray and desolate rock, in an ocean unapproachable and unknown. (2:732)

These visions are characteristic of what Mario Praz calls "romantic exoticism." As Praz explains, the exoticist transports himself in imagination outside the actualities of time and space and thinks he sees in whatever is past and remote from him the ideal atmosphere for the contentment of his senses.[13] It is not difficult to see how the dream world envisioned by the exoticist can easily become a solipsistic world. For the Romantic, exoticism is in effect a version of the urge toward subjectivity, and if the world elsewhere that the hero envisions exists neither in the past nor in some remote part of the actual present, then it can exist as a unique world created solely by the imagination. Such is the case with Pym. His visionary realm is typical of the ideality imagined by the exoticists whom Praz examines, a world characterized by "agolognia," an intimate and inseparable blending of pleasure and pain, love and hate, tenderness and sadism. Its attractiveness is enhanced by those very qualitites that would seem to make it repulsive, and there is a correlative delight in pain and melancholy, a "loveliness of terror," which is most beautiful when cursed and relished more as it becomes sadder and more painful.[14] These visions also reinforce Pym's strategy for achieving his escape from external reality, which is one of immolation, the infliction of pain upon the self in order to increase self-awareness until ultimately the hero is relieved of all consciousness. Pym finds a lustful joy in contamination, a perverse fulfillment in melancholy, in the absorption of a fatal, satanic energy. Furthermore, Pym relates that these dreams were not merely visions:

> Such visions or desires—for they amounted to desires—
> are common, I have since been assured, to the whole
> numerous race of the melancholy among men—at the
> time of which I speak I regarded them only as prophetic
> glimpses of a destiny which I felt myself in a measure
> bound to fulfill. (2:732)

The bulk of chapters two and three, which describe Pym's incarceration in the hold of the *Grampus,* contain his first extended venture into self-isolation following the retreat from society, a venture that proceeds in two stages, beginning, of course, with the fact of his isolation. This situation is at first pleasant enough. Pym has a few essentials—food, water, light, a watch, and several books—and he relates that "I thought I had never seen a nicer little room than the one in which I now found myself" (2:734). When the brig puts out to sea, however, Pym falls into a sound slumber, transitional to the second stage of his experience. When he awakes, a key dimension of the not self has vanished: "Striking a light, I looked at the watch; but it was run down, and there were, consequently, no means of determining how long I slept" (2:737). Food and water have diminished, books no longer hold an interest for him, light itself will soon be unavailable, and with time absent, Pym lapses into a world of dreams, visions that represent a fulfillment of his previously mentioned desires for catastrophe and immolation, for the entire dissolution of external reality: "My dreams were of the most terrific description. Every species of calamity befell me" (2:738).

At no point during this stage of the incarceration is there a clear distinction between dreams and reality. Pym, however, has not entered a world of pure selfhood. The dream world is invaded by his dog, Tiger, and Pym flounders momentarily in "indistinctness and confusion," until gradually his senses return. When this happens, he realizes the horror of his situation, and his first thought is for reentry into the world of time and human companionship. Frantically, he attempts to force open the trap door, only to find himself shut off from escape. For the remainder of

his incarceration Pym attempts to impose some sort of
order upon his world by utilizing the elemental items of
the not self that are at his disposal. His efforts, however,
are in vain. Again, all reality is characterized by illusion
and metamorphosis. The message from Augustus promises
deliverance, but delivers only despair when it appears to
be blank; and after Pym's hopes soar as a result of his
realization that he has not read the underside of the paper,
the words in their vagueness produce only "indefinable
horror." Tiger inexplicably turns on him, and, as in the
Ariel adventure, it is only a paradoxical turn of fate—his
"fit of perverseness" in smashing the cordial bottle on the
floor—that effects his rescue.

But when Pym emerges from the hold, it is only to re-
live, in a slightly different form, his previous experiences,
to repeat the pattern of encounter. The world he returns
to is a still more primitive world than the one he left before retreating into the hold; but rather than being more
receptive to the self, it is only more illusory and more evil.
Again, a mutiny has occurred; the social organization of
the *Grampus* has been destroyed, to be replaced eventually
not by a more simple order but only by a more intense
chaos. The movement toward a primitive order begins
with the mutiny; but the mutineers themselves soon begin
to vanish, and the ship itself slowly begins to disintegrate.
The overthrow of the mutineers by Pym, Peters, and
Augustus, accomplished largely through deception, re-
duces the number of men on board to four; and shortly
after this event, a gale begins reducing the *Grampus* to
the drifting hulk that it is soon to become.

During this storm Pym goes through the same routine
of mounting pain, isolation, and eventual loss of consciousness that he experienced aboard the *Ariel* and in

the hold of the *Grampus*. As suffering and anxiety increase, Augustus, Parker, and Peters pass out, leaving Pym alone in a state of consciousness. In this isolated condition Pym, too, lapses into partial insensibility, and dreams once again fill his mind. Now, however, Pym does not dream of catastrophe or the agologniacal awareness of the self in a fixed and stable atmosphere. Instead, the images that fill his mind are of the not self, images associated primarily with the land and the society that he has left behind; and now the flux, the metamorphoses, and the instability of reality appear not deceptive and treacherous but exceedingly attractive:

> The most pleasant images floated in my imagination; such as green trees, waving meadows of ripe grain, processions of dancing girls, troops of cavalry, and other fantasies. I now remembered that, in all which passed before my mind's eye, *motion* was a predominant idea. Thus, I never fancied any stationary object, such as a house, a mountain, or anything of that kind; but windmills, ships, large birds, balloons, people on horseback, carriages driving furiously, and similar moving objects, presented themselves in endless succession. (2:777)

The change in the nature of Pym's dreams is representative of an inversion that is taking place in the location of his being. By this point his visions of catastrophe and immolation do not need to be sublimated into dreams, for they are becoming actualized. As Pym moves toward the complete realization of his imaginative vision, his dreams represent a yearning for the instability of life associated with the not self that he has forsaken, and that, from his present perspective, appears more attractive than previously. When Pym regains consciousness, however, he finds that the pleasantness of these images has been a delu-

sion. The storm has abated, and he and his companions
are adrift on a wreck in a deadly calm.

The simple social order on the raft produces at first a
sense of community among the survivors. They help each
other adjust to the situation, both physically and with
words of consolation, and they engage in a mutual endeavor to dive into the hold to secure provisions. With
hunger and desperation, however, the community rapidly
dissolves, and Pym increasingly finds himself standing
alone against the others. It is he who must dive into the
hold, he who must revive the others when they lapse into
drunkenness, and finally he alone who opposes Parker's
suggestion that they resort to cannibalism, His disagree-
ment, however, is ineffectual, and the sense of community
deteriorates into the lowest and most beastly form of
human violation. Just as the social order becomes more
and more primitive, so, too, the natural not self becomes increasingly hostile and imposing. The wind and
sea are constant tormentors, alternating between storm
and calm. The marine life is grotesque: a gull deposits
on Pym's raft the remnants of a body it has been gnawing;
and sharks swim up on the hulk, finally clustering about
it to mutilate the dead body of Augustus, when Peters, no
longer able to endure its putrefaction, pushes it over-
board.

Throughout the entire episode on the wreck, all reality
remains deceptive. An approaching brig becomes a ghost
ship manned by corpses, a ship heading in Pym's direction unaccountably changes course, and a crisis that seems
to forbode utter destruction becomes a blessing, as the
bottom of the capsized hulk reveals a plentiful supply of
barnacles. Thus far, Pym has moved from an assumption
that man lives by order, law, and design in his private

life and in society to the realization that man survives
through deception, from an assumption of the coherence
and reality of the not self to a recognition that everything, even the most logically substantial, is an illusion.[15]
This entire section of *The Narrative* involves the dissolution, by degrees, of the elements of external reality; and
with each more primitive stage a new level of beastliness
and horror arises.

Whether the section of *The Narrative* from the point
where Pym and Peters are picked up by the *Jane Guy* to
the end forms an entirely new story, unrelated to what
has gone before and complete in itself, as L. Moffit Cecil
contends,[16] or whether, as Davidson and Patrick Quinn
maintain,[17] the tale as a whole has a structural unity, it is
evident that the story at this point takes on a new direction. For one thing, Pym's narration in this section is
rendered in a much different style from what has gone
before. Previously, the narrator has been largely the characteristic voice of Poe's tales, describing in grotesque and
vivid detail the most terrifying of human emotions. In
what follows, except for the episode at Tsalal, the narration is far less subjective; the voice is much more often
that of an impassive observer. Pym himself, in the text,
makes it clear that the past is to be erased and a new beginning to be undertaken:

> Peters and myself recovered entirely from the effects of
> our late privation and dreadful suffering, and we began
> to remember what had passed rather as a frightful
> dream from which we had been happily awakened, than
> as events which had taken place in sober and naked
> reality. I have since found that this species of partial
> oblivion is usually brought about by sudden transition,
> whether from joy to sorrow or sorrow to joy—the de-

gree of forgetfulness being proportioned to the degree
of difference in the exchange. (2:803)

Sudden transition there certainly is, but not in terms
of the basic concerns of *The Narrative*. The sharp break,
rather, occurs in regard to the level of encounter. The inversion suggested by Pym's pleasant dreams upon the raft
is now much nearer completion. Suddenly Pym's world
exists on a far more primitive base and is characterized by
a much more highly expanded concept of self. Whether,
as Harry Levin suggests, the cannibalism on the raft,
representative of the worst of human nature, forms a
climactic point in the tale, after which Pym can no longer
be at all concerned with the possibilities of humanity,[18]
or whether, as the textual evidence indicates, Poe began at
this point a substantially new piece of work, actually
makes little difference. In this section of the tale the hero
moves rapidly into a position of total selfhood, with only
a brief pause at the most primitive level of the not self
for a final repetition of the motif of encounter, exploration, rejection, and the final destruction.

Except in this final encounter, at Tsalal, there are no
characters to speak of in the remaining portions of *The
Narrative*. Peters is mentioned hardly at all and only in
an offhand manner. Captain Guy, "deficient in energy
and . . . spirit of enterprise" (2:803), is merely a pawn
in the hands of the narrator. When Pym expresses a desire
to go south, the *Jane Guy* goes south. Pym himself even
begins to disappear as a distinct character, becoming more
and more only a voice. Everything associated with external
reality recedes from importance, fading into the intense
chiaroscuro of a Pym-created and Pym-inhabited world, in
which the only reality is that of the creative imagination.

Pym remains only as a narrator, a voice engaged in the imaginative creation of a world made up entirely of the expanding self, a concept that in the latter pages of the tale becomes symbolized by the color white.

Only gradually, however, does this retreat into pure selfhood become manifest in *The Narrative,* and it is completed only in the final moments of the tale. In the course of the *Jane Guy's* cruise from the location off Cape St. Roque to the island of Tsalal, remnants of the metamorphic and illusory not self remain. The weather is in constant change: "A perfect hurricane will be blowing at one moment from the northward or northeast, and in the next not a breath of wind will be felt in that direction, while from the southwest it will come out all at once with a violence almost inconceivable" (2:804). Desolation Island presents "a deceitful appearance . . . caused by a small plant resembling saxifrage, which is abundant, growing in large patches on a species of crumbling moss" (2:805).

However, as the *Jane Guy* travels beyond the furthest previous reach of man's exploration, Pym is free to expel from his imaginative world any commitment to verisimilitude, either natural or psychological. Almost immediately, the motif of whiteness begins to pervade the tale, always associated with Pym's "discoveries," elements that have no counterpart in known reality. He observes, for example, the carcass of a strange variety of Antarctic Bear:

> It was three feet in length, and but six inches in height, with four very short legs, the feet armed with long claws of a brilliant scarlet, and resembling coral in substance. The body was covered with a straight silky hair, perfectly white. The tail was peaked like that of a rat, and about a foot and a half long. (2:819)

The motif of whiteness, however, disappears as the *Jane Guy* nears Tsalal. It is, in fact, overshadowed by a growing motif of blackness. The sea becomes "extraordinarily dark," the inhabitants of Tsalal are "jet black," clothed in the skins of a black animal, carrying black stones in the bottoms of their canoes. As the writer of the concluding "Note" makes sure to point out, "nothing *white* was to be found at Tsalal, and nothing otherwise in the subsequent voyage to the region beyond" (2:853). It is also at Tsalal that Pym reappears as a distinct character and the style once more becomes subjective. It is at Tsalal that Pym constructs, in the form of the most primitive aspects of man and nature, the scene of his final encounter with the not self, which is symbolized by the color black.

Tsalal seems at first to be an island paradise. The inhabitants are friendly, food is abundant, and Pym maintains that

> not one of us had at this time the slightest suspicion of the good faith of the savages. They had uniformly behaved with the greatest decorum, aiding us with alacrity in our work, offering us their commodities, frequently without price, and never, in any instance, pilfering a single article, although the high value they set upon the goods we had with us was evident by the extravagant demonstrations of joy always manifested upon our making them a present. The women especially were most obliging in every respect, and, upon the whole, we should have been the most suspicious of human beings had we entertained a single thought of perfidy on the part of a people who treated us so well. (2:830)

But faith in even the most primitive of human beings is a dangerous illusion:

> A very short while sufficed to prove that this apparent
> kindness of disposition was only the result of a deeply-
> laid plan for our destruction, and that the islanders
> for whom we entertained such inordinate feelings of
> esteem, were among the most barbarous, subtle, and
> bloodthirsty wretches that ever contaminated the face
> of the globe. (2:830)

Nor is primitive nature any different. Even the waters, the
rocks, and the mountains, all of which are weirdly strati-
fied, operate in hostility to Pym. When the deception of
primitive man and nature reaches its climax in the massa-
cre of the crew of the *Jane Guy,* Pym has examined and
rejected the last possibility of the not self:

> I was suddenly aware of a concussion resembling nothing
> I had ever before experienced, and which impressed me
> with a vague conception, if indeed I thought of any-
> thing, that *the whole foundations of the solid globe
> were suddenly rent assunder, and that the day of uni-
> versal dissolution was at hand.* (2:832, italics added)

All that remains is the possibility of human brotherhood
with Peters. But as Leslie Fiedler maintains, even in the
act of saving Pym, Peters remains the fiend and ogre that
he was apparently intended to be in Pym's initial description (see 2:751).[19] Pym, poised on the edge of a precipice,
falls—apparently into destruction, but actually into the
arms of Peters: "A dusky, fiendish, and filmy figure stood
immediately beneath me; and, sighing, I sunk down
with a bursting heart, and plunged within its arms" (2:
845). Even as a savior, Peters remains an ogre, and Pym,
having rejected this last possibility, withdraws as a character and begins his final movement into pure selfhood.
As Pym progresses toward the "pole," the black not self

recedes, merging first into the "light gray vapour" of the southern horizon and finally into the blinding whiteness of the apocalyptic imagination. The style ceases to be subjective, and Pym begins to vanish as a narrator as well as a character, having relinquished completely all ties with the not self: "I felt a *numbness* of body and mind—a dreaminess of sensation—but this was all" (2:851). Peters, too, has for all purposes ceased to exist: "(He) spoke little, and I knew not what to think of his apathy" (2:851). Their other companion "breathed, and no more" (2:851). The world now is exclusively and exhaustively a Pym world, and being such, it can no longer be communicated. The retreat from the not self that was foreshadowed in Pym's several earlier states of insensibility is now complete. The not self has been totally dismissed; the objectified self of Pym as character has been drawn into the mind, and with not even the material self as an object of consciousness, the narrator himself can no longer be conscious, having fully retreated into the stable, eternal experience of pure selfhood. The not self has been dismissed so completely that not even language is left, and *The Narrative* itself must cease.

The question of whether Pym finds ecstasy or annihilation at the end of *The Narrative* is an interesting and challenging one, but in the final analysis it is irrelevant. Pym, in the course of his journey, has examined not only the not self but also the self, and he has fully experienced the horrors of the isolated state. These horrors, however, whatever they may be, represent finally a more attractive alternative to Pym than any encounter with the not self. The realm of the imagination, divorced from eternal reality, has been chosen for better or worse, and whether it is dream or nightmare makes no difference to Pym.

Poe's poetry reveals two attitudes toward such an experience, suggesting that he himself had no single-minded opinion about it. Poems such as "To Helen" and "Israfel" describe a realm of positive ideality; thus, Israfel exists in a world

> Where deep thoughts are a duty—
> Where Love's a grown-up God—
> Where the Houri glances are
> Imbued with all the beauty
> Which we worship in a star.
>
> (1:43)

Just as in "To Helen" Poe celebrates the power of the imagination to actively create beauty, so in "Israfel" he laments:

> If I could dwell
> Where Israfel
>   Hath dwelt, and he where I,
> He might not sing so wildly well
>   A mortal melody,
> While a bolder note than this might swell
>   From my lyre within the sky.
>
> (1:43)

Poe does not describe the nature of external reality in this poem, except to say that it is "a world of sweets and sours," where "flowers are merely—flowers." The implication, however, is that this realm is maleficent to the poetic imagination. For Poe there can be no vital or meaningful relationship between the self and the not self. The poet's quest for fulfillment has a chance of being successful only when he can free his imagination from the constrictions of reality. The role of the poet is purely that of creator, molding poetic forms out of the material of his own individual soul, and in no way discovering or un-covering them in the not self, for they are simply not to be found there. The individual identity of the self, the fulfillment of the potentiality that is represented by Isra-fel, is something that can be realized only by a complete separation of self from not self. In other poems, however, this world of self appears as one in which the poet is trapped in some psychotic nightmare of his own creation. Thus, for example, Poe's "Dream-land" consists of

> Bottomless vales and boundless floods,
> And chasms, and caves, and Titan woods,
> With forms that no man can discover
> For the tears that drip all over;
> Mountains toppling evermore;
> Into seas without a shore;
> Seas that restlessly aspire,
> Surging into skies of fire;
> Lakes that endlessly outspread
> Their lone waters—still and chilly
> With the snows of the lolling lily.
>
>   (1:70)

Just as in Poe's poetry this darker vision appears more frequently, so in the ending of *The Narrative* the pros-pect seems to be predominantly one of annihilation. Yet this interpretation is not as indisputable as some critics maintain.[20] The closing paragraph does begin with a sug-gestion of impending doom, but the final sentences seem to imply that Pym does not fall into the terrifying chasm:

> And now we rushed into the embraces of the cataract, where a chasm threw itself open to receive us. *But* there

> arose in our pathway a shrouded human figure, very
> far larger in its proportions than any dweller among
> men, and the hue of the skin of the figure was of the
> perfect whiteness of the snow. (2:852, italics added)

Pym leaves no further clue to the meaning of the "shrouded
human figure," but considering the consistent association
between images of whiteness and the creative power of the
imagination, it seems reasonable to assume that the closing
lines are intended to represent the final movement into
pure selfhood, in which the hero is "saved" from destruction by the redeeming power of the imagination.

One final question must be entertained with regard to
The Narrative. Is it finished? This question has been a
challenging one for critics, but like the problem of inter-
preting the ending, it cannot be given a final or unquali-
fied answer, for, as Davidson maintains, it is both finished
and unfinished.[21] Thematically, the tale is complete. Pym
has escaped from reality by destroying it and has retreated into a solipsistic world, banishing the not self so
completely that not even language is left. There is nothing
left to say, and if there were, it could not be said. This
thematic conclusion, however, creates a structural problem; for if Pym has vanished from reality, when did he
write his narrative, and how did it fall into the hands of
the "anonymous editor"? To make at least a token attempt at a rational explanation for the existence of the
manuscript, Poe appended a "Note." Most scholars agree
that the "Note" was written primarily to arouse interest
and curiosity and increase the book's market value, and
that it does not stand as an integral part of the tale itself.
Nevertheless, without entering the philosophical morass
of the question of fictional closure, it is illuminating to

compare Poe's strategy with that of Melville in *Moby Dick.*

Technically, any piece of fiction related by a first person narrator, unless it is in diary form, must have a circular structure if it is to be considered complete.[22] Nineteenth-century convention demanded that the narrator at least indicate the manner in which he arrived at the point where he began to relate his adventures, the point where he changes from character to narrator. Within the work of art the reader should be able to follow him as he endlessly repeats this metamorphosis, the beginning of the tale both preceding and following the conclusion in an endless circle of action and words. Melville accomplishes this by having Ishmael describe his own survival in the "Epilogue" of *Moby Dick.* Poe, on the other hand, evades this responsibility by adding a "Note" written by an anonymous hand, which leaves Pym's whereabouts unknown. The "Note" remarks that Pym may have returned to the United States, but, as Davidson observes, the statement carries little conviction.[23] This tactic relieves Poe of the necessity of returning his hero to the world of space and time. For Melville, such a return posed no special problem, for Ishmael never leaves the metamorphosis and flux of reality. Pym, on the other hand, enters a world of pure selfhood, an eternal realm, and, as Davidson says, Poe "could not bring Pym back to reality again if reality no longer exists." [24] *The Narrative* stands as a record of the Romantic hero's recoil from a valueless, illusory not self into a world in which the self, for better or worse, is the only reality.

Five

PATERSON

THE POET AS TRAGIC HERO

Whitman in "Song of Myself" and Poe in *The Narrative of A. Gordon Pym* represent the polar forms of nineteenth-century American Romanticism: the aspiration toward a complete union of self and not self in a pantheistic whole, and the recoil of the self into the world of an isolated, solipsistic imagination. In the twentieth century the Romantic hero has tended to move in a range between these ideal types. Generally, the modern hero is unable to achieve a total reconciliation with the world in which he exisis, but at the same time he has been unwilling to reject totally the need for that reconciliation. Consequently, he moves along Emerson's "diagonal line," seeking redeeming moments of stability, fluctuating emotionally between the affirmations of Thoreau and the darker, more ironic and despairing vision of Melville's Ishmael. For both William Carlos Williams and Wallace Stevens, the two men with whom my final chapters are concerned, the Whitmanian urge toward confrontation and merger with external reality is still the starting point; but this urge often fails to find, either spiritually or culturally, an equivalent response in nature or society, and the hero consequently turns increasingly toward Poe's end of the scale, toward an affirmation of pure self and the world of the imagination.

The immediate, formative influences upon Williams and Stevens did not come from the Romantics, much less from the Transcendentalists; early contemporary criticism most often approached their work in the context of "Imagism," "Symbolism," and the broad currents of French and German aesthetics and epistemology. In recent years, however, a growing number of scholars have recognized and begun to trace the lines of similarity between these modern poets and the central concerns of both English Romanticism and the American poetic and heroic tradition.[1] Both Williams and Stevens are concerned with fundamentally the same problems as the earlier American Romantics, and the framework within which they approach these problems is essentially the framework of the Romantic tradition as it developed in American literature.

As with the nineteenth-century heroes, so with Williams and Stevens a dualistic conception of reality—represented for Williams by "ideas" and "things" and for Stevens by "imagination" and "reality"—is the starting point of all endeavor, and the heart of the heroic quest lies in the attempt of the self to achieve a unification of these dualities. As with the Transcendentalists, so with the modern Romantics language and style are the prime vehicles for achieving this unification, and the hero, the "central man," is the man of creative imagination. But of the great Transcendentalist triangle of self, not self, and divine spirit, divine spirit more often than not has been deleted, leaving the modern hero without the main strategy of the Transcendentalists' resolution, leaving the self in naked confrontation with the world, and producing a thoroughly naturalized Romanticism, stripped of a belief in any kind of prior, essential value. The modern hero, like Stevens' "Snow Man," begins by realizing his own "nothingness" and in the external world "beholds / Nothing that is not there and the nothing that is." [2]

In this sort of existential and naturalistic vision, toward which both Williams and Stevens are temperamentally inclined, the absence of divine spirit creates the need for a new religion, a new mythology. After the "death of gods" and with an awareness of nothingness, the desire of the mind for harmony and meaningfulness must be satisfied by a new order, but it must be an order that has its sources in man himself and the reality of his experience. In such a world art itself, and the ability of the artist to create himself as hero and produce his own transcendent unification, becomes increasingly more important and more essential to the heroic quest, so much so that in Williams and Stevens the Romantic tendency to identify self-fulfillment with artistic creation is brought to its culmination, within a framework that is purged of all supernaturalism. As Roy Harvey Pearce explains, the poetic act becomes the sole means of self-identification and self-preservation, for "esthetic experience is the only means we have of initiating the inquiry by which we arrive at propositions and is, moreover, the only means we have of realizing and believing in them." [3] But the poetic act is a process that demands constant change and self-adjustment and endless re-creation. Poetry must remain forever in process, with success achieved in redeeming moments only to grow stale and demand renewal. More than ever, for the modern Romantic, the heroic journey is a series of endless experiments.

In dealing with *Paterson,* as with the other works examined, it is helpful to distinguish between two levels of the heroic experience: on one level is the poet himself, William Carlos Williams, engaged in a quest to create the poem that will itself be an artistic unification of the dualities of his world; on a second level is the hero within the poem, whose experience is a reflection of the dramatic movement of the poet's consciousness. As Linda Wagner and other critics have observed, the hero within *Paterson* is not a simple consciousness moving toward a single goal, but rather a diverse, all-inclusive being, a composite of elements of nature, city, art, and the poet himself, whose own identity is never totally separate from the changing identities of the persona.[4] Indeed, the hero within the poem is often indistinguishable from the poet writing the poem; but the distinction must be maintained for analytical purposes, for it is the quest of the single consciousness of the poet to create his poem, more than the action of the metamorphic hero within the poem, that gives *Paterson* its sense of epical continuity. Moreover, the metamorphic nature of the hero within the poem grows directly from Williams's conception of his poetic quest; the metamorphic hero is a necessary part of Williams's attempt to fuse the dualities of his world into an artistic whole. The premise and key metaphor of *Paterson*—"that a man in himself is a city" [5]—determines the nature of the hero within the poem, but it is also, as Williams wrote in his *Autobiography,* "the result of an attempt to find an image large enough to embody the whole knowable world around me." [6] Thus, to understand the dual levels of the Romantic heroic experience in *Paterson,* it is necessary to begin with a brief survey of Williams's conception of poetry and its relationship to the central tradition of American Romanticism.

For Williams a poem (one is tempted to say, "the ultimate poem") is an independent object existing in its own right, depending upon external objects and at the same time free from them, thus allowing the object to be itself at the same time that it confirms its own independent existence.[7] The poem is not a representation of a thing, but a thing itself. It is compounded of words, which are themselves independent objects, whose sole significance and meaning lies in their power of referring to something else and thus, like the total poem, making both things, idea and object, real. Poetry then becomes "new form dealt with as reality in itself," and the result is "to enter a new world, and have there freedom of movement and newness." [8]

Such a "new world," however, is possible only when the word or image of the poem precisely embodies both the idea within the mind and the concrete object to which it refers. Thus, the central dictum of *Paterson,* as of all Williams's poetry, is "no ideas but in things." "Ideas," the conceptions and imaginative constructs of the self, can be brought to fruition only when they are located within, or have a basis in, the reality of the not self, in "things." For Williams there is to be no affirmation and no fulfillment unless it can be on these terms, and the accomplishment of this goal, to find in objects a concrete manifestation of conceptions, forms the heart of William's poetic quest. He makes this clear in the opening lines of the poem:

> "Rigor of beauty is the quest. But how will you find beauty when it is locked in the mind past all remonstrance?"

(p. 11)

As long as the conception remains "locked in the mind," it can never achieve actualization. Without the essential "marriage" of imagination and object, the idea conceived

by the self remains "divorced," full of potentiality but
destined to remain isolated and sterile, like the image
that recurs throughout *Paterson* of

> a bud forever green,
> tight-curled, upon the pavement, perfect
> in juice and substance but divorced, divorced
> from its fellows, fallen low—
>
> (p. 28)

The power of the self, which is located in imaginative
conceptions of the mind, will be wasted unless it can be
released from the mind and merged with the concrete
object. For the poet the consequence of isolated thought
is staleness and stagnation:

> and the craft,
> subverted by thought, rolling up, let
> him beware lest he turn to no more than
> the writing of stale poems . . .
> Minds like beds always made up,
>   (more stony than a shore)
> unwilling or unable.
>
> (p. 13)

While divorce negates the imaginative power of the
mind, it also has the effect of devitalizing the pure, existential reality to which the mind's conceptions must be
related, the "beautiful thing" to which Williams refers
throughout the poem. Like Emerson, Williams insists on
the need for perceiving a vital reality that lies hidden or
obscured beneath the surface of reality. The difference
between the modern and the nineteenth-century Romantic is that for Emerson this vital reality is a spiritual es-

sence that is immanent, but veiled, in material objects. For Williams the "beautiful thing" is wholly natural, the pure existential object, which has become obscured by the false names men have given it and the outworn conceptions by which they have sought to capture it. The "beautiful thing" of *Paterson* is represented by the female principle in all its forms, usually women themselves or flowers. It is the object with which the poet, the male principle of the poem, must unite to create marriage and bring about consummation. This core of reality is not necessarily "beautiful" in the conventional meaning of the word. It may (and does) consist of both beauty and ugliness, but it is "beautiful" to the poet because of its purity and vitality. In *Paterson I*, for example, an archetype of this principle is the "first wife" in the *National Geographic* picture, a basic force which supports its replicas. As Williams explains the meaning of the picture:

> Which is to say, though it be poorly
> said, there is a first wife
> and a first beauty, complex, ovate—
> the woody sepals standing back under
> the stress to hold it there, innate
>
> (p. 33)

However, the beautiful thing has been so maligned and perverted by the misnomers of modern language and so hidden beneath the false and artificial abstractions of society, that it is buried like the "musty bone" of the *Preface*. In Book I it appears as:

> a flower within a flower whose history
> (within the mind) crouching
> among the ferny rocks, laughs at the names

by which they think to trap it. Escapes!
Never by running but by lying still—

(p. 33)

Unless the poet can find this reality and bring himself
into marriage with it, it too will remain impotent and
sterile, and both self and other, thus divorced, will perish.
To quote again from the *Preface:*

(The multiple seed,
packed tight with detail, soured,
is lost in the flux and the mind,
distracted, floats off in the same
scum)

(p. 12)

The philosophy of language implied by the dictum "no
ideas but in things" has a direct parallel in American
Transcendentalism. The Transcendentalists posited an
essential creative energy emanating from a divine source
in two parallel currents, into the self and into nature,
thus creating a total correspondence of conceptions and
objects. It was the function of the poet to discover and
name the unity of idea and object. The word, or, more
specifically, the symbol, was to be a sign both of man's
idea and of a natural fact, both of which were, in turn,
signs of spiritual facts. Language united the parallel strands
of divinity and, by closing the circle, brought about the
awareness of the World Soul (Over-Soul). The elaborate
metaphysical framework constructed by the Transcendentalists and the belief in an immanent divine spirit are absent from *Paterson,* but the conception of a vital reality
to which the mind must penetrate to achieve a unification
of experience remains, along with a conviction that this

merger can be brought about only through language and only when the word or image precisely embodies both the conception within the mind and the concrete object.

Along with the Transcendentalists, Williams also emphasizes that this task can be completed successfully only when the poet directs his full attention to the local and immediate reality around him. For Williams a retreat from life in society is not a movement from a superfluous existence toward the possibility of a meaningful experience, but rather an evasion of the central terms of his quest as they are stated in another of the poem's apothegms:

> Be reconciled, poet, with your world, it is
> the only truth!
>
> (p. 103)

Just as it is impossible for the poet to create truly in isolation from the physical world, so for Williams any retreat from the local, the immediate, and the particular is out of the question. To deny the world in which the poet finds himself is not to escape to a more vital realm, but only to be divorced and to perish without meaning. Only by directing his full attention to the local and the immediate can the poet hope to achieve marriage. James Guimond has stressed Williams's belief that "although man's dilemmas are universal, the solutions must be local to be valid," [9] and Williams himself makes this position perfectly clear in the *Preface* to *Paterson,* establishing his own emphatic commitment to the local in contrast to the majority of his fellow poets, who "ran out" to areas felt to be more conducive to their imaginations:

> To make a start,
> out of particulars

and make them general, rolling
up the sum, by defective means—
Sniffing the trees,
just another dog
among a lot of dogs. What
else is there? And to do?
The rest have run out—
after the rabbits.
Only the lame stands—on
three legs. Scratch front and back.
Deceive and eat. Dig
a musty bone

(p. 11)

At times, when this local reality seems intransigent and
obtuse, the poet envies the expatriates, but he continually
affirms that their direction is an impossible one for him:

Moveless
he envies the men that ran
and could run off
toward the peripheries—
to other centers, direct—
for clarity (if
they found it)
            loveliness and
authority in the world—

a sort of springtime
toward which their minds aspired
but which he saw,
within himself—ice bound

(p. 48)

Like Whitman, whose poetry was a celebration of his
age and his immediate world at the same time that it was

a song of himself, Williams, by adopting Whitman's directive, by turning inland with an inclusive vision, conceives of his poem as a song of his own world.

The poet's task is to descend through the false and artificial mass of his environment to seek the beautiful thing and, if he can find it, to release it from the rubble that immures it, by bestowing upon it the proper name. By this creative act the poet will also free the conception from its imprisonment within his mind. The poetic act is often expressed in *Paterson* through the motif of descent and release, a movement of the poet away from "the ivory tower" and into an encounter with reality, followed by a penetration through the false, the artificial, and the superfluous to the essential core, and the metamorphosis of this prosaic and leaden reality into poetry. In *Paterson II,1*, to cite only one example from the earlier portion of the poem, the image is that of vitality at the bottom of an excavation, revealed when rain washes away the dirt that has covered it. Finding this essence, the poet is able to release the idea from his mind:

> AND a grasshopper of red basalt, boot-long,
> tumbles from the core of his mind,
> a rubble-bank disintegrating beneath a
> tropic downpour
>
> Chapultepec! grasshopper hill!
>
> (p. 62)

More obvious and important in this respect is the example of Madame Curie in Book IV, who released the precious radium during the metamorphosis of uranium to lead, finding essence in the midst of deterioration and decay:

> *Item*   .   with coarsened hands
> by the hour, the day, the week
> to get, after months of labor   .
>
> a stain at the bottom of the retort
> without weight, a failure, a
> nothing. And then, returning in the
> night, to find it   .
>   LUMINOUS!
>
> .   .   .   .
>
> Uranium, the complex atom, breaking
> down, a city in itself, that complex
> atom, always breaking down   .
> to lead.
>   But giving off that, to an
> exposed plate, will reveal   .
>
>   (p. 209)

Like Madame Curie, the poet must confront leaden reality, seek out its essence, and release the essence from the fixities that destroy it and make it worthless. Williams's concern is to uncover and release the beautiful thing, thereby saving not only himself and this vital core of reality but also the very world that has degraded and defiled them both. This redemption, furthermore, is perceived to be an act of which only the poet is capable.

The difficulty in the poetic process is that words have lost most of their power and the poem has become a dead thing. The imagination has become divorced from reality, and this divorce has implications for humanity as a whole. The language has become spoiled and corrupted, no longer affirming reality, but hiding it, a barrier between man and his consciousness of immediate contact with the world. Objects may still potentially contain revelations of beauty, but the failure of language means a failure of man's power to perceive the object and share its life. The loss of a proper language accompanies man's divorce from the not self. Authentic speech, on the other hand, sustains man's openness to the world. The state of poetry is a reflection of the state of society, and thus the poet's fate is of tremendous significance to society as a whole. And the poem itself (again, the ultimate poem?) is an object worthy of and demanding an endless quest to realize it. Only in proper, fresh, living language does man's interpenetration with the world exist, and therefore it is essential for society that the poet speak, not out of an obsolete tradition, but on his own terms, that he find a true language and create a true poetry. The poet, in undertaking this quest, becomes a hero attempting to redeem society from the effects of a corrupted language; he becomes, as Emerson said, "a liberating god."

By the terms set for himself, Williams is a physician in search of a cure for the disease that afflicts modern society and himself as an inseparable part of that society, a disease that prevents a fundamental, spiritual relationship between self and not self. The disease is a blindness to reality, and its most baneful symptoms are primarily three: a lack of any sustaining beauty, a language that is false and dead, and an intractability to genuine herosim. Society's only heroes are "false" heroes, men whose very lives have contributed to the pathology of the sickness; Cotton Mather, Benjamin Franklin, and especially Alexander Hamilton, to name only a few, are singled out. A major necessity in the attempt to break through the illness of society is the need for a hero who will take up the quest to bring reality to life by infusing the "particulars" of both the present and the past with the "strange phosphorous" of his own imagination. Williams himself attempts to satisfy this need.

To more fully understand Williams's heroic vision, it is helpful to consider *In the American Grain,* a book of essays that attempt to find in the past the qualities that make for true heroism. The entire book may be viewed in terms of a single perspective, the search of man for the New World, and in this respect it is especially relevant to *Paterson,* for this perspective serves admirably as a model for Williams's aspiration to a new poetry, the "new line" that, by utilizing a living language, will penetrate to reality and bring about another type of "new world." One finds in Williams a keen consciousness of his role as an experimenter with poetry, an explorer of a new realm, just as the explorers of *In the American Grain,* from Red Eric to Lincoln, are men in search of something new and fresh. In Williams's vision the New World and a new poetry become parables of each other.

The heroes of *In the American Grain* are men who are superior in degree, but not in kind, to other men and not superior to their natural environment, thus the typical heroes of what Northrop Frye has termed the "high mimetic mode" of literature.[10] Like the heroes of *In the American Grain,* the poet as hero is a leader, having enough in common with other men and enough to differentiate him from them to make his fate significant. Perhaps the most important quality pervading all the admirable figures of *In the American Grain,* that which lifts them above the ordinary, can best be called their "intensity." The intensity of the hero has two major related components: first, an emotive power capable of feeling greater joy and consequently also greater despair than the ordinary man, an ability and a willingness to reach the heights of joy and the depths of despair; second, the uncompromising spirit, unyielding purpose, and almost obsessive devotion that he brings to his quest and with which he continues his quest in the face of failure. The Spanish heroes, for example, are admired for their passionate nature, whereas the Puritan heritage is rejected for its "littleness," its tight control of the emotions and denial of the senses:

> They gave to it [the new world] parsimoniously in a slender Puritan fashion. But the Spaniard gave magnificently, with a generous sweep, wherever he was able. (*IAG,* p. 108)

Williams does admire the Puritan's vigor, but he sees it as a misdirected intensity, springing from a perverted source and focused upon a single static vision:

> True enough, I said, there is abundant vigor. . . . Fiery particles, the Puritans. . . . Their sureness which you praise is of their tight tied littleness, which, firm as it was, infuriates me today. It is their littleness that explains their admirable courage. (*IAG,* p. 110)

Similarly, the historical figures in *Paterson*—Altgeld, Curie, Brueghel, Toulouse-Lautrec, for example—are people who brought to life an immediacy of energy and imagination. A major villain in *Paterson,* as in *In the American Grain,* is Alexander Hamilton. In *In the American Grain,* he is juxtaposed to Aaron Burr, who possessed "a springtime of the soul, a mounting desire that makes him seem, beside the harness animals of that dawning period, like a bird in flight" (*IAG,* p. 196). Hamilton is one of the harness animals, a man of misdirected intensity, who aspired "to harness the whole, young, aspiring genius to a treadmill" (*IAG,* p. 195). In *Paterson,* Hamilton's ideas are contrasted throughout *II,2* with those of Klaus Ehrens, wandering prophet and preacher, in terms of the acquisition of money versus its rejection for the spiritual elements of life. Again, Williams makes the important contrast between the acts of "harness" and "release." Madame Curie releases the power of uranium; Klaus seeks release from money and all that it represents in order to realize the spiritual truths of life; the poet must release the beautiful thing to begin the process of unification and reconciliation; Hamilton wanted to make *Paterson* the capital of the country because it had natural power and beauty that could be harnessed. Like the Puritans, Hamilton has vigor of purpose; but his vigor exists without being affected in the least by the emotions and without a passionate sense of the reality of its object, and it is thus only another form of wasted power and divorce. Like Ahab, Hamilton and the Puritans attempt to impose themselves upon reality, to remake it according to their own specifications. Intensity, for Williams, implies the desire "to MARRY, to touch— to *give* because one HAS, not because one has nothing. And to give to him who HAS, who will join, who will make, who will fertilize . . . : to hybridize, to crosspollenize" (*IAG,* p. 121). Concomitant with this, of course, is a highly charged emotional nature, a freedom of the emotions, and an outward-looking inclusiveness, unlike that of the Puritans, who denied themselves the heights of joy that they might avoid the depths of despair and who made of their world a closed system of "tight, tied littleness." It is this characteristic of intensity, coupled with a local directive, that gives the poet the potential of a redeeming culture-hero.

The creation of a multiple, inclusive protagonist, one who contains elements of both self and not self is a major part of Williams's attempt to realize his own heroic potential. James Guimond has pointed out the contrast between the hero of Williams's epic and "Mr. P." of the early "Paterson" (1927).[11] Mr. P. also declares, "no ideas but in things," but the things that surround him do not easily lend themselves to the poetic thoughts that he wishes to have, and thus he remains aloof, going away "to rest and write." As a hero, Mr. P. is a sensitive, imaginative protagonist; but as a projection of the self, he is purely individual and renders a poem of his own consciousness in purely subjective terms. In *Paterson,* Williams escapes this subjectivity by the use of an environmental rather than a personal stream of consciousness, in which his personal experiences are fused with those of his city, and self and other coexist in the form of the expanded metaphor.

Nevertheless, the actual heroic movement within *Paterson* begins with the protagonist in isolation from reality. At this point the not self appears as a force that deadens his creative efforts and forces him into his own subjectivity; it is ambiguous, recalcitrant, overwhelming, and torrential. The overwhelming, torrential quality of the not self is often represented in the poem by the rushing of the wind or, more commonly, by the roar of the Passiac River as it crashes over the falls at Paterson. It is this roar of a collective, social consciousness that keeps Paterson the giant asleep and withdrawn from reality in *I,1:*

> Paterson lies in the valley under the Passiac Falls
> its spent waters forming the outline of his back. He
> lies on his right side, head near the thunder
> of the waters filling his dreams!
>
> (p. 14)

Like Mr. P., the hero is aloof, asleep, immersed in the
subjectivity of his dreams and his imagination. He, too,

> has gone away
> to rest and write. Inside the bus one sees
> his thoughts sitting and standing. His
> thoughts alight and scatter—

(p. 18)

The poet is a creator, but here he is a creator who fails
and his creations are merely "automatons":

> Immortal he neither moves nor rouses and is seldom
> seen, though he breathes and the subtleties of his
>   machinations
> drawing their substance from the noise of the pouring
>   river
> animate a thousand automatons. Who because they
> neither know their sources nor the sills of their
> disappointments walk outside their bodies aimlessly
>   for the most part,
> locked and forgot in their desires—unroused.

(p. 14)

In such a situation the poet's ideas are sterile, in isolation
from each other and from their essential source:

> Who are these people (how complex
> the mathematic) among whom I see myself
> in the regularly ordered plateglass of
> his thoughts, glimmering before shoes and bicycles?
> They walk incommunicado, the
> equation is beyond solution, yet
> its sense is clear—that they may live
> his thought is listed in the Telephone
> Directory—

(p. 18)

The poet realizes that such art contains no truth and that both self and not self can be fully realized only through direct confrontation. Thus, Paterson endeavors to awake and bring about the essential encounter with reality, to immerse himself in his world and out of this immersion to create a fusion of self and other, thereby imparting life to both.

In *I,2* he struggles to awake, confident of his approach, but at a loss to find the beautiful thing. With his method, the "how" that he fears may degenerate into a "howl," he begins to search, unsure of where to look, and the ambiguous and deafening roar of the not self almost forces him to retreat and resume his uncreative slumber:

> There is no direction. Whither? I
> cannot say. I cannot say
> more than how. The how (the howl) only
> is at my disposal (proposal) : watching—
> colder than stone .
>
> . . . .
>
>   with the roar of the river
> forever in our ears (arrears)
> inducing sleep and silence, the roar
> of eternal sleep . . challenging
> our waking—

(p. 28)

Nevertheless, Paterson does awake and force himself to face the torrent and attempt to "comb out" meaning and essential sounds from the vast and deafening wall of noise. In undertaking his quest, Paterson becomes a wanderer, endlessly searching throughout his world for the beautiful thing, as Williams the poet endlessly attempts to create his poem. There are moments of success and affirmation, but no vision can be accepted as final and fixed. In the closing pages of Book I, for example, Paterson seems able to embrace the sordidness of the world, assert its essence, and affirm a formal correspondence in his mind, but he is unwilling to allow himself to rest with such a partial victory, and he continues to wander and search:

> Things, things unmentionable,
> the sink with the waste farina in it and
> lumps of rancid meat, milk-bottle-tops: have
> here a tranquility and loveliness
> Have here (in his thoughts)
> a complement tranquil and chaste.
>
>   He shifts his change:
>
>   (p. 51)

Like the Transcendentalists, Williams realizes that any single vision or poetic creation, if it is fixed, cannot be correct for long and will soon become stagnant and stale. This fixity is one of the things that Williams finds most grievously wrong with modern American culture and literature. Elsewhere, for example, he claims that "the greatest characteristic of the present age is that it is stale —stale as literature." [12] Within *Paterson* the prime example of the failure of any final vision is the figure of Sam Patch. For the poet, Patch's leaps become an attempt to marry idea and thing, to complete the word by embodying it in an act: "a speech! What could he say that he must leap so desperately to complete it" (p. 27)? Patch meets with initial success, but his act becomes a formula and his language, remaining static, becomes, like the volumes in the library of Book III and the outworn tradition that

Williams insists on rejecting, frozen, hidebound, sterile,
and "stale as a whale's breath. . . ." Appropriately, when
Patch's body is recovered after his last fatal plunge, it is
frozen in an ice-cake. Patch accomplished a marriage, but
because it remained static it became false.

The figure of Mrs. Sarah Cummings is complementary
to that of Patch and represents another type of stasis.
Whereas Patch's demise is the result of a marriage that
became fixed and false, Mrs. Cummings apparently chooses
annihilation in preference to what she realized was her
own false marriage or the continuous attempt that is
necessary to create a true one:

> She was married with empty words:
>   better to
>   stumble at
>   the edge
>   to fall
>   fall
>
>   and be
>
>   —divorced
>
> from the insistence of place—
>   from knowledge,
> from learning—the terms
> foreign, conveying no immediacy, pouring down.
>   —divorced
> from time (no invention more), bald as an
>   egg   .
>
>   (pp. 102–3)

Either type of stasis, acceptance of a single vision or renunciation of the continuing quest, is unsatisfactory to
the poet, although here he seems, like Ishmael in his de-

spair, to look almost longingly toward death, the "divorce from time," a realm in which continuous invention is no longer necessary.

The word *invention* is perhaps the central idea in Williams's concept of continuing re-creation. As Guimond points out, the idea is applicable in all three senses of its meaning: to construct newly, to discover, and to come into.[13] Each of these activities demands the endless motion of continual re-creation. Not only must the poet engage in a constant search for the elusive and hidden beautiful thing but, if he is to retain his creativity, he must also be seeking constantly to refine and develop his vision and techniques. Reality itself is in continual motion, its essential nature in constant alteration. Thus, the poet maintains:

> Certainly I am not a robin nor erudite,
> no Erasmus nor bird that returns to the same
> ground year by year. Or if I am   .   .
> the ground has undergone
> a subtle transformation, its identity altered.
>
> (p. 29)

If the poet assumes that his quest is complete once he has found and named the beautiful thing, he is mistaken and accepts a "partial victory," which, like the partial victory of Sam Patch, will lead into stasis and stagnation. Realizing this fact at the beginning of *I,3,* the poet reprimands himself:

> How strange you are, you idiot!
> So you think because the rose
> is red that you shall have the mastery?
> The rose is green and will bloom,

> overtopping you, green, livid
> green when you shall no more speak, or
> taste, or even be. My whole life
> has hung too long upon a partial victory.
>
> (p. 41)

Only through motion and continual invention can stagnation and "recurring deadliness" be avoided. The mind and art of the poet must be in endless metamorphosis:

> Without invention nothing is well spaced,
> unless the mind change, unless
> the stars are new measured, according
> to their relative positions, the
> line will not change, the necessity
> will not matriculate: unless there is
> a new mind there cannot be a new
> line, the old will go on
> repeating itself with recurring
> deadliness:
>
> .   .   .   .
>
> without invention the line
> will never again take on its ancient
> divisions when the word, a supple word,
> lived in it, crumbled now to chalk.
>
> (p. 65)

The poem itself must always be changing. It must be endlessly created and re-created, and though this endless effort is perceived to be the source of all value, it is also, as for Ishmael and at times Whitman, a source of exhaustion and despair. At the end of *II,2*, for example, the poet, addressing the beautiful thing as it has become successfully metamorphosed into his poem, describes this facet of his experience:

> The world spreads
> for me like a flower opening—and
> will close for me as might a rose—
> wither and fall to the ground
> and rot and be drawn up
> into a flower again. But you
> never wither—but blossom
> all about me.
>
>   (p. 93)

At this point, however, the poet, rejoicing in his success, remembers the necessity for endless re-creation:

> In that I forget
> myself perpetually—in your
> composition and decomposition
> I find my   .   .
>
>   despair!
>   (p. 93)

Despite moments of success, the prevailing mood of *Paterson* is one of defeat and failure, through which the hero doggedly continues his search, examining all things, endlessly attempting to achieve marriage, always rebounding from defeat to seek out the beautiful thing. The hero's determination is, of course, a major attribute of his intensity; and it is again useful to compare the heroic vision of *In the American Grain,* for most of the heroes discussed favorably there are admired largely for their endurance and perseverance in the face of failure and adversity.

Columbus, De Leon, De Soto, Boone, and others are all figures devoted to a quest that meets time and again with failure. Williams perhaps brings these historical figures closest to his own identity when he invokes his muse to sing of Raleigh:

> Of the pursuit of beauty and the husk that remains, perversions and mistakes, while the true form escapes in the wind, sing O Muse; of Raleigh . . . , and say, there is a spirit that is seeking through America for Raleigh: in the earth, the air, the waters, up and down, for Raleigh, that lost man: seer who failed, planter who never planted, poet whose works are questioned, leader without command, favorite deposed. (*IAG*, pp. 59–62)

The "spirit that is seeking through America for Raleigh" is the poet himself, and the search for Raleigh is simultaneously the search for the heroic qualities he exhibits and for the object of his pursuit, the "true form." And just as Raleigh is left with only the husk of his dream, so the poet in *Paterson* often finds himself left with only the husk of his poem, divorced, blocked, faced with the failure of language. For example, at the end of *II,1* Paterson, identifying himself, as in the *Preface,* with a male dog, finds himself prohibited from even entering the park-world of society unless confined "on a leash":

NO DOGS ALLOWED AT LARGE IN THIS PARK
(p. 77)

And Williams the poet, Paterson the wanderer, the dog, thus restricted and denied central freedom, finds himself at the beginning of *II,2*

> Blocked.
> (Make a song out of that: concretely)
> (p. 78)

Here is the nucleus of Williams's heroic vision: to be blocked and to rebound, to make a song out of the blocking, to be defeated and to resume the quest, just as Raleigh, defeated again and again, never gave himself over to self-defeat, but even at the close of his life was determined to return to "England again and force the new king to keep his promise and behead him" (*IAG*, p. 62). Columbus presents a similar example: "Bewildered, he continued, voyage after voyage, four times, out of his growing despair; it seemed that finally by sheer physical effort a way must be found—till the realization of it all at last grew firmly upon him" (*IAG*, p. 11). So Paterson continues, out of his growing despair, continually seeking; and Williams continually attempts to create his poem.

Like Ishmael, Williams becomes subject to a compound despair. On a simple level is the exhaustion derived from the continuous "composition and decomposition" demanded by the quest. More acute is the despair arising when the hero begins to doubt the validity of his own approach. The two types of despair follow one another in direct succession. *II,2* closes with the hero in despair of his endless flux, and *II,3* begins with a lyric suggesting that at the core of the not self there is not a beautiful thing but only a "nul," a void that renders his quest completely meaningless, "defeats it all." The vital force of the "first wife" who "holds the others up" is now perceived as:

> that rock, the blank
> that holds them up
>
> which pulled away—
> the rock's
>
> their fall.

(p. 95)

And the poet's quest itself seems destined only to con-
tribute its petty share to this great universal void

> that's past all
> seeing
>
> the death of all
> that's past
>
> all being   .

(p. 95)

However, with his characteristic self-honesty, the poet
refuses to allow himself to wallow in despair. He chides
himself:

> But Spring shall come and flowers will bloom
> and man must chatter of his doom   .   .

(p. 95)

He begins again, with a new strategy, to create out of his
despair, to look even there for positive qualities:

> No defeat is made up entirely of defeat—since
> the world it opens is always a place
>   formerly
>   unsuspected. A
> world lost,
>   a world unsuspected
>   beckons to new places
> and no whiteness (lost) is so white as the memory
> of whiteness   .
>
> .   .   .   .
>
> The descent
>   made up of despairs

> and without accomplishment
> realizes a new awakening :
> which is a reversal
> of despair.
>
> (pp. 96–97)

Nevertheless, as Paterson wanders further through the park, grows more conscious of his failure, and lapses further into despair, he becomes tempted, like Ishmael, to "lower his conceit of attainable felicity." In his despair he reconsiders a withdrawal from the not self and reliance upon an art of the purely independent imagination. In Book I Paterson reflected:

> The thought returns: Why have I not
> but for imagined beauty where there is none
> or none available, long since
> put myself deliberately in the way of death?
>
> (pp. 30–31)

In Book III, where his despair is greatest, the attractions of such a purely imaginative art are especially strong. Indeed, it is with the evasive intention of seeking relief from the roar of reality that has penetrated even into his own mind that Paterson retreats into the library:

> Spent from wandering the useless
> streets these months, faces folded against
> him like clover at nightfall, something
> has brought him back to his own
>
> mind   .
>
> .   .   .   .
>
> Books will give rest sometimes against
> the uproar of water falling

            and righting itself to refall filling
            the mind wtih its reverberation
                                    shaking stone.
                                    (pp. 118–19)

However, in the tranquility of the library he finds not
a suitable environment for his creative spirit but rather a
trap. He realizes that to remain there will result in stagnation and spiritual death:

            The place sweats of staleness and of rot
            a back-house stench   .   a
            library stench

            It is summer! stinking summer

            Escape from it—but not by running
            away. Not by "composition." Embrace the
            foulness

                                    (p. 126)

The escape must be neither another retreat nor further
writing, for writing at this point would be worthless.
Divorced from life, the poet has become stale, and "composition" isolated from its source is useless. Here the
dilemma of the poet is clearly stated. The not self is torrential and its overwhelming roar is deadening to his
creative capacity, but the self, withdrawn from this reality
into a state apparently more conducive to creativity, loses
its power and can create only false and stale poems. Thus,
finding it useless to pursue an art that is purely imaginative, the poet, in his despair, is drawn to the other polar
alternative: to give up the attempt at creation and surrender his individual identity. Finding it impossible to
create amidst the not self and worthless to create in isolation, he goes so far as to renounce his quest entirely:

Give it up. Quit it. Stop writing.
"Saintlike" you will never
separate that stain of sense,

.   .   .   .

—never separate that stain
of sense from the inert mass. Never.
Never that radiance

.   .   .   .

                    Give up
the poem. Give up the shilly-
shally of art.

.   .   .   .

Quit it. Quit this place. Go where all
mouths are rinsed : to the river for
an answer
              for relief from "meaning"
                    (pp. 131, 132, 132, 135)

Paterson, however, refuses to give himself over to this temptation. Throughout Book III the poet's despair is mingled with continued efforts to arrive at a true and valuable creativity. Both the dilemma and the approach that is necessary to resolve it are concisely stated in the verse that introduces part two. The poet first describes the problem:

The writing is nothing, the being
in a position to write (that's

where they get you) is nine tenths
of the difficulty:

.   .   .   .

to write, nine tenths of the problem
is to live.

                    (pp. 137–38)

Following this statement the poet describes the approach that he will use in Book III:

> —the cyclonic fury, the fire,
> the leaden flood and finally
> the cost—
>
> (p. 138)

The poet's solution is to make creation and immersion in life continuous cycles of the creative process. This solution is not a new one for Paterson. It is the very process of "composition and decomposition" described at the end of Book II, by which the poet will attempt to resolve the dilemma of living / creating, in which the cost of full contact with the not self is a deadening of the creative self and the cost of withdrawal is a "false language." Through a confrontation with "the cyclonic fury, the fire, and the leaden flood" of the not self, through an immersion in the very life that threatens to destroy his creative power, the poet hopes to emerge with something of meaning and value, the beautiful thing that will become his poem. This resolution, however, has its costs, too: it is an endless process. If any value is to be found, it is only to be derived from this constant and cyclical motion, and no value can be considered fixed and final. Once "composed," the poem must be "decomposed" as the poet immerses himself in life to find the source of a new composition. The primary symbol of this process, of course, is Madame Curie, whose experience comprises a statement of the value that lies only in metamorphosis and flux. For radium, "that stain of sense," can only be released through the decomposition of uranium to lead. If this motion were to cease, the radium, the beautiful thing, would no longer be released, but would remain locked within the "inert mass." Since the motion of this symbolic parallel is a destructive or decaying motion that is at the same time creative, it is not surprising that Williams's own images are those of a power that is both creative and destructive. The initial metaphor of the not self is fire, and Williams makes full use of its dual potentialities; for fire in *III,2* represents both the fire of creative passion and the destructive, raging torrent of the not self. By immersing himself in this torrent, the poet hopes to "beat fire at its own game," by metamorphosing its destructive force into his own creative power and releasing from it the beautiful thing. The poet does "embrace the foulness," and he manages to wrest from it a mauled bottle, "the glass warped to a new distinction, reclaiming the undefined. . . . Annihilation ameliorated":

> Hell's fire. Fire. Sit your horny ass
> down. What's your game? Beat you
> at your own game, Fire. Outlast you:
> Poet Beats Fire at Its Own Game! The bottle!
> the bottle! the bottle! the bottle! I
> give you the bottle! What's burning
> now, Fire?
>
> (p. 143)

The experience allows an affirmation:

> Beautiful thing, your
> vulgarity of beauty surpasses all their
> perfections!
>
> (p. 145)

But it is and can be only a momentary affirmation; for the beautiful thing is soon lost, and the creative fire becomes again a destructive, deafening roar, like the wind and the waterfall:

> the waterfall of the
> flames, a cataract reversed, shooting
> upward (what difference does it make?)

The language,

> Beautiful thing—that I
> make a fool of myself, mourning the lack
> of dedication
> > mourning its losses,
> > > (p. 146)

Williams again realizes that no single vision can be considered final. In all the books of the library he sees volumes forged in the fire of creative passion, now silent, containing nothing of the beautiful thing that their writer dreamed they would include, the writer himself a

> white-hot man become
> a book, the emptiness of
> a cavern resounding
> > (p. 149)

The books are worthless now, for they were assumed to be complete and have become static, and the library consequently must be destroyed. Like radium, that which is valuable can only be discovered through endless "composition and decomposition." At the beginning of part three Williams makes this idea explicit:

It is dangerous to leave written that which is badly written. A chance word, upon paper, may destroy the world. Watch carefully and erase, while the power is still yours, I say to myself, for all that is put down, once

it escapes, may rot its way into a thousand minds, the
corn become a black smut, and all libraries, of necessity,
be burned to the ground as a consequence.

Only one answer: write carelessly so that nothing that
is not green will survive. (p. 155)

Once again, Paterson must immerse himself in the decay
and destruction around him, seeking language. This time
it is the "leaden flood" of crass particulars, dead words,
perverted poetry, and cold statistics. Once again, he must
endure the process of "decomposition" in hopes that the
beautiful thing may be released. This time, however, no
success emerges:

When the water has receded most things have lost their
form. They lean in the direction the current went. Mud
covers them

—fertile(?)mud.

If it were only fertile. Rather a sort of muck, a detritus.

(p. 167)

The poet now despairs of the task of composition:

How to begin to find a shape—to begin to begin again,
turning the inside out : to find one phrase that will
lie married beside another for delight   .   ?
—seems beyond attainment   .

(p. 167)

Again, he speculates a void rather than an essential core
at the heart of reality:

Go down, peer among the fishes. What
do you expect to save, muscle shells?

(p. 170)

However, he again fights off his despair and rededicates himself to the endless process of his quest for language:

> Does the pulp need further maceration?
> take down the walls, invite
> the trespass. After all, the slums
> unless they are (living)
> wiped out they cannot be re-
> constituted   .
>
> The words will have to be rebricked up, the
> —what? What am I coming to   .
>   pouring down?
>
> (p. 170)

At the end of Book III Paterson again faces the falls, the torrent of the not self, determined to "comb out" the essential language that is hidden there and "make of it a replica" in his poem.

But despite his courage and dedication, the dominant overtones of *Paterson* remain those of failure and defeat. Much more often than not, the poet finds himself, as at the beginning of *II,2,* "blocked." Like most of the heroes of *In the American Grain,* the predominant result of his effort is defeat. However, if the poet is blocked, if Raleigh is inevitably separated from his true form, if the flower of a New World that Columbus envisioned must be perverted to bitter fruit, Williams raises a basic question at the beginning of *II,2:*

> By whom?

What, in other words, makes for the poet's failure? What makes for the tragic nature of the situation? There would seem to be two possible answers: either the hero fails be-

cause of some innate incapability, or the failure is occasioned by some force external to, and more powerful than,
himself. Williams raises the question here, but offers no
answer, perhaps because there is no unequivocal answer.
Indeed, a major portion of Paterson's wandering consists
of an examination of both self and not self in an attempt
to identify the root causes of the failure.

At times, the poem reveals a genuine sense of doubt as
to the poet's capabilities. In the early portions of Book I,
while Paterson is asleep, for example, the divorce is certainly caused by the poet's isolation from reality. Here the
flower, the female principle, seems receptive, but the male
force is unable to complete the consummation:

> They begin!
> The perfections are sharpened
> The flower spreads its colored petals
>   wide in the sun
> But the tongue of the bee
>   misses them
> They sink back into the loam
>   crying out
> —you may call it a cry
> that creeps over them, a shiver
>   as they wilt and disappear:
> Marriage come to have a shuddering
>   implication
>
> (p. 20)

In Book II the same image is repeated, here in more
specific terms, as Paterson, overwhelmed by the roar of the
falls and displaying a lack of courage, seems on the verge
of retreat and again refuses to engage in consummation
with the beautiful thing:

> —the language is worn out.
>
> And She —
>> You have abandoned me!
>
> —at the magic sound of the stream
> she threw herself upon the bed—
> a pitiful gesture! lost among the words:
> Invent (if you can) discover or
> nothing is clear—will surmount
> the drumming in your head. There will be
> nothing clear, nothing clear   .
>
> He fled pursued by the roar.
>
> (pp. 103–4)

The letters, too, primarily those from Cress, often operate to accuse the poet of a basic inability to create on his own terms. For example, this passage from the end of Book II describes Paterson's failure to combine the cycles of his creative process:

> You've never had to live, Dr. P—not in any of the by-ways and dark underground passages where life so often has to be tested. The very circumstances of your birth and social background provided you with an escape from life in the raw; and you confuse that protection from life with an *inability* to live—and are thus able to regard literature as nothing more than a desperate last extremity resulting from that illusionary inability to live. (I've been looking at some of your autobiographical works, as this indicates.) (p. 111)

The possibility that the hero is blocked by his own shortcomings corresponds roughly to the first of two "reductive" theories of tragedy that have been delineated by Northrop Frye.[14] This theory holds that the tragic process is the result of some moral flaw in the tragic hero. However, if Paterson's lack of ability is at the root of his failure, the situation would not be truly tragic, but rather "absurd," caused not by a "moral flaw" but by a ludicrous gap between the hero's pretensions and his abilities. This, indeed, would at times seem to be the case with Paterson, for often he appears as a rather pretentious, sometimes clumsy, and sometimes pompous buffoon. The second of the passages cited directly above is an example of this, and the hero remains somewhat mock-heroic throughout Book II. Indeed, Guimond holds that for the entirety of Book II Paterson is possessed of "a fastidious disgust and erudite contempt" for his townspeople, which makes true communication with them impossible.[15]

However, while Paterson seems at times to be an absurd hero, Williams the poet cannot be considered absurd, largely because of his awareness of his own shortcomings. Since Paterson, in all his metamorphoses, is a projection of the poet's self-image, his occasionally absurd nature must be taken as a mark of Williams's admirable honesty with himself. This mock-heroic self-portrayal allows the poet to stand back and take an objective view of himself, and it keeps him from becoming carried away with his own heroism. It serves as a reminder, as do several of the poet's conversational partners in *In the American Grain* (particularly in the essays "Pere Sebastian Rasles" and "The Virtue of History") of the poet's limitations. In "Pere Sebastian Rasles," Williams describes his role as that of a Saint George, and it is this same quality that characterizes the mock-hero in *Paterson*. This type of self-examination is also important in its function as a caution against the traps posed by sentimentality and self-pity, emotions that would seem to be natural when one conceives of oneself as a defeated hero, but that can have no place in Williams's mature poetics, for they are obviously obstructions in the poet's search for a true and living language. The letters from Cress also contain reminders against these emotions. Full of self-pity, Cress is presented as an example of allowing failure "to have so disastrous an effect upon me" (p. 81). The letters are often strategically placed to follow an episode where the poet has reached a low point of despair, as if to warn him of the danger and urge him away from it (see pp. 59, 80, 93, 105). The letters from E. D. have a similar function, and much of the violence in the poem may also be a caution against this tendency. Thus, the gap between the hero's pretensions and his capabilities, though it can hardly be considered a moral tragic flaw, does not render the hero absurd, because Williams realizes his limitations and throughout the poem is courageously attempting to overcome them.

Furthermore, there are also many instances where the blame for the hero's failure to find and release the beautiful thing seems to lie not within but rather outside the hero, in a reality that is dense and oppressive and a society that is constantly operating to thwart him. Throughout *Paterson* society is portrayed as tending to destroy anything that is valuable, the beautiful thing in all its forms. Many of the brief passages in Book I and II illustrate this process: the spoilation of the pearl (p. 17), the capture of the Sturgeon (p. 19), the forced expatriation of "Jackson's whites" (p. 21), the slaughter of the Eels (p. 47), the attempted destruction of the Mink (p. 64), the separation of Musty and her beau (p. 78), and, of course, the various passages concerning Hamilton and his designs for Paterson in *II,2*.

This is also the view of the tragic situation that prevails

in *In the American Grain*. In describing the failure inherent in the perversion of the beauty of Tenochtitlan, for
example, Williams maintains:

> Bitter as the thought may be that Tenochtitlan, the bar
> baric city, its peoples, its genius wherever found should
> have been crushed out because of the awkward names
> men give their emptiness, yet it was no man's fault. It
> was the force of the pack whom the dead drive. (*IAG*,
> p. 27)

The hero is consistently seen as having a substantial dignity that remains after he is defeated by men or things
"smaller" than himself. Williams, for example, writes of
Columbus, who "heroically, but pitifully . . . strove to
fasten to himself that enormous world that presently
crushed him among its multiple small disguises" (*IAG*,
p. 10), and of "Raleigh, beloved by majesty, plunging his
lust into the body of the new world—and the deaths, misfortunes, counter coups, which swelled back to certify that
ardor with defeat" (*IAG*, p. 59).

Williams was also not the least bit reticent to lay a good
deal of the blame for the decadence of language and the
perversion of the beautiful thing on stale tradition and
academicism in the literary arts. The reality of Daniel
Boone, for example, has been overshadowed, and he "has
. . . remained buried in a miscolored legend and left for
rotten" (*IAG*, p. 130). In *Paterson*, Williams speaks out
against the universities: "clerks / got out of hand forgetting for the most part / to whom they are beholden" (p.
44); and against the school headed by Ezra Pound: "Leadership passes into empire; empire begets in- / solence; insolence brings ruin" (p. 50). In his attempt to refurbish a

"usable past," Williams feels particularly stifled by tradition. In *Paterson III,* for example, he describes:

> Dead men's dreams, confined by these walls, risen,
> seek an outlet. The spirit languishes,
> unable, unable not from lack of innate ability—
>
> (barring alone sure death)
>
> but from that which immures them pressed here
> together with their fellows, for respite   .
>
> (p. 123)

It would seem, then, that just as the heroes of *In the American Grain* fail not wholly for internal reasons, so the poet fails largely because of the obduracy of the not self. Much of the poetry in Book II immediately following the question "By whom?" supports this view. Paterson surveys the crowd of the poor in the park and observes their oppression:

> Cash is mulct of them that others may live
> secure
> .   .   and knowledge restricted.
>
> An orchestral dullness overlays their world
>
> .   .   .   .
>
> We leap awake and what we see
> fells us   .
>
> (pp. 78, 79)

Later, after watching Klaus Ehrens, he asks:

> Is this the only beauty here?
> And is this beauty—

                    torn to shreds by the
                    lurking schismatists?

                                                (p. 88)

Toward the end of Book II the not self is portrayed as
almost totally hostile, impotent, and destructive:

     .   reversed in the mirror of its
own squalor, debased by the divorce from learning,
its garbage on the curbs, its legislators
under the garbage, uninstructed, incapable of
self instruction   .

       a thwarting, an avulsion   :

—flowers uprooted, columbine, yellow and red,
strewn upon the path; dogwoods in full flower,
the trees dismembered; its women
shallow, its men steadfastly refusing—at
the best   .

       The language   .   words
without style! whose scholars (there are none)
       or dangling, about whom
the water weaves its strands encasing them
in a sort of thick lacquer, lodged
under its flow   .

                                                (pp. 99–100)

Perhaps the strongest sense of the intransigence of the not
self occurs in Book III, where Williams suggests:

Let's take a ride around, to see what the town looks like

   Indifferent, the indifference of certain death
   or incident upon certain death

```
      propounds a riddle (in the Joyceian mode—
                              or otherwise,
      it is indifferent which)
                    A marriage riddle:
      So much talk of the language—when there are no
      ears.

      .   .   .   .   .   .   .   .   .   .   .   .

      What is there to say? save that
      beauty is unheeded     .     tho' for sale and
      bought glibly enough

                    But it is true, they fear
      it more than death, beauty is feared
      more than death, more than they fear death

                    Beautiful thing

      —and marry only to destroy, in private, in
      their privacy only to destroy, to hide
                        (in marriage)
      that they may destroy and not be perceived
      in it—the destroying
                                        (pp. 129–30)
```

Thus, at many times it seems that it is a society "without ears," unable to receive a true language even if the poet should create one, that maligns the beautiful thing and makes for the failure of the poet and the tragedy of the situation. From this perspective Frye's second "reduction" would seem to be relevant. This theory maintains that all tragedy exhibits the omnipotence of an external fate. However, this theory, too, is limited in its applicability to *Paterson*. Frye has observed that the relation of the tragic poet to his hero is that he knows his hero will be in a tragic situation, but exerts all his power to avoid the sense of having manipulated that situation for his own purposes. As Milton's Adam was to God, so the hero must be sufficient to stand, yet free to fall. The poet exhibits his hero to us as God exhibits Adam to the angels. If the hero is not sufficient to stand, the mode is not tragic but merely ironic. But as Frye also points out, this argument carries little weight, for God must have known in the instant he created Adam that he was creating a being who would fall.[16] In the same way, if Williams conceives of his hero, who is a projection of himself, as fated or predestined to defeat, he must concede that his own poetic goal is unattainable before he even begins to write. Such a concession would render him only an ironic or, more accurately, an absurd hero, and would deprive his quest of any tragic meaning.

In short, it is the very fact that the question "By whom?" cannot be answered definitely, and the resulting ambiguity concerning the location of the tragic principle, that enables the hero to rise to true tragic stature. Since the cause of failure lies neither in an ineluctable fate nor in some flaw of character or innate incapability of the self, the hero can undertake his quest as if his goal were possibly attainable, with a sincere belief in his sufficiency to stand, the only terms in which the hero can be considered truly a tragic one and in which his quest can have any tragic significance. Paterson's quest, then, becomes twofold. First, of course, is the attempt to unite idea and object, find and release the beautiful thing with a true and living language, bring society, in spite of itself, into a marriage with its spiritual essence, and cure it of its blindness to Reality. Beyond this goal *Paterson* also contains a constant examination and reexamination of both the self and the not self, a search for the cause of the poet's failure to realize his goal. Paterson is at once exploring all facets of his world in search of an equivalent response and at the same time constantly surveying, evaluating, and attempting to refine and develop his own selfhood.

Perhaps the most lucid portrayal of the ambiguity concerning the poet's failure is the "Idyl" of *IV,1,* a verse play with the following cast of characters: Phyllis, as the beautiful thing; Corydon, as the false poet; Phyllis's father, along with Corydon, representing a crass and debasing society; Paterson, as himself. Phyllis, in self-imposed exile from her home due to the actions of her father, has come to New York, where she finds work administering to the needs of the lonely Corydon. Corydon wants to write a poem about Phyllis, but Corydon's poem is a travesty, for it contains nothing of either Corydon, Phyllis, or any type of truth. Her style is imitative: "I think that's Yeats . . . No, I think *that's* the Yeats" (p. 197). Rocks, splattered with pigeon-droppings, are transformed into sheep, and any form of truth is carefully banished, because "this is a POEM" (p. 195)! Corydon takes pleasure in Phyllis's virginity, and obviously there is no chance for any type of consummation between them.

Paterson, however, hardly fares better. At first the failure seems due to Paterson's own inability to communicate or to accept Phyllis as she is, to embrace her ugliness as well as her attractiveness. He is disappointed at discovering that she is "just broad shouldered," and he voices his disapproval of her heavy thighs. Paterson's technique, too, seems to fail him; he is too rough and too coarse in the art of seduction. But Phyllis herself seems to be recalcitrant. Understandably hostile toward Corydon, she also resists Paterson, who at this point seems deserving: "I don't know why I can't give myself to you. A man like you should have everything he wants" (p. 189). Phyllis, warped by society's fear of consummation and touch and maligned by both her father and Corydon, is simply unable to give herself to Paterson. The entire scene of *IV,1* is characterized by a notable lack of sexuality, and all four of the characters exist in a state of impotency and isolation from each other.

Whatever its causes, however, the poet's failure is also a failure of society; as Phyllis explains at the end of *IV, 1,* only when she is successfully married will consummation be possible for anyone. Society and the beautiful thing, as well as the poet, are victims of the failure of language, but it is only the poet who lends a tragic dignity to the situation. By virtue of his heroism, because of his intensity and the fact that he has creative potential that he is unable to exercise and can know beauty that he cannot possess without having it become perverted, he removes the failure from the level of the merely ironic or absurd to the level of the tragic. Frye elaborates on this distinction between irony and tragedy:

> Irony does not need an exceptional central figure; as a rule, the dingier the hero the sharper the irony, when irony alone is aimed at. It is the admixture of heroism that gives tragedy its characteristic splendor and exhilaration. The tragic hero has normally had an extraordinary, often a nearly divine, destiny almost within his grasp, and the glory of that original vision never quite fades out of tragedy.[17]

Certainly, a sense of the "paradise lost" or "something beyond" pervades both *In the American Grain* and *Paterson,* appearing as a vision of unspoiled natural beauty, the virgin New World or the "beauty and clearness of the

river around the falls at Paterson before its rape by the
drastic combination of raw politics, raw technics, and raw
business," [18] or as a lost, vital language that would make
possible the full realization of reality. The poet, having
this vision and striving toward it, becomes a mediator between society and the "something beyond," and the fact
that his vision is inevitably elusive or despoiled does not
negate its importance. William describes this succinctly
in *In the American Grain:*

> Poets, through their energy, receive such a stamp of the
> age upon their work, that they are marked, in fact, even
> in the necessities of their defeat, as having lived well in
> their time. Poets are defeated but in an essential and
> total defeat at any time, that time is stamped in char-
> acter upon their work, they give shape to the formless
> age as by a curious die,—and so other times recognize
> them, the positives that created the forms which give
> character and dignity to the damp mass of the over-
> powering resistance. (*IAG*, p. 186)

Thus, the poet, even in his failure and concomitant contemporary isolation from society, is in this sense the redeemer of society by virtue of the order and value, however minimal, that he has been able to wrest from the
frustrations of his encounters.

Paterson was originally planned to be "a long poem in
four parts," but obviously the nature of the hero's quest
precludes any type of completion. A fifth book was necessary, and when Williams died, fragments of a projected
sixth book were found among his papers. Just as the hero's
quest must be endless, so *Paterson* the poem could have
no end. In a way, *Paterson V*, with its emphasis on graphic
art, myth, and the imagination, might be seen as a devi-

ation from some of the essentials of Williams's tragic
vision, a dismissal of society and a search for meaning and
permanence not through merger with the not self but
through development of the imaginative self. If this is
what Williams has done in Book V, it represents a radical,
but understandable, change in the terms of his quest and
negates much of its tragic significance. It is to take up a
strategy that has been repeatedly rejected in Books I–IV.
But Book V represents no real alteration. Rather it is a
turn toward graphic art and myth as a means of expression
and communication, to "take the world of Paterson into
a new dimension . . . to give it imaginative validity" (pp.
7–8). As Louis Martz has noted, through the tapestries, the
central image of Book V, Williams is defending and ex-
plaining his own technique by suggesting an analogy of the
tapestries to *Paterson*.[19] Both are based upon a combination of the vulgar and the ideal, the local and the mythical.
"Book V suggests that we might regard *Paterson* as a kind
of tapestry, woven out of memories and observations, composed by one man's imagination, but written in part by
his friends, his patients, and all the milling populace of
Paterson, past and present."[20] Book V is not a retreat
from Williams's concern with building a world that unites
self and not self, but rather an illustration of how he tried
to do it and a statement of the significance of the attempt.

The sense of end, failure, and defeat is strong in Book
V. The poet is writing "in old age":

> Paterson has grown older
>
>   the dog of his thoughts
> has shrunk
> to no more than "a passionate letter"

                        to a woman, a woman he had neglected
                        to put to bed in the past   .

                                                    (p. 268)

Like the unicorn of the tapestries, his imaginative power
has been debased by the long encounter with society, and
he bears scars and "a collar round his neck / hid in the
bristling hair" (p. 247). In his identification with the unicorn, there is a sense of the immanence of death, alone,
without merger:

                              The Unicorn
          has no match
                    or mate   .   the artist
                                        has no peer   .
          Death
                    has no peer:
          wandering in the woods,
                    a field crowded with small flowers
          in which the wounded beast lies down to rest   .

                                                    (p. 246)

   Yet with the realization of the failure and defeat of
Paterson in his attempt to find, release, and marry the
beautiful thing, Williams himself arrives at the moment
of recognition characteristic of tragedy. It is a recognition
that has been implicit in Books I–IV and *In the American Grain:* that if the artist is true to the terms of his
quest, bringing to poetry his own expanded and inclusive
imagination, an imagination not turned away from society
but projected "inland" in an attempt to embrace the
myths and the facts of his age, then he achieves a discovery
of his own reality, which will be also a discovery of the
reality of his age.

With this final recognition Williams can reassure himself of the validity of his own poetics. Thus, after describing a particularly displeasing section of the tapestry, which portrays beauty defiled in the butchering of the unicorn, Williams realizes that the unsatisfying effect, apparently a failure of the tapestry, is not really a failure, but the reflection of a deeper tragic meaning; the perversion of the tapestry, like the perversion of beauty and the failure of his poem, avails itself of a positive affirmation, and he tells his hero:

>   Paterson,
>   keep your pecker up
>   whatever the detail!
>   Anywhere is everywhere:
>   You can learn from poems
>   that an empty head tapped on
>   sounds hollow
>   in any language! The figures
>   are of heroic size.
>
>   (p. 273)

Because his poetic imagination has been an embracing one, a "living fiction" like the tapestries, the poet can affirm the tragic necessity of plural melodies:

>   saying   .
>
>   The measure intervenes, to measure is all we know,
>
>   .   .   .   .
>
>   We know nothing and can know nothing   .
>   but
>   the dance, to dance to a measure

> contrapuntally,
>> Satyrically, the tragic foot.
>>> (pp. 277–78)

"Contrapuntally," with its connotations of plurality, implies all the necessary dualities and contradictions of the poet's situation: language found and distorted, beauty possessed and perverted, composition and decomposition, failure, defeat, and endless renewal, the timeless balance of good and evil in the world, and a poetry that must embrace all these things and can do so only imperfectly—thus the element of absurdity or mock-heroism suggested even here by the pun involving the Satyrs. By recording these pluralities in the measure of his own inclusive artistic vision, the poet leaves behind him in his defeat the spirit of his own imagination in an art that affirms the value achieved in wresting from the Satyric dance of existence an occasional, radiant "stain of sense." With this affirmation the poet gives substance to his society and finds his own identity in assuming the role of tragic hero.

Epilogue

WALLACE STEVENS

THE HERO IN AN AGE OF DISBELIEF

In all of the works examined here, there is a tendency for the heroic experience to become a drama of the self in the act of creation, as if only language and style can bring about the necessary balanced union of the Romantic duality and produce self-realization. Even in *Moby Dick* and *The Narrative of A. Gordon Pym,* where the heroes (as characters) are twice removed from their authors, the heroic experience lies ultimately not in the dramatic action but in the underlying drama of creation. This tendency of American Romanticism to identify self-fulfillment with artistic creation and to make the heroic journey the drama of the creative self reaches a culmination in the work of Wallace Stevens. Although Stevens engaged in a good deal of thought about the nature of the hero and heroism, in the poems themselves heroic figures are notably sparse. In the longer poems only Crispin stands forth as a sustained protagonist, and "The Comedian as the Letter C" is more a mockery of Crispin's heroic pretensions than a statement of the possibilities of true heroism. But, like Walt Whitman, Stevens is a poet who is best read at large, and behind the whole canon of his work stands the man himself, a genuinely heroic figure, whose quest is manifest in the very work that reflects and records its results.

Toward the end of his life Stevens was asked for a brief
biographical sketch and a statement of the main ideas of
his work to accompany a reprinting of "The Auroras of
Autumn" in the summer 1954 issue of *Perspectives, U.S.A.*
"The author's work," he wrote in reply, "suggests the possibility of a supreme fiction, recognized as a fiction, in
which men could propose to themselves a fulfillment. In
the creation of any such fiction, poetry would have a vital
significance. There are many poems relating to the inter-
actions between reality and the imagination, which are to
be regarded as marginal to this central theme." [1] Here, in
a nutshell, are the basic concerns of Stevens's work, and
yet the characteristic humility implicit in this description
belies the integral unity that these concerns had come to
have in his mind. For example, the remark that "in the
creation of any such fiction, poetry would have a vital
significance," is an understatement, for to Stevens the
aesthetic act is our only source for such a fiction, and, as
he had written to Henry Church, "in the long run, poetry
would be the supreme fiction" (*L*, p. 430). Furthermore,
the interaction of reality and the imagination is hardly
"marginal" to Stevens's conception of poetry; on the contrary, it is the very foundation of poetry, because it is the
essence of the life of the mind. In Stevens's development
of the relations between these three concerns—the interaction of imagination and reality, poetry, and the idea of a
supreme fiction—we have a most articulate statement of
the posture of the American Romantic sensibility and its
implications for the hero in the contemporary world.

For Stevens, as for the earlier Romantics, the dualism of
self and everything that is not self is the starting point of
all thought and all experience. With Stevens, however,

man and his world stand not in transcendent, spiritual unity but rather in dramatic opposition, in the bare confrontation of the human imagination with a meaningless, chaotic reality. The initial situation in which Stevens finds himself in the world is well expressed by the "Snow Man" of his early poetry:

> One must have a mind of winter
> To regard the frost and the boughs
> Of the pine-trees crusted with snow;
>
> And have been cold a long time
> To behold the junipers shagged with ice,
> The spruces rough in the distant glitter
>
> Of the January sun; and not to think
> Of any misery in the sound of the wind,
> In the sound of a few leaves,
>
> Which is the sound of the land
> Full of the same wind
> That is blowing in the same bare place
>
> For the listener, who listens in the snow,
> And, nothing himself, beholds
> Nothing that is not there and the nothing that is.
>
> (CP, pp. 9–10)

Like the snow man, Stevens begins with only an awareness of his own solitary consciousness and a world whose existence is independent of his own. As J. Hillis Miller explains, "Stevens is left in a world made of two elements: subject and object, mind and matter, imagination and reality. Imagination is the inner nothingness, while reality is the barren external world with which imagination carries on its endless intercourse." [2]

The position of the snow man, however, is one that
Stevens finds unsatisfactory and impossible to sustain. The
mind, which "can never be satisfied," cannot remain passive, and even in a valueless world it demands orientation
and belief. Stevens exists in a world that is not part of the
self, but that must, for the sake of belief, be made part of
it. The dualities of his vision must be related, not because
such relation has ultimately some transcendental rationale,
but simply because man's inner rage for harmony and
order demands it. But relation and reconciliation are difficult to obtain, and Stevens consequently oscillates between two extremes, seeking a satisfactory middle ground.
"Sometimes I believe most in the imagination for a long
time," Stevens writes, "and then, without reasoning about
it, turn to reality and believe in that and that alone" (*L*,
p. 710). As Roy Harvey Pearce writes:

> The poems may move toward one of two ends: toward
> celebrating the power of the subject, the mind which
> not only wills but makes its knowledge; or toward cele-
> brating the givenness of the object, the reality which
> is unchanging and unchangeable, perdurably out
> there. . . . The utopian alternatives are pure intro-
> spection and pure abstraction—knowledge of pure act
> as against knowledge of pure substance.[3]

Both the pure affirmation of reality and the celebration
of imaginative power are present in Stevens's early poetry.
In "Ploughing on Sunday," for example, the persona celebrates a purely naturalistic triumph over the outworn con-
ventions of the sabbath day, finding all the value he needs
in cocks' tails, the sun and moon (neither of which are
here symbolic), the wind, the rain, and the land:

Remus, blow your horn!
I'm ploughing on Sunday,
Ploughing North America.
Blow your horn!

Tum-ti-tum,
Ti-tum-tum-tum!
The turkey-cock's tail
Spreads to the sun.

The white cock's tail
Streams to the moon.
Water in the fields.
The wind pours down.

(*CP*, p. 20)

At the other extreme stands Hoon, an extremely subjective figure, encased in the purple that is for Stevens generally suggestive of imaginative power. For Hoon the world is all self:

Out of my mind the golden ointment rained,
And my ears made the blowing hymns they heard.
I was myself the compass of that sea:

I was the world in which I walked, and what I saw
Or heard or felt came not but from myself;
And there I found myself more truly and more strange.

(*CP*, p. 65)

Ultimately, of course, neither alternative can be accepted, and most of Stevens's work is devoted to the quest for some sort of meaningful and satisfactory reconciliation. Like the earlier Romantics, Stevens insists that the resolution be one that unites self and not self without denying the fundamental, existential facticity of either, one that links the parts of the duality without destroying the duality itself. In "Effects of Analogy" he writes:

> We could not speak of our world as something to be distinguished from the poet's sense of it unless we objectified it and recognized it as having an existence apart from the projection of his personality, as land and sea, sky and cloud. He himself desires to make the distinction as part of the process of realizing himself.[4]

Without this dualism, Stevens realizes, there can be neither a concept of individual selfhood nor a fundamental belief in the existence of anything beyond the self. To realize himself, the poet must preserve and give life to the duality, but in this task he is threatened from both ends: by the over-idealizing tendency of the mind, which seeks to make all of the not self a projection of its own creative power, and by the pressure of reality, which deadens the power of the mind.

Stevens, as much as Emerson, is aware of the dangers of idealism. For Stevens awareness of this danger is based in a realization of the fact that the mind inevitably colors whatever it sees, that "things seen are things as seen."[5] Hoon, to Stevens, is not so much a bizarre figure as he is the representation of a very real tendency of the mind. It is this tendency that Stevens calls the "romantic" in a "pejorative" sense, or, at times, the "false romantic." By these terms he means a personal identification with the objective world, making external reality a part of the self, or vice versa. This, to Stevens, "belittles" the imagination and results only in "minor wish-fulfillment," without a clear awareness of either the self or the world. The poet must guard against this tendency and strive to see the external world in its pure singularity, without reference to its possible role as a mirror for mankind. Stevens, for example, invokes a star in "Nuances of a Theme by Williams":

> Lend no part to any humanity that suffuses
> you in its own light.
> Be not chimera of morning,
> Half-man, half-star.
> Be not an intelligence,
> Like a widow's bird
> Or an old horse.
>
> (CP, p. 18)

Like Williams, Stevens insists on preserving the integrity of the world as object. Like Williams, too, he realizes that the difficulty of seeing reality as it is results not only from the fact that we must view it through the lens of our own mind but also from the fact that we tend to view it through the names given it by society and history. For Stevens, as for Williams and also for Emerson, true reality is obscured by false language and outworn conceptions, and the poet consequently must strive to pierce beneath them; he must "live in the world but outside of existing conceptions of it" (*OP*, p. 164).

The main strategy in Stevens's attempt to overcome both of these obstacles to a full realization of external reality (and, thus, also to a full realization of self) lies in becoming, in the language of "Notes toward a Supreme Fiction," a "thinker of the first idea." As he explained to Henry Church: "If you take the varnish and dirt of generations off a picture, you see it in its first idea. If you think about the world without its varnish and dirt, you are a thinker of the first idea" (*L*, pp. 426–27). Like Williams and the Transcendentalists, Stevens insists on the existence of a vital reality to which the mind must penetrate. "There is inherent in the words *the revelation of reality*," he writes, "a suggestion that there is a reality of or within or beneath the surface of reality" (*OP*, p. 213). However, like Williams and in contrast to the Transcendentalists, the reality that Stevens must find and reveal is not a spiritual essence immanent in the material world, but rather the pure, existential object itself, known free of its "varnish and dirt."

Thus, Stevens begins the "Notes" with basic instructions:

> Begin, ephebe, by perceiving the idea
> of this invention, this invented world,
> The inconceivable idea of the sun.
>
> You must become an ignorant man again
> And see the sun again with an ignorant eye
> And see it clearly in the idea of it.
>
> (*CP*, p. 380)

There is, of course, an apparent paradox here. Ideas, conventionally, are thought or *conceived*, and Stevens is demanding that the ephebe *perceive* an *inconceivable* idea. What Stevens means is this: since "things seen are things as seen," we can only perceive the sun as an object through the filter of our mind and thus can never know it as existing independently of ourselves. Yet it is precisely a realization of this independence that must be achieved, and thus what the ephebe must do is to abstract from his perception of the sun the *idea* of the sun as an independent, existential reality. Such an idea is "inconceivable" in the sense that it must be recognized as something that the mind itself, any mind, did not and could not create, as something independent of the conceiving powers of thought. Only then can the poet know reality in its individuality and freshness, and only when he can achieve this kind of knowledge can he fulfill one of the vital functions of his art, as Stevens describes it in his essay "On Poetic Truth":

> Poetry has to do with reality in that concrete and individual aspect of it which the mind can never tackle altogether on its own terms, with matter that is foreign and alien in a way in which abstract systems, ideas in which we detect an inherent pattern, a structure that belongs to the ideas themselves, can never be. It is never familiar to us in the way in which Plato wished the conquests of the mind to be familiar. On the contrary its function, the need which it meets and which has to be met in some way in every age that is not to become decadent or barbarous is precisely this contact with reality as it impinges on us from the outside, the sense that we can touch and feel a solid reality which does not wholly dissolve itself into the conceptions of our own minds. (*OP,* pp. 236–37)

The initial task of the poet, then, is the revelation of reality and, as it was for Williams, so for Stevens the poet's task is one with vital implications for society as a whole.

But the necessity to confront reality and to preserve a sense of a reality not ourselves represents only one side of the dilemma in Stevens's mind. Equally necessary is the need for the self to resist that aspect of reality which can deaden the mind, what Stevens calls the pressure of reality, "the pressure of an external event or events on the consciousness to the exclusion of any power of contemplation" (*NA,* p. 20). In "The Noble Rider and the Sound of Words," Stevens describes the contemporary age as "violent," and suggests that the preservation of self lies in the ability to resist this violence:

> I am thinking of life in a state of violence, not physi-
> cally violent, as yet, for us in America, but physically
> violent for millions of our friends and for still more
> millions of our enemies and spiritually violent, it may
> be said, for everyone alive.
>   A possible poet must be a poet capable of resisting
> or evading the pressure of the reality of this last degree,
> with the knowledge that the degree of today may be-
> come a deadlier degree tomorrow. (*NA,* pp. 26–27)

By resistance or evasion, Stevens does not mean a retreat
from reality into a more felicitous realm of imagination.
Although he calls the act "escapism," he insists that he
does not mean the term in the "pejorative" sense, which
"applies where the poet is not attached to reality, where
the imagination does not adhere to reality, which, for my
part, I regard as fundamental" (*NA,* p. 31). Instead of
moving away from reality, the imagination becomes "a
violence from within that protects us from a violence from
without" by "pressing back against the pressure of reality"
(*NA,* p. 36).

The task of the poet is not merely to reveal a reality not
ourselves but to mediate it for us, to transform it into
something in which we can believe and find a fulfillment.
Such transformation is possible only through a conjunc-
tion of reality and the imagination, only when both halves
of the duality are preserved in the process of uniting them.
The poet, like "the man with the blue guitar," must play
"a tune beyond us, yet ourselves":

> A tune beyond us as we are,
> Yet nothing changed by the blue guitar;
>
> Ourselves in the tune as if in space,
> Yet nothing changed, except the place

> Of things as they are and only the place
> As you play them, on the blue guitar,
>
> Placed, so, beyond the compass of change,
> Perceived in a final atmosphere;
>
> For a moment final, in the way
> The thinking of art seems final when
>
> The thinking of god is smoky dew.
> The tune is space. The blue guitar
>
> Becomes the place of things as they are,
> A composing of senses of the guitar.
>
> (*CP,* pp. 167–68)

In suggesting that " the blue guitar / Becomes the place of things as they are," Stevens is referring to the process that he will later call "abstraction." In "The Noble Rider and the Sound of Words," he writes that the measure of the poet is "the measure of his power to abstract himself, and to withdraw with him into his abstraction the reality on which the lovers of truth insist. He must be able to abstract himself and also to abstract reality, which he does by placing it in his imagination" (*NA,* p. 23). The imagination abstracts things as they are from the surrounding chaos, the pressure of reality, and forges them into a new truth, "a composing of senses of the guitar." The result is an abstraction, which is a "fiction" in the sense that it does not exist without the words that describe it; yet it is a credible fiction, whose truth is "not so much that it is actually so, as that it must be so" (*NA,* p. 53). Only in such abstract description is true revelation of things as they are to the imagination possible. In a later poem the truth of the "composing of senses of the guitar" becomes the abstract truth of "description without place," the truth of "words of things that do not exist without the words" (*NA*, p. 32):

> Description is revelation. It is not
> The thing described, nor false facsimile.
>
> It is an artificial thing that exists,
> In its own seeming, plainly visible,
>
> Yet not too closely the double of our lives,
> Intenser than any actual life could be,
>
> A text we should be born that we might read,
> More explicit than the experience of sun
>
> And moon, the book of reconciliation,
> Book of a concept only possible
>
> In description, canon central in itself,
> The thesis of the plentifullest John.
>
> (CP, pp. 344–45)

Elsewhere Stevens has more to say regarding the actual mechanics of "abstraction." The process begins with the perception of resemblance, "a partial similarity between two dissimilar things" (*NA*, p. 77), which the imagination makes brilliant. "To confront fact in its total bleakness," Stevens writes, "is for any poet a completely baffling experience. Reality is not the thing but the aspect of the thing" (*NA*, p. 95). When the poet abstracts the aspect of a thing seen as a "first idea" into his imagination and views it there in its relationship to other things, the result is a new abstraction. This is the beginning of the process by which the proliferation of resemblance extends an object into virtually unlimited artifice, as, for example, the pineapple of "Someone Puts a Pineapple Together." Beginning with the pure idea of the pineapple, the "root of a form," the unnamed character of the poem abstracts this idea into his mind and allows his imagination to operate on it:

> Divest reality
> Of its propriety. Admit the shaft
> Of that third planet [imagination] to the table and then:

1. The hut stands by itself beneath the palms.
2. Out of their bottle the green genii come.
3. A vine has climbed the other side of the wall.

4. The sea is spouting upward out of rocks.
5. The symbol of feasts and of oblivion . . .
6. White sky, pink sun, trees on a distant peak.

7. These lozenges are nailed-up lattices.
8. The owl sits humped. It has a hundred eyes.
9. The coconut and cockerel in one.

10. This is how yesterday's volcano looks.
11. There is an island Palahude by name—
12. An uncivil shape like a gigantic haw.

> (*NA,* p. 86)

The result is a poetry of "things which do not exist without the words," a poetry of abstractions that, by virtue of being abstract, are able to "exhibit affinities in the *actual* structure of objects by which their significance is deepened and enhanced" (*OP,* p. 237). Stevens concludes in "Effects of Analogy": "Thus poetry becomes and is a transcendent analogue composed of the particulars of reality, created by the poet's sense of the world, that is to say, his attitude, as he intervenes and interposes the appearances of that sense" (*NA,* p. 130).

Poetry itself, then, created through the interaction of

reality and the imagination, becomes for Stevens the means of reconciling self and not self, the irreducible halves of the Romantic duality. It is a reconciliation created by man out of his own human needs, without the aid or guidance of any kind of spiritual energy, a "fiction" in which man proposes to himself a fulfillment. In the past—to the Transcendentalists, for example—belief in God had offered such a fulfillment at the same time that it offered a divine rationale for the ultimate harmony of self and not self. But for Stevens there is no divine source for such a union, and the only harmony that can exist is the harmony that man himself creates through the operation of his own sensibility on the real world. "After one has abandoned a belief in god," he writes in his "Adagia," "poetry is that essence which takes its place as life's redemption" (*OP,* p. 158).

This is so because the idea of God is itself a poetic idea, but one, Stevens feels, that has grown stale and lost its power. As Stevens explains in a memorandum to Henry Church:

> The major poetic idea in the world is and always has been the idea of God. One of the visible movements of the modern imagination is the movement away from the idea of God. The poetry that created the idea of God will either adapt it to our different intelligence, or create a substitute for it, or make it unnecessary. (*L,* p. 378)

What Stevens is suggesting is that the idea of God, the supreme fiction by which we have lived but which no longer suffices, is a product of the transcendence implicit in the process of abstraction in which bare self and bare not self are linked together through the creative power of the imagination. Once begun, it is the process of abstraction based on resemblance that is the source of our thinking about the ideal. Stevens suggests that "since, as between resemblances, one is always a little more perfect than another and since, from this, it is easy for perfectionism of a sort to evolve, it is not too extravagant to think of resemblances and of the repetitions of resemblances as a source of the ideal" (*NA*, p. 81). Through the poetic process we are able to project a state in which all oppositions and contradictions would be resolved, an ideal state of total harmony, a supreme fiction to replace the outworn fiction of God. In a world stripped of all essential, prior value, the imagination takes over for Stevens as the agent and sole creator of value. "If the imagination is the faculty by which we import the unreal into what is real," writes Stevens, "its value is the value of the way of thinking by which we project the idea of God into the idea of man" (*NA*, p. 150).

Equally, it follows that the value of imagination is the value of the way of thinking by which we might project the idea of the *hero* into the idea of man. "The trouble with humanism" Stevens wrote to Hi Simons, regarding the "MacCullough" canto of "Notes," "is that man as God remains man" (*L*, p. 434). In other words, in creating the supreme fiction of God, traditional humanism fails to recognize that God is but a version of man, that man is the being who has given the gods reality, who "put into their mouths the only words they have ever spoken" (*OP*, p. 167); consequently, man is demeaned by his own fiction and the fiction is apotheosized at the expense of its creator. What Stevens demands is a much more radical humanism that frankly recognizes man himself as the source of his fictions, a humanism that must have its roots in the idea of the heroic possibility of man. In the "MacCullough" canto, Stevens asks:

> Can we compose a castle-fortress home,
> Even with the help of Viollet-le-Duc,
> And set the MacCullough there as major man?
>
> *(CP,* p. 386)

The "castle-fortress-home" suggests a supreme fictional place, and MacCullough, as Stevens told Simons, is "any name, any man" *(L,* p. 434). The answer to the question is negative, because any particular man, such as Mac-Cullough, can only be himself, and as such is inevitably something less than the possible heroic image that man is able to project for himself: "the MacCullough is Mac-Cullough. / It does not follow that major man is man." *(CP,* p. 387) "Major man" is more than any single, individual man; rather, it is an abstraction from the reality of the common man. Thus, Stevens continues in "Notes":

> The major abstraction is the idea of man
> And major man is its exponent, abler
> In the abstract than in his singular,
>
> More fecund as principle than particle,
> Happy fecundity, flor-abundant force,
> In being more than an exception, part,
>
> Though an heroic part, of the commonal.
>
> *(CP,* p. 388)

The idea of the hero is itself a fiction, but a necessary fiction, perhaps the essential one; for unless we believe in the possibilities of man, no further belief is possible. "Unless we believe in the hero," Stevens asks, "what is there /

To believe?" (*CP*, p. 275). The person who can give us this belief in ourselves is, of course, the poet, the man of imagination. So the "ephebe" must make of the common man "looking for what was [a supreme fiction to believe in] where it used to be [outside of humanity itself]" the "final elegance," the idea of human heroism that will enable man to believe in himself:

> It is he. The man
> In that old coat, those sagging pantaloons,
>
> It is of him, ephebe, to make, to confect
> The final elegance, not to console
> Nor sanctify, but plainly to propound.
> (*CP*, p. 389)

Like MacCullough, the comical vagabond presented here is the basis of the idea of major man; yet, in their "singular," as "particles" rather than principle, these figures are much more absurd than genuinely heroic. This sense of the absurdity of the particular exists throughout Stevens's poetry, and it forms a crucial paradox in his work. On the one hand, he demands that the poet must give us an awareness of our heroic potential, must create for us the idea of the hero. On the other hand, Stevens is so keenly aware of the breach between the abstract idea of the hero and any particular hero whom he might create that he finds it virtually impossible to write dramatically heroic poetry or to dramatically create heroic protagonists. Consequently, in Stevens's work, the only sustained *action,* by which the hero must ultimately be measured, is the poet's own incessant "propounding," the "never-ending meditation" of his poems.

Needless to say, in such a vision the poet, or as Stevens

at times insists, "any man of imagination," becomes the "central man," the only remaining hero in Stevens's work. Because the poetic act not only "gives to life the supreme fictions without which we are unable to conceive of it" (*NA,* p. 31) but also gives us the only grounds we have for believing in them, the poet becomes a heroic figure in his own right, and the heroic journey becomes the process of poetic creation. The final goal of the quest, for Stevens, is a poem that will constitute in itself both a ground for belief and an object to believe in, what Roy Harvey Pearce calls an "ultimate poem." As Pearce writes, "the poem he sought—and, especially toward the end of his life, with superbly lucid awareness of what he was seeking—was one of a creative process purified in such a way that all men could share in it. It was to be a poem in which all men could come to behold, stripped of its antecedents and consequences, that which made them human." [6] But as Pearce also explains, "the ultimate poem is a poem which, like the ultimate man, exists only by virtue of the mind's ability to abstract forward, as it were, and to partake, through the abstraction, of its own potentiality to make more poems and to realize itself in all its humanity." [7] Such is the final goal of Stevens's heroic quest, as it is of Williams's: the creation in art of an ultimate poetry and the full realization of the self as the fully heroic "major man"—the ultimate poet,

> The impossible possible philosophers' man,
> The man who has had the time to think enough,
> The central man, the human globe, responsive
> As a mirror with a voice, the man of glass,
> Who in a million diamonds sums us up.
>
> (*CP,* p. 250)

But even as he aspires to this end, Stevens, like Williams, realizes that the "ultimate poem" cannot be a poem to complete all poems; it is not the sort of thing that, once created, can avail itself of a final certainty. A supreme fiction "must change," for it must constantly be refreshed and renewed through contact with bare reality. As Marie Boroff explains, "the mind can find satisfaction only if what it affirms is felt as true, but the truth is perpetually changing in both its aspects, the perceiving consciousness and the world as perceived." [8] The poetic achievement is a momentary "agreement with reality" (*NA*, p. 57), a triumph of the creative imagination, but a triumph that is highly unstable and must be continually recreated if it is to remain a victory and not become outworn and thus a defeat. The ultimate poem must always be in a state of process; the creative effort of the heroic self can have no final conclusion.

The poet's achievement, as a heroic figure, lies not in what he completes but rather in his ability to continually affirm the possibility of such a supreme fiction as the ultimate poem. Receiving the National Book Award in 1955, Stevens told the audience: "It is not what I have written but what I should like to have written that constitutes my true poems, the uncollected poems which I have not had the strength to realize" (*OP*, p. 246). Here is the same sense of an ultimate success toward which the poet has vainly struggled that characterizes *Paterson* and becomes a major factor in the development of Williams's tragic vision. But, although a melancholy, elegiac, sometimes sacramental tone dominates much of Stevens's later poetry, his heroic vision never becomes a fully tragic one. This is not to say that Stevens ignores or denies the presence of evil or tragedy in the world, but rather that in his conception of his own poetry he finds that the ability to come to grips with the *mal* of the world takes him beyond tragedy to an essentially comic vision. "Pain is human," Stevens writes in "Esthetique du Mal" (*CP*, p. 314), which is to say that death, evil, unseemliness, disorder, and disease are part of "things as they are." As Daniel Fuchs writes, for Stevens man is a creature who can find beauty in imperfection and arduousness, and the self is born and realized in difficulty, complexity, and struggle.[9] In this sense, tragedy is simply part of being human, part of "the unalterable necessity of being this unalterable animal":

> It may be that one life is a punishment
> For another, as the son's life for the father's.
> But that concerns the secondary characters.
> It is a fragmentary tragedy
> Within the universal whole. The son
> And the father alike and equally are spent,
> Each one, by the necessity of being
> Himself, the unalterable necessity
> Of being this unalterable animal.
> This force of nature in action is the major
> Tragedy.
>
> (*CP*, pp. 323–24)

As such, evil and tragedy can become sources of fundamental beauty. By clearly recognizing that they are an inextricable part of the human condition and creating an imaginative "agreement" with them through the poetic assertion of consciousness, Stevens is able to achieve a comic affirmation of the possibilities of the mind.

Consequently, the poet's response, as Stevens instructs the "ephebe" in "Notes," must be neither to "console" man for his lot, nor to "sanctify" him for his power to endure, but "plainly to propound" his possibilities. And although the poet-as-hero must inevitably fall short of his ultimate goal, such failure is insignificant beside the substantial success achieved in redeeming moments and implicit in the poet's ability to envision the possibility of that goal. Stevens, for example, continues his 1955 National Book Award address:

> Humble as my actual contribution to poetry may be and however modest my experience of poetry has been, I have learned through that contribution and by the aid of that experience of the greatness that lay beyond, the power over the mind that lies in the mind itself, the incalculable expanse of the imagination as it reflects itself in us and about us. (*OP*, p. 246)

More than any of the other American Romantics, Stevens is willing to accept and affirm his human limitations, and, as Fuchs writes, "he finds infinite possibilities in man's admission of his finite capabilities." [10] The discovery of possibility is a cause for affirmation and is reason in itself to continue the quest of creative effort; and the momentary achievement of "single, certain truth," even though such truth must change and be endlessly renewed and can be known only in "uncertain light" (*CP*, p. 380), is a cause for celebration.

In describing modern poetry as "the poem of the mind in the act of finding / What will suffice," (*CP*, p. 239), Wallace Stevens also describes the essence of the Romantic search, and in "the never-ending meditation" (*CP*, p. 465) of his own poetry, the heroic drama of American Romanticism becomes explicitly what it has always been implicitly: the drama of the creative self seeking harmony, fulfillment, and belief. It is a drama that must continually be renewed, for the balanced agreement with reality that the hero seeks is a triumph of imaginative vision which, to be true, must constantly be re-created. In such an experience value lies not in that which is fixed, final, or permanent but in the redeeming moments of crystalization that a man can wrest from his endless experiments with the world.

Notes

PREFACE

1. *English Romantic Poets: Modern Essays in Criticism,* ed. M. H. Abrams (New York, 1960), p. 6.

INTRODUCTION

1. "Victor Cousin," *The Transcendentalists,* ed. Perry Miller (Cambridge, Mass., 1967), pp. 109–10. Subsequent references to Brownson's essay are from this edition and will be found in the text.

2. *The Puritans,* ed. Thomas H. Johnson and Perry Miller (New York, 1938), p. 31.

3. Ibid., p. 40

4. *The Transcendentalists,* p. 10.

5. "Of Some of the Sources of Poetry among Democratic Nations," in *American Poetry and Poetics,* ed. Daniel G. Hoffman (New York, 1962), p. 335.

6. *A Study of English Romanticism* (New York, 1968), pp. 17–18.

7. *Emerson's Angle of Vision* (Cambridge, Mass., 1952), p. 151.

8. *The Selected Writings of Ralph Waldo Emerson,* ed. Brooks Atkinson (New York, 1950), p. 6. All subsequent references to Emerson's writings, unless otherwise noted, are from this edition and will be found in the text.

9. *Emerson's Angle of Vision,* p. 31.

10. *The Romantic Imagination* (New York, 1961), p. 273.

11. *Selections from Ralph Waldo Emerson,* ed. Stephen E. Whicher (Cambridge, Mass., 1957), p. 449.

12. *Emerson: A Statement of New England Transcendentalism As Expressed in the Philosophy of Its Chief Exponent* (New York, 1917), p. 36.

13. *American Renaissance* (New York, 1941), p. 62.

14. *American Renaissance,* p. 52.

15. *Emerson: A Statement of New England Transcendentalism,* p. 52.

16. Matthiessen, *American Renaissance,* pp. 41–42.

17. *Emerson's Angle of Vision,* p. 113.

18. *American Renaissance,* p. 70.

19. Paul, *Emerson's Angle of Vision,* pp. 34 ff.

CHAPTER I

1. "Thoreau in the Context of International Romanticism," *Nature's Nation* (Cambridge, Mass., 1967), p. 177.

2. Ibid., p. 177.

3. *Emerson and Thoreau: Transcendentalists in Conflict* (Middletown, Conn., 1966), *passim.*

4. *Thoreau* (Cambridge, Mass., 1939), p. 205.

5. *A World Elsewhere: The Place of Style in American Literature* (New York, 1966).

6. For the most comprehensive treatment of Thoreau's indictment of society, see Sherman Paul, *The Shores of America* (Urbana, Ill., 1957).

7. *The Variorum Walden,* ed. Walter Harding (New York, 1962), p. 37. All subsquent references to Thoreau's work, unless otherwise noted, are from this edition and will be found in the text.

8. *The Shores of America,* p. 301.

9. Ibid., p. 297.

10. A. B. Hovey, *The Hidden Thoreau* (Beirut, Lebanon, 1966), pp. 102 ff.

11. *Emerson and Thoreau,* p. 143.

12. *A World Elsewhere,* p. 18.

13. *The Hidden Thoreau,* pp. 98–99.

CHAPTER II

1. Without suggesting that there are rigid lines between them, I have grouped the following sections together in my discussion: 1–6, 7–16, 17–32, 33–43, and 44–52. The reasoning behind these particular divisions is made clear in the text.

2. Walt Whitman, "Song of Myself," *Leaves of Grass,* Comprehensive Reader's Edition, ed. Harold W. Blodgett and Sculley Bradley (New York, 1965), p. 30. Unless otherwise noted, all subsequent references to Whitman's writing are from this edition and will be found in the text.

3. *The Uncollected Poetry and Prose,* ed. Emory Holloway, 2 vols. (New York, 1932), 2:36.

4. For this interpretation see Gay Wilson Allen, *Walt Whitman Handbook* (New York, 1962), p. 252.

5. Ibid., pp. 264–69.

6. Although nearly all critics agree that Whitman was a mystic, and the vision portrayed in section 5 certainly has all the earmarks of a mystical experience, I think the term is an unfortunate one for discussing Whitman's art. Not only is it inherently ambiguous, but it suggests a kind of finality or perfect certainty that is alien both to Whitman's dynamic experience and to Romanticism in general so far as it implies, in Emerson's words, nailing "a symbol to one sense, which was a true sense for a moment, but soon becomes old and false." Furthermore, as Richard Chase writes, "there may be sometimes a kind of mysticism at work in Whitman's poetry. But it is hardly ever distinguishable from merely vague thought and diffuse metaphor—and therefore it seems more gratuitous or honorific than accurate to refer to it as mysticism. . . . And in fact the more one reviews the evidence and the more one reads the poems, the less likely does the "mystical experience" seem and the less relevant to an understanding of such poems as "Song of Myself" does it become, even if it occurred" (*Walt Whitman Reconsidered* [New York, 1955], pp. 48–49). Along with Chase, it seems to me that although Whitman's moments of imaginative insight and awareness may have a mystical tenor about them, mysticism itself is important, if at all, only as an element in the formation of his vision, and that "Song of Myself" can be understood better in the context of Romanticism than as an account of a mystical experience, dynamic (as Allen suggests in *Walt Whitman Handbook,* pp. 246 ff.), inverted (cf. James E. Miller, *A Critical Guide to "Leaves of Grass"* [Chicago, 1957], pp. 6–35), or otherwise.

7. Although basically similar to Emerson's doctrine of spirit manifesting itself in endless mutations of form, the vision of "Song of Myself" is somewhat different in the emphasis that it places on the importance of the bodily form, both metaphysically and imaginatively; for to Whitman this is the essence of individual identity, though it is an essence that cannot exist independently of its cosmic element, the soul.

8. *Studies in Classic American Literature* (New York, 1923), p. 245.

9. "Whitman Justified: The Poet in 1860," *Whitman: A Collection of Critical Essays,* ed. Roy Harvey Pearce (Englewood Cliffs, N.J., 1962), p. 45.

10. "Whitman's Style: From Mysticism to Art," ibid., p. 92.

11. *Walt Whitman Reconsidered,* pp. 65–66.

12. See Gay Wilson Allen, *The Solitary Singer: A Critical Biography of Walt Whitman* (New York, 1955), pp. 191–259, passim.

13. *Walt Whitman Handbook,* pp. 136–73, is a discussion of the composition of the 1860 edition.

14. Allen points out that many of Whitman's manuscripts, first drafts, and unpublished poems reveal a depth of pessimism and despair that he rarely allowed to emerge in *Leaves of Grass.* See *Walt Whitman Handbook,* pp. 142–56, and *The Solitary Singer,* pp. 216–28.

CHAPTER III

1. "From Edwards to Emerson," *Errand into the Wilderness* (New York, 1964), p. 197.

2. For a brief account of Melville's early religious training, see Newton Arvin, *Melville* (New York, 1950), pp. 30–35.

3. *The Letters of Herman Melville,* ed. Merrell R. Davis and William H. Gilman (New Haven, Conn., 1960), pp. 130–131.

4. Herman Melville, *Moby Dick,* ed. Charles Feidelson, Jr. (New York, 1964), p. 181. All subsequent references to this edition will be found in the text.

5. Herman Melville, *Pierre, or the Ambiguities* (New York, 1930), p. 385.

6. Cited by Lawrance Thompson, *Melville's Quarrel with God* (Princeton, N.J., 1952), p. 143.

7. "The Image of Society in *Moby Dick," "Moby Dick" Centennial Essays,* ed. Tyrus Hillaway and Luther S. Mansfield (Dallas, 1953), p. 64.

8. This attitude is called "armed neutrality—the way of wisdom" by Merlin Bowen, *The Long Encounter* (Chicago, 1960), p. 235. Bowen describes it as "resistance without defiance and acceptance without surrender."

9. My interpretation of this passage is derived largely from Charles Feidelson, Jr.'s annotation to the text.

10. The classic interpretation of Ishmael is that he is basically a humanitarian and a Christian. Such is the view put forth by F. O. Matthiessen, *American Renaissance,* and Howard K. Vincent, *The Trying-Out of "Moby Dick"* (Cambridge, Mass., 1949). Yet the oppo-

site interpretation, that Ishmael is mainly an ironic figure who denies both God and Christian values, has also been widely defended. See, e.g., Thompson, *Melville's Quarrel*, and Ted N. Weissbuch and Bruce Stillians, "Ishmael the Ironist: The Anti-Salvation Theme in *Moby Dick*," *Emerson Society Quarterly* 31 (January 1963):71.

11. "The Function of the Cetological Chapters in *Moby Dick*," *American Literature* 28 (May 1956):175.

12. Ibid., p. 173.

13. *Pierre*, p. 202. See also Harry Levin, *The Power of Blackness* (New York, 1958), pp. 165 ff.

14. *The Heresy of Self-Love* (New York, 1968), p. 210.

15. Ibid., pp. 210–11.

16. Feidelson's annotation to the text, pp. 272–73.

17. Melville to Hawthorne, 1851, *Letters*, pp. 124–25.

18. *Ishmael's White World: A Phenomenological Reading of Moby Dick* (New Haven, Conn., 1965), pp. 115 ff.

19. In *The Confidence Man* (New York, 1964), Melville was to bring his total concern to bear on the negative aspect of this protean hero. He writes there that the truly "original" character is "like a revolving Drummond light, raying away from itself all round it" (p. 261). Such a figure tends to become, like the confidence man, void of individual identity.

20. Feidelson notes this in his annotation to the text, p. 618.

21. The wide variety of opinions concerning Ishmael is nowhere more evident than in interpretations of this vexing incident. The most common view is that the survival is also a salvation, an affirmation of an ethical universe in which Ishmael survives by virtue of some morally desirable trait of character, such as: his humanitarianism, as in James Dean Young, "The Nine Gams of the *Pequod*," *Discussions of "Moby Dick*," ed. Milton Stern (Boston, 1960), p. 105; his Christian conscience, as in Vincent, *Trying-Out*, and Matthiessen, *American Renaissance*; his ability to retain spiritual balance and a sense of proportion, as in Bowen, *Long Encounter*, Robert E. Watters, "The Meanings of the White Whale," *Discussions*, p. 79, Edward Rosenberry, *Melville and the Comic Spirit* (Cambridge, Mass., 1955), and William Elery Sedgewick, *Herman Melville: The Tragedy of Mind* (Cambridge, Mass., 1944). On the other side of the coin is the view put forth most definitively by Thompson, *Melville's Quarrel*, in which the survival is viewed as an emblematic confirmation of Ishmael's suspicions of God's indifference. Weissbuch and Stillians, "Ishmael the Ironist," see Ishmael as representing the

continuity of Ahab's search for ultimate truth; Brodtkorb, *Ishmael's White World,* sees Ishmael as an artist, surviving for the existentially sufficient reason that what transcends death in time is art.

CHAPTER IV

1. Campbell's position is stated most clearly and emphatically in *The Mind of Poe* (Cambridge, Mass., 1933).

2. "Poe," *In the American Grain* (New York, 1956), pp. 319–20. All subsequent references to this edition will be found in the text, preceded by the abbreviation *IAG.*

3. *The Power of Blackness,* p. 104.

4. Poe's statement is cited by Edward H. Davidson in his introduction to *Selected Writings of Edgar Allan Poe* (Boston, 1956), p. xxi.

5. *Poe: A Critical Study* (Cambridge, Mass., 1957), p. 157.

6. "Chartless Voyage," *Texas Studies in Literature and Language* 8 (Spring 1966):63.

7. No firm consensus exists regarding *The Narrative.* For D. H. Lawrence, *Studies in Classic American Literature* (New York, 1953), it is a study in the disintegration of the self. Harry Levin, *The Power of Blackness,* sees it as the archetypal American story of a boy's initiation into (the horrors of) manhood. For Patrick F. Quinn, "Poe's Imaginary Voyage," *Hudson Review* 4 (Winter, 1952):562, it is an elaboration on the themes of deception and revolt. For Leslie Fiedler, *Love and Death in the American Novel* (New York, 1960), it is primarily a combination of the death wish and the search for the mother. Edwin Fussell, *Frontier: American Literature and the American West* (Princeton, N.J., 1965), sees it as a search for the unknown in Poe's own personal version of the American West. For Edward Davidson, *Poe,* it is a study of the emergence and growth of the knowing and thinking self.

8. "Chartless Voyage," p. 80.

9. *The Complete Poems and Stories of Edgar Allan Poe,* ed. Arthur Hobson Quinn and Edward H. O'Neill, 2 vols. (New York, 1946), 2:724. All subsequent references to this edition will be found in the text, preceded by the volume number.

10. *Wordsworth's Poetry, 1787–1814* (New Haven, Conn., 1964), p. x.

11. *The Romantic Imagination,* p. 196.

12. *The Power of Blackness,* p. 111.

13. *The Romantic Agony,* trans. Angus Davidson (London, 1933), pp. 200–201.

14. Ibid., pp. 26 ff.

15. Davidson, *Poe,* pp. 168–69.

16. "The Two Narratives of Arthur Gordon Pym," *Texas Studies in Literature and Language* 5 (Summer 1963):232.

17. See Davidson, *Poe,* and Quinn, "Poe's Imaginary Voyage."

18. *The Power of Blackness,* p. 114.

19. *Love and Death,* p. 376.

20. Notably Leslie Fiedler, *Love and Death,* p. 374.

21. Davidson, *Selected Writings,* p. xxiv.

22. At times *The Narrative* does take diary form. However, Pym adds a footnote to his first such usage that makes it quite clear that *The Narrative,* in its present form, was not composed as a journal; rather, the dates were affixed at a later time: "For obvious reasons I cannot pretend to strict accuracy in these dates. They are given principally with a view to perspicuity of narration, and as set down in my pencil memorandum" (2:819).

23. Davidson, *Selected Writings,* p. xxii.

24. Ibid., p. xxiv.

CHAPTER V

1. I am thinking particularly of Harold Bloom, *The Visionary Company* (New York, 1961), Frank Kermode, *The Romantic Image* (New York, 1964), and Roy Harvey Pearce, *The Continuity of American Poetry* (Princeton, N.J., 1961).

2. Wallace Stevens, *The Collected Poems of Wallace Stevens* (New York 1954), p. 10. All subsequent references to this edition will be found in the text, preceded by the abbreviation *CP.*

3. *The Continuity of American Poetry,* p. 394.

4. See Linda Welsheimer Wagner, *The Poems of William Carlos Williams: A Critical Study* (Middletown, Conn., 1964), p. 104.

5. William Carlos Williams, *Paterson* (New York, 1963), p. 7. All subsequent references to this edition will be found in the text.

6. *The Autobiography of William Carlos Williams.* (New York, 1964) p. 391.

7. William Carlos Williams, "Spring and All," *William Carlos Williams: A Collection of Critical Essays,* ed. J. Hillis Miller (New York, 1966), pp. 10–11.

8. Ibid., p. 24.

9. *The Art of William Carlos Williams: A Discovery and Possession of America* (Urbana, Ill., 1968), p. 175.

10. *Anatomy of Criticism* (Princeton, N.J., 1957), p. 34.

11. *Art,* pp. 62–63.

12. "Spring and All," p. 24.

13. *Art,* p. 181.

14. *Anatomy of Criticism,* pp. 209–10.

15. *Art,* p. 185.

16. *Anatomy of Criticism,* p. 211.

17. Ibid., p. 210.

18. Kenneth Burke, "William Carlos Williams" in *Williams: A Collection of Critical Essays,* p. 55.

19. "The Unicorn in *Paterson:* William Carlos Williams," in *Williams, A Collection of Critical Essays,* pp. 70 ff.

20. Ibid., p. 75.

EPILOGUE

1. *Letters of Wallace Stevens,* ed. Holly Stevens (New York, 1966), p. 820. All subsequent references to this edition will be found in the text, preceded by the abbreviation *L.*

2. "Wallace Stevens' Poetry of Being," in *The Act of the Mind,* ed. Roy Harvey Pearce and J. Hillis Miller (Baltimore, 1965), p. 145.

3. "The Last Lesson of the Master," in *Act of the Mind,* pp. 126–27.

4. *The Necessary Angel* (New York, 1951), pp. 118–19. All subsequent references to this edition will be found in the text, preceded by the abbreviation *NA.*

5. *Opus Posthumous* (New York, 1966), p. 162. All subsequent refercences to this edition will be found in the text, preceded by the abbreviation *OP.*

6. *The Continuity of American Poetry,* p. 378.

7. Ibid., p. 408.

8. *Wallace Stevens: A Collection of Critical Essays,* ed. Marie Boroff (Englewood Cliffs, N.J., 1963), p. 11.

9. *The Comic Spirit of Wallace Stevens* (Durham, N.C., 1963), pp. 160–61.

10. Ibid., p. 156.

Index